the celestial proposal

our invitation to join the God kind

jane catherine rozek

Cataloging Data for *The Celestial Proposal: Our Invitation to Join the God Kind* (**ISBN**: 978-0-9919917-0-9) is available from Library and Archives Canada.

Cover and chapter images: Fotosearch (Stock Photography, Publitek Inc.), www.fotosearch.com. Most are from the Rolffimages collection. Chapter One, Chapter Three, and Chapter Ten are from the Farconville, Veneratio, and Albund collections.

Quoted scripture: The New Student Bible/New International Version, Philip Yancey and Tim Stafford, Expanded & Updated Hardcopy Edition, (Zondervan, March 1992).

Author's photograph: Kristine Zerr

ISBN: 0991991702
ISBN-13: 9780991991709

Published in Canada
Books of Life Publishing House
760 Cantina Court, Kelowna, BC, V1W 4X6, Canada
www.booksoflifepublishinghouse.com

dedication

To my mother in her ninetieth year,
who took me to Sunday school as a child and
quietly taught me simple celestial standards.

To my daughter, a very brave spiritual explorer,
who activates celestial principles with creativity and zeal.

endorsements

"Identifying faith as a force for shifting manifest reality, Jane Catherine Rozek untethers Bible verses from their historic, traditional moorings. Calling the Bible an "empowering formula for activating faith as a power source," she reboots scripture to read like a science fiction thriller with God as an extraterrestrial collective of "Great Ones" and Jesus as our "Superhero."

Updating humanity's understanding of the Bible is a thankless task, so taking on this particular challenge requires courage. That it falls short of a fully coherent reframing does not reflect badly on the author. This mash-up of Bible + sci fi + metaphysics has introduced new lines of thought for meditation and consideration."

—Bobbye Middendorf, Reviewing Editor, ForeWord Reviews

"*The Celestial Proposal* is a challenging, carefully conceived new look at the Christian faith through fresh eyes. [It] will challenge and intrigue both Christian (at least those willing to consider the faith from a bold, new angle) and New Age readers."

—Thom Lemmons, author of *Blameless* and *Jabez, A Novel,* and coauthor (with Jan Beazley) of *King's Ransom*

"I can, in all faith, proclaim this is a good book. I have been waiting for it most of my life and admire your ability to read between the lines of man's words and define God's message. You have a truly blessed gift, in my humble opinion. Perhaps you're one of God's messengers, to bring the good news from a different approach from the one most of us seem to have trouble with: organized religion."

—Maria Trautman, author of *The Path to Survival*

"There are many nonfiction books that tell, inform, and instruct. And then there are those rare ones, such as yours, that provoke thought. From the very beginning, in a gentle, conversational tone, your use of deep questions immediately immerses the reader in thought. As you naturally weave scripture verses throughout the book, you seem to have a self-revelation (as you mention being "surprised" by this or that), which is highly contagious and engaging."

—Faith Rose, author of *Now to Him*

"There is a spice in your writing style that I envy. A fresh look at an old truth wrapped in a seeker sensitive package guaranteed to pull people off the fence out of apathy!! Great work."

—David McGrinn, theologian, pastor, and author of *God, Why was I Born Gay? Biology, the Bible, and the Homosexual Debate*

"The author is a seasoned writer, and the style is clear and readable. This is one of the more interesting submissions we have seen so far this year. We want to commend you for thinking "outside the box" as you put it...."

—The Writer's Edge

contents

acknowledgments

I would not have chosen to write this particular book, but the task has relentlessly pursued me throughout the diverse chapters of my life's journey. I diligently searched for answers to the hard questions and they were given to me. I looked for a purpose, I needed empowerment, and these were other gifts I received. All that was asked of me was to share the concepts I had learned. Yet, sometimes we pour such amazing truths out from our hearts, we hardly know what we've written. My overflowing gratitude goes to God and to the presence of Spirit for guiding me in putting all the pieces together to discover the plan for the grand adventure we call life.

I want to thank Rebekah J. Antkow-Rozek, my first editor, with deep appreciation for helping me to understand the scope of what I wrote and to find the structure to present it. Without her assistance, this book never would have come to fruition.

I also want to express my thanks to Thom Lemmons, professional freelance editor, for diligently working with me to further refine the manuscript with his keen editorial skill.

Special appreciation goes to my stepfather Bob Ohm, my good friend Mary Smith, and my early supporters on Authonomy. com for their kindness in proofreading and giving editorial suggestions.

My heartfelt thanks also goes to my spouse, Sean Pegg, for his support and for helping with the final editing, but best of all, showing me how to savor again the beauty and the joy of living.

Thanks to all of you who have encouraged me. You know who you are!

introduction

Around midnight one foggy evening, I stood on the edge of a bluff overlooking the Columbia River far below and tried to connect with a higher power. Clouds covered the gorge and levelled themselves so it seemed as though I could step out and walk upon the surface. My life also lay before me like a vast journey of undulating ups and downs—there would be some joy, yes, but also lots of heartache. Did I even want to play the game?

"Why am I here? What's the purpose of life anyway?" I whispered intently over the sea of gray.

We all ask these age-old, mind-niggling questions at some point in our lives. It was at this time I began a personal search for those elusive answers. With perseverance I discovered them quite unexpectedly, right where they were said to be: in the ancient writings of an old, black Bible. At first the answers seemed bizarre and in such contrast to the standard beliefs of the denominations of Christianity I knew. I was young and idealistic enough to strip away all the religious terminology and put the words into a contemporary context. The conclusions were only logical but yet simply amazing.

I was raised with strong, mainstream Christian values. Yet to commit fully to an invisible God presence in our world, I first had to decide if having a Christian kind of faith would actually benefit my life. I believed if a God Source were real, it would also exist outside of corporate church doctrines. My premise then, was to read the words of the Bible without any preconceived religious ideas to see if they still made sense. Perhaps I was naive in my focus. However, when I read these powerful passages they made more sense to me, in our scientific age of space exploration, to take them literally than to accept what orthodox Christianity has expounded.

Like many others, I had been influenced earlier by the book *Chariots of the Gods* by Erich von Dåniken, who first dared to link a presence of God to God-beings who literally came down from the heavens. This did not seem to be a far stretch to me. In fact, it seemed perfectly logical since God was said to be from heaven.

I later discovered that my other perceptions were certainly not unique either. C. S. Lewis' book *Mere Christianity* is a classic but his book *The Screwtape Letters* presents a fascinating way to personify the forces of evil as other worldly entities. It explains to me why life is a struggle and why the world is in such a mess. Other best-selling books—such as Zecharia Sitchin's well-known series, *The Earth Chronicles*, which document his research into ancient texts and artifacts—provide even more reasons to consider that our traditional picture of God may be in need of a major overhaul. I also believe it's time we wake up to the larger plan for planet Earth in the spiritual evolution of humanity, as James Redfield maintains in the *Celestine Prophecy* series.

However, please take note: my own specific viewpoint *does not* take away any validity whatsoever from the priceless truths found in biblical text, nor does it eliminate the truths found in other religions. All belief systems in a higher power have merit and exist for cultural differences on the road to enlightenment.

I purposely write about these things in a bold way to inspire you to think outside the box and color outside the lines. Jesus Christ and his message were definitely controversial and outside the religious norm in his day. So if my thesis makes you want to question and research, then personal growth will happen even if you are not in agreement.

This book is for non-believers who still search for answers.

This book is for those who believe in a God and are willing to strip away the religious terms to read the ancient textbook for what it actually says. Truth doesn't change with the use of non-Christian terminology. Truth stands still and simply waits for us to understand.

This book is for Christians who realize we can't put God into a preconceived box and that God doesn't actually live in houses built by men.

This book is for those with New Age philosophies who are searching for the original roots to wisdom.

It's for all who are brave in heart and open of mind, for we are now involved in the most fantastic interactive reality game of all—*the game of life.* To get to the ultimate level, we must play it seriously with all the skills we have.

I hope you plan to read on. I encourage you to draw your own conclusions, map out your own spiritual journey, and forge your own philosophy for living life on planet earth. Just do it quickly, because the real reason you are reading these pages right now is because you are needed.

—Jane Catherine Rozek, 2013

the personas

1

a bold new
perspective

*A stunning, updated version of spiritual
faith is presented. Old terminology is
redefined into contemporary context so we may
accurately understand ancient biblical truths.*

What Is God?

One late afternoon while flying in a small prop plane in northern British Columbia in Canada, I was reminded how easy it is to look through the rotating propeller and view the fields and forest below in perfect clarity. The speed of the propeller made the metal blades invisible to me, but they were very much a powerful reality. I thought: Is this a simple analogy for how other-dimensional entities might exist in our physical realm? Are there invisible realities whirling at higher levels of energy, engaged and active in our world yet unseen by humanity?

The scientific community long ago dissected the components of the atom down to a central nucleus composed of positively charged protons and neutral neutrons. They thought this core was surrounded by negatively charged electrons that gyrate around it, all held together by an electromagnetic force. Now in the age of quantum physics the smallest particles of matter are really not even seen as particles anymore but more like waves. Ultimately, matter is composed of vibrating energy. Everything we touch, whether it's a wispy cloud or a hard rock, is composed only of a certain density of pulsating energy. Even the different atoms of our flesh are each made of infinitesimal amounts of electromagnetic energy. These are powers and laws we cannot see, but we know undoubtedly they exist. So what is this invisible energy that holds together and defines the molecules of all physical things in our world? Who designed it and set it all into motion?

Only in the twenty-first century are we able to grasp the meaning of certain concepts that were recorded so long ago in the Bible. Incredibly, there is a description of physical matter that lines up with today's scientific definition:

> *By faith we understand that the universe was formed at God's command so that what is seen was not made out of what was visible. (Hebrews 11:3)*

Who formulated the actual laws of nature that operate so efficiently in the universe? If it's the source we call "God," then this God would have to be a vastly intelligent, omnipotent, celestial entity, above and beyond time and space itself. This God would have to come from outside our three dimensional world. If we accept that an invisible, all-powerful God entity really does exist, what does it mean to us? What is this celestial force really doing? What is God? These were the thoughts that started me searching.

I found the most powerful, all-encompassing statement in the whole Bible comes right at the beginning. God seems to be speaking to others and proclaims: "Let us make man in our image, in our likeness, and let them rule..." (Genesis 1:26). My first surprise then, is that "God" is a title referring to more than one entity. There had to be others, or God would have been talking to himself. I learned that the English word *God* is translated from the term *elohim* in the original Hebrew writings. According to *The New Strong's Exhaustive Concordance of the Bible*, the singular word *eloah (Strong's* Hebrew word #432) is translated as *God* or *a god*. The word *elohim (Strong's #430)* is derived from and is the plural of *eloah*. *Elohim* can be translated as *Gods* in the ordinary sense but is also specifically used as the supreme *God*. It sometimes refers to magistrates, or judges, those who are great and mighty (James Strong, *Strong's Exhaustive Concordance of the Bible with Greek and Hebrew Dictionaries*, (Royal Publishers, 1979), *Strong's* Hebrew Numbers 430 and 432, http://biblesuite.com/hebrew/430.htm).

Then, in the later chapters of the Bible, I read about three God-beings symbolized in human terms by the words *Father, Son,* and *Holy Spirit*. This concept also portrays God as being more than one and is defined as the idea of a Holy Trinity, a concept we so often struggle to comprehend. So for me, God becomes a plural word for Gods who do great things.

From this reasoning, I decided to use the term, *the Great Ones*, in this book to remind us that God is more than one personality. We can think of God as a collection of benevolent, celestial God-beings: the Source, the Son and Spirit. They are vastly more powerful and intelligent than we can imagine. Yet I think the two terms can be interchangeable: God and the Great Ones.

At first it is difficult to remember that when we're speaking of God, we're talking about a collection of Great Ones. Yet we feel quite at ease with this kind of terminology when we say that man was created and "they" populated the earth, or when we say "the deer is a beautiful creature and they run in the forest." When we change our perspective from God-singular to God-plural in the same way, many pieces begin falling into place in our exploration of celestial matters.

Already we're starting to define what God is. Logically we can also consider that God is not solely a male entity. When human beings were somehow genetically engineered, "...God created man in his own image...male and female he created them" (Genesis 1:27). To be able to create male and female humans in their likeness, God or the Great Ones must consist of both genders. In one sense God acts with maternal feelings, saying, "Can the mother forget the baby at her breast? ...I will not forget you..." (Isaiah 49:150). We even refer to the unseen guiding force of life on earth as Mother Nature. Yet we read that "in *him* was life" (John 1:4, emphasis mine). So although the pronoun *he* will be used in this book, God is not actually gender-specific at all, nor only one personality. God is the source and the unity of the Great Ones.

Throughout the Bible, God and the angels always come down from heaven. In all cultures of the world, there are creation stories with gods coming out of the heavens. In fact the earliest recorded Sumerian and Greek stories have supernatural gods interacting with human kind. Did you know that all races of people have a innate automatic gesture of delight and triumph? We all raise our hands to the sky in victory!

The Great Ones, God, Jesus Christ, and Spirit—none of them are from our planet. They come from the heavens, or what in today's world we refer to as *outer space*. Using modern terminology we can think of them as celestial in origin, or dare we even say *extraterrestrial* because they do not come from our terrestrial planet earth. Why do we look at the concept of extraterrestrial life as always being dreadful? If there are super-intelligent, advanced God-beings that visited earth thousands of years ago, doesn't it seem logical to assume their morals and values may also be superior?

Let's conclude that God must indeed be celestial and definitely not from our planet if he exists. But the twenty-first century questions are: Who else is out there? What else might be here? The ancient scriptures explain phenomenal prehistory events, by simply saying, "...there was war in heaven" (Revelations 12:7). If there are two opposing celestial forces still working behind the scenes of our reality, what are they fighting over? There must be something of value to them. That war between celestial beings may have spilled over into our world, resulting in an invisible battle taking place for the domination of planet earth and the human race. I believe war between these gods continues onto our timeline, and the chaos on earth is evidence of it.

Even bigger questions arise: are these celestial beings for us or against us, and with which power in the battle are we aligning ourselves? In other words, as a species of Homo sapiens, are we victims or are we warriors? A great, mind-rocking celestial drama between good and evil seems to be playing out, and the whole planet is the stage!

I think we have a major part in the grand story. Down through the pages of human history, there have been many celestial interventions designed and set up for our human species by these Great Ones we call God. Some of these interventions, seen through a Judeo-Christian perspective, were the prophets of old, the chosen tribes, the moral laws, and then a unique, otherworldly ambassador bringing a proposed alliance. This was good news indeed!

Yet in space exploration programs today, humanity is still searching for contact with intelligent beings from outer space. In startling clarity the scriptures I read in the Bible state they have actually already arrived! Think of it. In recent history they have come as non-aggressively as we can possibly imagine—through the birth of a baby born to a human mother. The angels at the birth of Jesus were sent as messengers from the Great Ones to announce their coming ambassador and their peaceful motives for our planet. They chose to come in harmony and sincerity instead of with huge, menacing, intergalactic warships and threats to kill us off and take over the world. Their intention is to offer assistance, not to one nation or brand of religion but to save our world and the human species as a whole.

According to these same scriptures, something else has also entered our physical realm. Their ambassador, Jesus Christ, announced the coming arrival of another invisible member of the God family. Another entity called Holy Spirit was also sent into our dimension. Spirit was to be an invisible counsellor designed to form an inner intimate fusion within our minds. An otherworldly essence taking up residence within us? This would be kind of scary. Yet access to Spirit is supposed to assist us in developing the spiritual maturity to become a subspecies of the God Kind. Are these Great Ones proposing an alliance so we might enter the celestial portal to immortality? I believe this is their Celestial Proposal presented to us!

Our mental picture of God, the world religions in general, and especially the conventional belief system of the Christian faith may need to be updated. When all the sanctimonious language is stripped away, and when most of the manmade, traditional perceptions of religion are wiped clean, what is left? If we envision God's celestial forces as the ultimate evil-fighting heroes of the universe, would the principles of original Christianity still fit? I say yes, and they are deeply enriched with meaning!

Come, let's go back to the beginning of these biblical concepts using a modern framework for understanding ancient truths. The main characters and the basic plot to the story of God's plan for humanity warrant a second look. Unfortunately, Christianity has almost become a sort of optical illusion—a mosaic of extraordinary truth obscurely embedded within the common tapestry of the history of religion. Let's open the doors in our minds, blow the dust off an old Bible, and try to understand where a supernatural, omnipotent, space-age creator would like to take us, for we have been and still are being contacted by something far greater than ourselves.

An Ancient Textbook

The Bible is an ancient textbook. It is our manual for a grand adventure into a spiritual journey. But we must read what it really says. Fascinating, ancient passages come to light when manmade, traditional perceptions of religion and sanctimonious language are stripped away. Yet using contemporary language to understand scripture passages doesn't change the validity of the basic Christian principles. It simply makes the concepts a whole lot more relevant and applicable to our personal lives. One must simply update old religious terminology and the truth stands there waiting to be discovered.

What comes to light? The greatest story ever to unfold: a grand, historical account of celestial visitations to earth by the God Kind. Documented in black and white, a *celestial proposal* emerges for humankind. Underlying it all is this: the Great Ones are *purposing* a plan—for the human race to align ourselves to their standards and join the ranks of immortal beings!

If we are going to find the answers to our questions in these age-old passages, there are a few things to keep in mind. First, the Bible is translated into all major languages, and even in English there are many versions. We can now access some of these online through the Internet (for example at www.biblegateway.com). I have quoted the New International Version (1992) in this book because it has been a trusted and I think an accurate translation, but you may want to look up passages in any contemporary version.

At first when you read from the Bible, each scriptural passage is a piece of information that can be exquisite in meaning and detail, but it is hard to see where and how they all fit together. It's like a big jigsaw puzzle that is supposed to be breathtakingly beautiful, but the box with the complete picture on it has been lost a long time ago. The Bible verses that I have quoted are some of these odd and interesting pieces. However, when putting a jigsaw puzzle together, we have to try to match each piece from all the angles, and it must fit in with all the pieces surrounding it.

When you study these scriptural pieces individually, the words come alive, and you can almost believe a great persona is trying to communicate directly with you—specifically and personally to you. I can read the same passages for years, and then read them one day and suddenly see a totally new depth that applies to me in a unique and profound way. It's kind of magical! I invite you to look closely at each scripture quoted here with a new perspective so that you too may find the perfect place to fit it more clearly into your mind.

The two great testaments, the old and the new, can be taken as documented narratives by authors testifying about God's earlier interactions with humanity. Together they provide the history of direct contact between the celestial Great Ones and mortal humans. The Old Testament sets out the celestial laws of these Great Ones to advance and mentor specific tribes of ancient people. There were laws of obedience set out in a governing alliance in exchange for celestial protection and power. In the first half of the Bible, humanity's attempts to live up to the standards of the Great Ones seemed to me rather unsuccessful despite the vivid demonstrations of the concept of God's power.

In later chapters of the New Testament, I found the same purposeful intent to mentor us through principles of successful living, but expressed in a different way. The focus was to instruct us in their celestial laws through the concept of love. The Great Ones long for us to align ourselves to their standards so we may learn how to love. How could they get this message to us? How would we recognize an invisible, otherworldly, living being? They had to somehow enter our physical world.

The Great Ones intervened by melding celestial seed with a female human to birth a "Son of God and Son of Man," as Jesus Christ was called. He was the answer—their ambassador. His mission was to demonstrate how to operate in celestial standards so we might save ourselves from self-destruction. Through Jesus's living example, celestial law was spread throughout the world in the simplified commands to love God and to love one another. Giving celestial standards to humankind has always been the whole theme of the Bible.

Actually, this ancient textbook can be seen as a definitive how-to manual for developing spiritual maturity. Although the passages that now make up biblical scripture were written across many centuries by a diverse assortment of people, the design, flow, and continuity of the collection is astounding. Sure, over time the Bible has been manipulated by many brands of religion, but its essence of truth is still the basis for understanding God's purpose and plan for us.

In fact, by following a logical, straight line of events from the Old Testament to the new, we can find an amazing blueprint for the very purpose of our lives. This celestial blueprint defines the proposed steps to a spiritual evolution for our human species. It is what I call, *The Celestial Proposal.*

Our world is a small, orbiting ball populated by the human race. Our world today still needs celestial intervention desperately. The Great Ones come back to our planet in compassion, in order to teach, rescue, and save us, individually and corporately, from self-destruction. They come back with an invitation for immortal citizenship in their celestial realm.

This is my narrative of how the proposed celestial plan began and how it is still happening.

2

a design for the human species

God's characteristics are reflected in our makeup.

Godlike Form

If you have ever watched the birth of a child, you have seen the force of life glowing and centering upon a uniquely created human being. The birth of an animal happens the same way. First comes the body; it takes a breath, and then a visible source of life suddenly enters it. Another living creature is born in the timeless miracle of life itself. Even in the plant kingdom, seeds swell and burst open, and new green shoots reach up out of the earth.

What vast, colorful beauty and complexity it all has! In never-ending, continuous patterns, nature is on full throttle from the passing of winter to the rebirth of spring. Who tells the Canadian goose to fly south in migration? Who instructs the bear to go into hibernation? Who guides the salmon up the same river to spawn? In all these things, order, rhythm, and purpose testify to the incredibly astute and detailed presence of an intelligent creator. Certainly, biological diversity is evolving on our planet, but the simple evolutionary theory of our "climb from slime" does not ring true in the face of such orderly function. It seems very unlikely that random selection can adequately explain the operational blueprint we have in our universe either.

Even if we tried or were able to provide alternatives, the laws that govern and hold together the universe are truly superior to anything we can set into motion. At best, our efforts have only led to the further pollution and deterioration of our planet and its population. If we, in all our intelligence, cannot even preserve our world's balanced state of nature, it seems inconceivable that such an amazing phenomenon could have happened by random selection. Yet, the natural beauty and order of planet earth remains consistent around us.

For since the creation of the world God's invisible qualities, his eternal power and divine nature, have been clearly seen, being understood from what has been made, so that men are without excuse. (Romans 1:20)

In my beautiful homeland of Canada, I have been most privileged to see a river run so thick with salmon I could have walked across the blue-green and red, underwater carpet of churning movement. I have heard wolf packs serenading each other in scales of wild harmony, echoing from one end of a meadow to the other. I have trampled wildflowers glistening in the morning dew. When each of us has a chance to connect with nature and let its loveliness, colors, patterns, life force, rhythms, and reason enlighten our minds, we witness the work of a very passionate designer. The question is, how do we fit into this earthly garden of design—and why are we in the garden?

All great products usually come with instruction manuals, and this amazing planet is no exception. A tantalizing essay at the very beginning of Genesis begins the explanation of our purpose on earth:

> *God made the wild animals according to their kinds, the livestock according to their kinds, and all the creatures that move along the ground according to their kinds. And God saw that it was good.*
>
> *...So God created man in his own image, in the image of God he created him; male and female he created them.*
> *(Genesis 1:25, 27)*

How surprising, I thought upon reading this. The Great Ones made all the wild animals according to their own individual kinds, but then they made humans like themselves. The human species takes on their image and likeness. Doesn't this sound as if we are made in the God Kind mode, although maybe not quite finished or of the same quality? We certainly must be related!

In the twenty-first century, we have the ability to clone sheep and other animals from tissue samples taken from one and grown to become another. Today, with techniques like gene splicing, we can genetically modify an organism. Is it so outrageous then to consider that these invisible Great Ones somehow genetically modified themselves with physical flesh? They formed Adam in their likeness from the "dust of the ground," or from the living material they found on the earth. Then, as the story continues, they took bone tissue from Adam's rib to make a female version— the woman Eve—by a similar process. According to the Bible, these were the first two humans created in our world (Genesis 2:21-22).

By what form and shape were we actually designed? What does God look like? Ezekiel was 30 years old and by his account recorded in the Book of Ezekiel, he remembered the very day he saw what he believed to be a God-being. He stated that in the years of King Jehoiachin's exile, on the fifth day of the fourth month by the Kebar River, he saw a brilliantly lit object come down out of the sky. It looked like glowing metal but the most bizarre were the living creatures within the object. (Ezekiel 1:1-5). Yet, this was not what made him fall to his knees in worship.

> *Above the expanse over their heads was what looked like a throne of sapphire, and high above on the throne, was a figure like that of a man. I saw that from what appeared to be his waist up he looked like glowing metal, as if full of fire, and that from there down he looked like fire; and brilliant light surrounded him. Like the appearance of a rainbow in the clouds on a rainy day, so was the radiance around him.*
>
> *This was the appearance of the likeness of the glory of the Lord. When I saw it, I fell facedown.... (Ezekiel 1:26-28)*

The brilliantly glowing figure was "like that of a man," but this description doesn't sound like the old, historical, God-the-Father figure at all.

In the last days of his life, the apostle John also saw a vision of a celestial God-being that looked like a man. It is recorded in the last book of the Bible:

> His head and hair were white like wool, as white as snow, and his eyes were like blazing fire. His feet were like bronze glowing in a furnace, and his voice was like the sound of rushing waters. In his right hand he held seven stars and out of his mouth came a sharp double-edged sword. His face was like the sun shining in all its brilliance. (Revelation 1:14-16)

Three other eyewitnesses claimed they too had observed a similar supernatural occurrence. They saw Jesus Christ, that powerful enigma of a man, become altered into an essence of spirit, radiating with vibrant light right before them.

> After six days Jesus took with him Peter, James and John the brother of James, and led them up a high mountain by themselves. There he was transfigured before them. His face shone like the sun, and his clothes became as white as the light. (Matthew 17:1)

In all these accounts, God-beings are portrayed as having human shape but also as possessing magnificent celestial power. They are swathed in a radiating, blinding, supernatural light and are seen with faces, arms, and legs. We say they have human form, though actually we have their form. We were designed in their image. Physical form seems rather irrelevant however, with regard to invisible spirit entities. So what other characteristics do we have in common with the Great Ones who created us? Are we just superior animals with godlike shape? How do we differ from the rest of the animal kingdom? What makes us special or unique? It's true that animals and humans have similarly functioning brains that act like the central processing units of computers. In fact some animals have brains that are larger than ours. Yet there are vast differences in the programming found in each of them.

The Gift of Self-Will

As creators the Great Ones must also be the computer programmers. Genesis, the first book in the Bible, states that they created all species according to different kinds, as though those kinds were already determined with different parameters of existence. What if the Great Ones designed each class of living entity with a set of characteristics simply by installing different DNA programs? These are the boundaries in which we live. The brains of animals are programmed according to set patterns of activity. We call these patterns *instinct,* and they determine how animals react to their environments. The problem is they remain stuck in these instinctive programs endlessly. In other words we might train animals, but they cannot decide to train themselves.

We humans were made quite differently, and this is the second important likeness we share with the Great Ones. It seems possible that our creators designed our minds to be like their own. The Great Ones gave us a most important component: self-will, which makes us more godlike by enabling us to make choices. This gift was the awakening of our self-consciousness. It is as though we can program our own computers' defaults. We don't operate by instinct but by reasoning. We were given what scientists are currently trying to achieve with state-of-the-art computer technology—artificial intelligence. This is the unique difference between us and all the other animals. Self-will over our own lives is the major likeness we have to the Great Ones, for truly we are like gods, and we are powerful because of it.

Created to Create

The third unique and important way we resemble our creator is our self-expressive creativity. Gods create, and it is a basic human nature to create also. Animals may only create things when they are programmed to do so. For example, beavers build dams and create ponds. However, although these animals can fell huge trees and build wonderful, intricate homes with underwater entrances, they cannot choose instead to build log cabins.

Humanity's drive to create is innate and compulsive. We relentlessly produce new things, new methods, and even new philosophies. From toddlers' imaginary conversations to the autobiographies of the aged our personal worlds are created. From the small gatherings of tribal herdsmen to empire-building corporations, great dominions have been achieved. We have been given the creative qualities of our designers and the self-will to use them. In a sense we get to create our own lives. We get to choose how we interpret our surroundings and use the data to create the manner in which we want to live. This is the correlation we have to the God Kind. The Great Ones created us to be like their species and to create things on earth. But this still does not answer the question of why we were called into being. What is our purpose for being able to create here?

The account of creation is recorded in the book of Genesis, and perhaps this story from antiquity will give us some answers. What we find are magnificent, all-powerful celestial God-beings that created earthlings in their image along with all the living things in the world around them. The first man and woman, Adam and Eve, were such superbly created human specimens with such perfect physical anatomy that Adam is recorded to have lived to be 930 years of age (Genesis 5:5)! There were likely genes for all colors and kinds of human characteristics in Adam and Eve's makeup, for we are told they were the parents of the entire human race. They lived in utopian Eden, the beautiful and bountiful garden, which is portrayed with fairytale-like splendor. They named all the animals and had dominion over them. It is said that God walked and talked to this man and woman in the garden, teaching them the living laws of the Great Ones. God looked around after the creation of humanity and saw "it was very good" (Genesis 1:31).

Now, if the Great Ones wanted a proliferation of robots—beings that would be merely efficient and productive—then wouldn't this saga have ended right there? But our designers must have wanted something more. What they wanted was unique in all of creation. They desired creatures that looked like them but that would also act like them.

This is not a new concept in theology. Most believers will recognize this truth, though couched in different terminology. Jesus came to announce specifically that we could become children of God—children born not of natural descent, nor of human decision or a husband's will, but born of God (John 1:13). Jesus clearly stated that our purpose is to become part of the God-family. The Great Ones created us in their image and likeness for the sole purpose of procreating themselves in physical form! Just as we find joy in recognizing ourselves in the upturned faces of our small children, so too were we created to delight our celestial creators. In whatever way we can grasp the significance of this truth, it was and is God's purpose for creating humankind. In other words if God has a dream, then we are it!

Capacity to Love

There is another major character trait the Great Ones have and are trying to pass on to us. It is something most difficult to create.

In the clearest of concepts, we are told that "God is love." It is the simplest definition.

> And so we know and rely on the love God has for us. God is love. Whoever lives in love lives in God, and God in him. (1 John 4:16)

Sometimes during encounters of spiritual connection and meditation, the experience of being surrounded by love can indeed be overwhelming. It has been described as peak experiences of undeniable, sheer inner joy. Connected to God's love, we have the confidence to face anything in life through the knowledge that we never stand alone. The Great Ones are *for* us just as all good parents unquestionably love and nurture their small children. They want to see us happy and try to bless us by bringing good things into our lives.

Do we appreciate that there exists such a thing in our reality as pure, wholesome, unselfish giving? God doesn't have to be so kind to us. Do we appreciate the splendor in the beautiful nature of the physical world around us? The creator of our three-dimensional world didn't have to create exquisiteness in living things, down to the smallest colorful detail in a flower stamen. God didn't have to give us a kaleidoscope of seasons—the sunny days of summer, the golden glow of autumn, the striking simplicity of a frosty winter scene, and the sweet birth of spring. God didn't have to give to us a child's innocent laughter, a young woman's beauty, or a close friend's smile of pleasure and mirth. By design the caress of a lifetime partner's wrinkled and gnarled hands doesn't have to warm the heart. But from God's great nature, it was designed in that way. We may indeed choose to align ourselves with these omnipotent, intelligent God-beings, for love is their essence and their nature. Their prime desire is to bathe us in it!

In the biblical definition, God doesn't just love; God *is* love. The word used in the original Greek is *agape*, meaning "affection and benevolence." It comes from the root word *agapeo*, meaning "to love in a moral or social sense." The old-fashioned word *charity* fits this definition too, but to update it perhaps we can say agape love is "having a generous, giving attitude toward others." This type of love originates from our creators with bighearted, bountiful compassion toward us. It is quite different from the love that expects something in return, which we find in so many of our worldly personal relationships. God's agape love is pure and goes far beyond and above what we understand. This unconditional love is so great that God even loves those who are truly unlovable from our perspective. He doesn't have to choose to love; God is love. The plural parts and manifestations of God—they are love. Love is intrinsic to God's nature.

The Great Ones have defined themselves to us using the highest, purest emotion that humankind is capable of understanding. This has to be the foundational bedrock to our whole concept of God. Love is not finite. It cannot be measured or manufactured. It has no physical substance, yet every person alive knows what it is. If God is love, if love makes up the very essence of God, then no negative emotion can exist within God. Hate cannot exist in the presence of God because Love is what defines the parameters of God. This is the most important likeness he wanted to create in us. His plans called for developing progeny capable of loving because, according to the definition of God, that is what God-beings consist of. That is who they are.

However, the desire and capacity to love cannot be mass produced. It is also impossible to create them within robotic creatures. How does one create perfect robots that can love? How could a program be written for robots to love and to have compassion not only for others but for themselves, with healthy pride and happiness? Is love still love when it is forced or commanded? No, by its very nature it cannot be. If one is forced to love, it is not love at all. Love requires us to make a choice. This is the very reason why God had to give us self-will. Many have explained this as having free moral agency. In other words we have minds of our own, self-will that robots cannot have and still be robots under someone's control. Self-will had to be in the blueprints of our design in order to produce godlike progeny. God wants us to feel authentic love and to be able to choose to give love, not just to have instincts or robotically programmed reactions.

Love involves making choices in life—choosing to give out to others rather than to take away from them. It involves a choice of behaving kindly instead of selfishly. Love has to be developed, learned, and it has to be voluntary. Because of the very nature of love, the Great Ones could not instantly create this characteristic in us by fiat, for it is a learned emotional trait of preference.

Designed for Power

What are these Great Ones like, and how would it feel to be one of them? If we're related to their species, what other characteristics might we have? Of course we ought to be powerful! We have been given supreme power to fill and cultivate the earth, to have dominion over the plant and animal kingdoms of our world.

> *Then God said, let us make man in our image, in our likeness, and let them rule over the fish of the sea and the birds of the air, over the livestock, over all the earth, and over all the creatures that move along the ground.*
>
> *...God blessed them and said to them, "Be fruitful and increase in number; fill the earth and subdue it. Rule over the fish of the sea and the birds of the air and over every living creature that moves on the ground." (Genesis 1:26, 28)*

We have been given the authority to subdue the planet in whatever way we choose: to create plains of fertility or dust bowls of wastelands; to harness water for an abundant power supply or to pollute it to poison; to split atoms for energy purposes or for devastating destruction. We have the ability and the motive to train, control, breed, and experiment with all life forms down to the smallest virus and to the very DNA of our own genetic code. How must we appear to the lowly beasts that seem to cringe, stare in awe of us, and run away? We have the means to subdue or kill at our whim even the most ferocious creatures. We must appear to them like earth-gods! And that is what we are. The ancient texts clearly state that God set us apart and gave us dominion over all the terrestrial creatures on our planet.

In the blueprints for the creation of humankind, we can see we are undoubtedly the intended masters in a physical realm of natural beauty. This was always known in ancient wisdom and written down in the old and new collection of our ancient texts.

I said, 'You are "gods"; you are all sons of the Most High.' But you will die like mere men.... (Psalms 82:6)

Jesus answered them, "Is it not written in your Law, 'I have said you are "gods"'? (John 10:34)

There is always a problem with empowerment, however. How do we ensure appropriate use of the power God has given us? Although we are designed to wield power in our world, this godly characteristic could not be fully extended to us. Any source of power can be used to enhance the human condition wonderfully but can also be used selfishly to the detriment of humankind.

Time As a Process

There was a dilemma in producing humans as the God Kind: God could not create us as a finished product. What a paradox! Amazingly, we had to be left incomplete in this aspect so we might desire to learn to love and to wield power appropriately. In infinite intelligence, the Great Ones saw that only a process of development could create these final characteristics. In human terms, that process is called life. God created the dimension of time for us to develop these foundational godlike characteristics; learning how to love and handle power takes time, hence to develop spiritual maturity we are given a lifetime.

And so, the ultimate gifts of time and experiences were given to us, all wrapped up in a lifetime. A well-known folk song uses simple verses of scripture:

> ...a time for everything and a season for every activity under heaven:
>
> a time to be born and a time to die,
>
> a time to plant and a time to uproot,
>
> a time to kill and a time to heal,
>
> a time to tear down and a time to build,
>
> a time to weep and a time to laugh....
>
> a time to keep and a time to throw away,
>
> a time to tear and a time to mend,
>
> a time to be silent and a time to speak,
>
> a time to love and a time to hate,
>
> a time for war and a time for peace. (Ecclesiastes 3:1-8)

Under all the skies of our planet, in all kinds of cultures right now, human reality is being lived. Every conceivable experience exists with infinite options limited only by time and our five senses. We have been given life on a beautiful planet, and we are accountable. The Great Ones don't want just to save us. They want to help us gain spiritual maturity in order to take our place in the celestial order of god-beings. This is their proposal to us, and this is why they created us. It is their intent and the purpose of our existence. Each of us has been given a free ticket to play the game of life with a full spectrum of human conditions and emotions from which to learn. This is life—a gift to us from the Gods!

3
celestial beings
behind the scenes

We have company! Angels are designated
messengers and a subspecies of celestial beings.
A third of the angels resist in deadly opposition,
standing fast against God's plan for humanity
to be given rights to immortality.

Mystical Messengers

Just as there is a vast difference between humankind and the animal kingdom, a wide chasm exists between the echelon of the
Great Ones and our human species. Now that we have a better
understanding of what man is and what God might be, there are
other classes of creatures we need to discuss in order to become
skilled at playing the game of life.

Many portrayals in the Bible of God and other intelligent
beings don't reflect traditional Christian ideas at all. Instead they
make these entities look more like a collection of science-fiction
heroes. These scriptures are not usually the ones discussed in
churches on sunny Sunday mornings, Yet these strange verses
started me wondering what the Christian hype was really all
about.

People who lived during the lifetime of Jesus Christ also wondered what otherworldly entities were all about. The disciple
John was what you would call an eyewitness, and he had been a
close friend of Jesus. Near the end of his life, he was jailed on the
rocky island of Patmos, which was like Alcatraz for exiled criminals. While there he had a vision of what the God Source and his
attendants look like. The things John claimed to see definitely
don't match the traditional picture of God. But imagine what a
scene of power and richness this biblical description would make
if it were turned into a movie:

> At once I was in the Spirit, and there before me was a
> throne in heaven with someone sitting on it. And the
> one who sat there had the appearance of jasper and
> carnelian. A rainbow, resembling an emerald, encircled the
> throne. Surrounding the throne were twenty-four other
> thrones, and seated on them were twenty-four elders.
> They were dressed in white and had crowns of gold on
> their heads. From the throne came flashes of lightning,
> rumblings and peals of thunder....

> *In the center, around the throne, were four living creatures, and they were covered with eyes, in front and in back. The first living creature was like a lion, the second was like an ox, the third had a face like a man, the fourth was like a flying eagle. Each of the four living creatures had six wings and was covered with eyes all around, even under his wings. Day and night, they never stop saying: "Holy, holy, holy is the Lord God Almighty, who was, and is, and is to come." (Revelation 4:2-8)*

This scene sounds as if it comes straight out of some fascinating science-fiction plot, complete with bizarre creatures, but it comes from the last book in the Bible. In this scene great deference was shown to this Lord God Almighty. Even if these celestial beings were only symbolic, why would they all harbor such unprecedented allegiance?

Hundreds of years earlier, the prophet Ezekiel described seeing something very similar by the banks of the Kebar River while he was in exile as a captive in Babylon. This account was mentioned earlier in Chapter One but if we continue to read, it's as though he were seeing a UFO and extremely bizarre, extraterrestrial creatures.

> *I looked, and I saw a windstorm coming out of the north—an immense cloud with flashing lightning and surrounded*

by brilliant light. The centre of the fire looked like glowing metal, and in the fire was what looked like four living creatures. In appearance, their form was that of a man, but each of them had four faces and four wings....

Each of the four had the face of a man, and on the right side each had the face of a lion, and on the left the face of an ox; each also had the face of an eagle.... (Ezekiel 1:4-14)

According to Ezekiel's description, the bizarre creatures also had feet like calves, human hands under their wings, and were integrated with moving wheels which could lift off from the ground. They seemed to move by means of "a wheel intercepting a wheel"; "they sparkled like chrysolite" and the wheels were "full of eyes all around" (Ezekiel 1:16-18). This experience was so real to Ezekiel that he dedicated his life as a priest to warn the Israelite nation of impending national disaster.

Later he had a second spiritual encounter with the same vivid and memorable celestial beings (Ezekiel 8:1-4). These creatures were called *cherubim*; we know them now as angels. Some fifteen hundred years earlier, they had been represented in the instructions to build the Ark of the Covenant for God: images of cherubs were to be hammered out in gold and set at the ends on the cover of the Ark, which later held the Ten Commandments.

Even more intriguing is that from the very beginning, there were celestial creatures named cherubim who guarded the gate to the Tree of Life after Adam and Eve were exiled from the paradise of the Garden of Eden (Genesis 3:24). I find it so fascinating that these strange, living species appear from the beginning of these ancient passages to the very last chapter. Are we to write off all these descriptions as imaginary?

Of the sixty-six books in the Bible, thirty-four mention angels. Since we are taking the Bible as an important source of information on spiritual reality, we may want to accept that these creatures do exist. But what are angels? Where do they fit in? What is their purpose for existence?

The word *angel* simply means "messenger," according to Bible concordances and Greek dictionaries. A messenger is one who is sent with an announcement. When God wills something to occur, it is put into effect sometimes in this way:

> *The decision is announced by messengers, the holy ones declare the verdict, so that the living may know that the Most High is sovereign over the kingdoms of men.... (Daniel 4:17)*

Angels are sent out with messages to initiate the action that God desires to happen. Their function is like that of ambassadors to foreign countries—and so they are! Many paragraphs in the Old Testament start with the words "the angel of the Lord went before him...." Other passages say, "...the angel of the Lord said unto him...." This was the notification that the prophets were about to receive information God wanted us to know. Even in the New Testament the angels act as messengers. God sends them into our realm to carry out his will.

Throughout the Bible different angels announce messages of coming events according to God's great plans. How does God identify what is about to happen? The Great Ones don't exist in spans of time as we know it because they have created time for us to live in so that we might develop our spirituality. They live both in and out of time. God knows everything that is going to happen because without the limits of time, anything that is going to happen, in a sense, has already happened—it just *is*. When God declares it, it is created. So then we can view angels as messengers who come from the timeless realm of eternity to our physical, human timeline.

When speaking of angels, we use the pronoun *it* because although they are intelligent beings, they are not male or female. There are no descriptions in the Bible of the gender of angels. They cannot marry or procreate, but they are immortal (Luke 20:36). They were not made in God's image or likeness in the same way humans were—nor can they create things on their own with godlike autonomy. They can only travel into our reality with messages for us from God, administering what they are commissioned to do. They are servants, but they are powerful, formed from spirit, and immortal, whereas we may only be given immortality after a biological life.

Different kinds of angelic beings are mentioned in the ancient writings. Recall, for example, the strange and bizarre-looking cherubim (which is the plural of *cherub*). The Bible also speaks of the *seraphim* (the plural form of seraph). What these entities look like in spirit form is not that important, since it may be inexplicable to our merely human physical senses. But the fact that special titles were used to differentiate between these creatures may suggest their characteristics are unique within the angelic realm.

At least three angels are mentioned by name: the archangel Michael, another called Gabriel, and Lucifer, whom we will discuss later. Michael and Gabriel seem to be of higher status than the rest. Just as there are billions of people inhabiting the earth, there are innumerable multitudes of angels in the spirit realm. Here is an interesting passage portraying that:

Then I looked and heard the voice of many angels, numbering thousands upon thousands, and ten thousand times ten thousand. They encircled the throne and the living creatures and the elders. (Revelation 5:11; also see Psalms 68:17)

Clearly there are a few different celestial beings in this scene from the heavenly realm: angels, living creatures, elders, and the one on the throne.

When Jesus Christ died on the cross, he could have appealed to his celestial father to send more than twelve legions of angels to attend him (Matthew 26:53). That would have been more than sixty-four thousand angels, according to how the Roman army organized legions at the time. Angels are usually invisible to us because they exist in the spirit realm, which is what we might call an alternate reality or a different dimension. On occasion, however, they are capable of taking on visible form.

There is an appealing and humorous example of this back in ancient scriptures. A man named Balaam was going on a trip to negotiate with adversaries, and apparently God wanted to use him in order to write a different kind of history. Three times an angel appeared to the donkey Balaam rode and stood in the way to get Balaam to turn around. When the animal saw the angel blocking the way, he refused to move, and Balaam beat her severely. The third time the donkey bolted into a wall, crushing Balaam's foot. So what happened next? God and the angels must have a sense of humor, because it soon appeared to Balaam that the donkey was talking to him! Whether this incident was a clear voice in Balaam's mind or an audible voice, you will have to decide, but here is the account from the written word:

> Then the Lord opened the donkey's mouth, and she said
> to Balaam, "What have I done to you to make you beat
> me these three times?"
>
> Balaam answered the donkey, "You have made a fool of
> me! If I had a sword in my hand, I would kill you right now."
>
> The donkey said to Balaam, "Am I not your own donkey,
> which you have always ridden, to this day? Have I been in
> the habit of doing this to you?"
>
> "No," he said. Then the Lord opened Balaam's eyes, and
> he saw the angel of the Lord standing in the road with
> his sword drawn. So he bowed low and fell facedown.
> (Numbers 22:28–31)

In another passage in the Old Testament, God was trying to communicate with a man named Gideon, and he sent an angel as his messenger. The angel told Gideon to go out to battle and save the nation of Israel. He heard the message, but he questioned how he could save Israel, as his clan was the weakest—and he was the least in his clan. He didn't quite believe the message was really from God and asked for some kind of verification.

> "If now I have found favor in your eyes, give me a sign that it is really you talking to me."
>
> When Gideon realized that it was the angel of the Lord, he exclaimed, "Ah, Sovereign Lord! I have seen the angel of the Lord face to face!"
>
> But the Lord said to him, "Peace! Do not be afraid. You are not going to die." (Judges 6:17, 22-23)

A better-known verse in the New Testament states that an angel became visible to the women at the tomb of Jesus after he had died and been buried:

> There was a violent earthquake, for an angel of the Lord came down from heaven and, going to the tomb, rolled back the stone and sat on it. His appearance was like lightning, and his clothes were white as snow. The guards were so afraid of him that they shook and became like dead men. The angel said to the women, "Do not be afraid, for I know that you are looking for Jesus, who was crucified. He is not here; he has risen, just as he said. Come and see the place where he lay. Then go quickly and tell his disciples: 'He has risen from the dead and is going ahead of you into Galilee. There you will see him.' Now I have told you." (Matthew 28:2-7)

Celestial beings giving us messages have been sighted many times in our history. They have carried on actual conversations with men and women. We are even instructed to be hospitable to those we don't know—because they might be angels:

> Do not forget to entertain strangers, for by so doing some people have entertained angels without knowing it. (Hebrews 13:1-3)

From the 291 times that angels are referred to in our sourcebook, it seems their physical appearance usually causes awe and fear in human observers. It is indeed a paranormal encounter! They are described as servants of the God Source, as "mighty ones who do his bidding, who obey his word" (Ps. 103:20). If an angel visits someone, there is little doubt that person has had an encounter with a celestial entity—one that is alien to usual human experience. The truth is real angels can be big and scary rather than little or cute. Angel paraphernalia and figurines do not represent the reality of these celestial beings. Angels are powerful; they require our acknowledgment and respect.

In the Western world, many people find it so easy to ridicule and despise any person with authority. We even swear by and slander the powerful personalities of God and Jesus Christ, but it isn't so in the spirit realm.

> *This is especially true of those who follow the corrupt desire of the sinful nature and despise authority. Bold and arrogant, these men are not afraid to slander celestial beings; yet even angels, although they are stronger and more powerful, do not bring slanderous accusations against such beings in the presence of the Lord. But these men blaspheme in matters they do not understand. (2 Peter 2:10-12)*

It seems we should give high regard to celestial beings. Yet this does not mean we are to worship angels, for this is not required or even permitted:

> *Do not let anyone who delights in false humility and the worship of angels disqualify you for the prize. Such a person goes into great detail about what he has seen, and his unspiritual mind puffs him up with idle notions. (Colossians 2:18)*

In other words angels are not our role models. We don't have to be afraid of them or idolize them. They are to be respected as powerful celestial entities. They are different from us, but they are not necessarily above us. In fact we are told:

> *"Do you not know that we will judge angels? How much more the things of this life!" (1 Corinthians 6:3)*

Here's another interesting portrayal of what angelic entities are like and how they sometimes show themselves to us. Once again this was set in the land of early Palestine. A wife of a herdsman was given a message that she would become pregnant, and she was overjoyed.

> Then the woman went to her husband and told him, "A man of God came to me. He looked like an angel of God, very awesome. I didn't ask him where he came from, and he didn't tell me his name. But he said to me, 'You will conceive and give birth to a son.'" (Judges 13:6-7)

The man, Manoah, and his wife later encountered the strange being again and invited him to dinner even though they were not sure who he was. The angel refused the food but suggested they make it a sacrificial offering.

> Then Manoah inquired of the angel of the Lord, "What is your name, so that we may honor you when your word comes true?"
>
> He replied, "Why do you ask my name? It is beyond understanding." Then Manoah took a young goat, together with the grain offering, and sacrificed it on a rock to the Lord. And the Lord did an amazing thing while Manoah and his wife watched: As the flame blazed up from the altar toward heaven, the angel of the Lord ascended in the flame. Seeing this, Manoah and his wife fell with their faces to the ground... The woman gave birth to a boy and named him Samson. (Judges 13:17-20, 24)

What is interesting is this angel didn't want to be honoured. When they asked his name, the angel stated it was simply "beyond understanding." Instead the messenger encouraged them to worship only God. From this it seems that an angel sent from God doesn't need acknowledgement or recognition; the angel is just the messenger.

Powerful Angels

Since the task of angels is to administer what God wants done, angels can be sent to help us.

> For he will command his angels concerning you to guard you in all your ways.... (Psalms 91:11)
>
> Are not all angels ministering spirits sent to serve those who will inherit salvation? (Hebrews 1:14)

It is also true that they are commissioned especially to look after young children. Jesus gave us these instructions:

> See that you do not look down on one of these little ones. For I tell you that their angels in heaven always see the face of my Father in heaven. (Matthew 18:10)

Isn't it comforting to know that there are angels all around us, and that we individually have angels who guard and guide us? A whole other dimension coexists with our reality, and angels seem to be involved intimately in our lives.

Down through biblical history, there are a multitude of examples of this. A powerful angel rescued Shadrach, Meshach, and Abednego from a fiery furnace (Daniel 3:25-28). A commanding angel shut the mouths of the lions for Daniel when he was thrown in their den (Daniel 6:22). When one of the first passionate Christian leaders was thrown into jail for spreading the good news about Jesus, a strong and influential angel rescued him (Acts 12:6-11).

However, angels do not do these miracles. They are simply ministering spirits sent to those who believe in God, because that is what God intends for them to do. The authority and power comes from God. They were made to administer the actions he articulated. They are only his assistants and do his bidding.

In the story about Balaam and the donkey, the angel was able to halt the man's progress, and the angel said something after the incident that was at first shocking to read. He calmly stated:

> I have come here to oppose you because your path is a reckless one before me. The donkey saw me and turned away from me these three times. If she had not turned away, I would certainly have killed you by now, but I would have spared her. (Numbers 22:32–33)

The character of angels is fascinating! This one seemed to become impatient with the man and saw an injustice done to the animal. In other words the angel didn't have loyalty to the man but to his mission.

Scripture seems to indicate that angels do not have to care for us unconditionally, as we would desire to believe. No scripture talks about loving angels. The ability to love as we know it may not even be in their makeup, for there is no indication that they were designed in God's likeness. God is love, and angels are sent to administer acts of love, but this does not ascertain that the angels themselves feel love in a human sort of way at all.

In fact angels can also be sent out to stop human action from continuing, and this can actually lead to human deaths. There are, unfortunately, numerous examples of terrifying angels, including this example:

> That night the angel of the LORD went out and put to death a hundred and eighty-five thousand men in the Assyrian camp. When the people got up the next morning—there were all the dead bodies! (2 Kings 19:34-36)
>
> So the Lord sent a plague on Israel from that morning until the end of the time designated, and seventy thousand of the people from Dan to Beersheba died. When the angel stretched out his hand to destroy Jerusalem, the LORD was grieved because of the calamity and said to the angel who was afflicting the people, "Enough! Withdraw your hand." (2 Samuel 24:15)

These passages of ancient scripture don't match up with our current images of small, angelic, childlike icons at all, do they? The presence and purpose of angels on earth have been skewed by misunderstanding. Our sourcebook reveals that powerful angels will also assist with the task of setting up God's kingdom at the end of our age. It states that:

> As the weeds are pulled up and burned in the fire, so it
> will be at the end of the age. The Son of Man will send
> out his angels, and they will weed out of his kingdom
> everything that causes sin and all who do evil. (Matthew
> 13:40-41)
>
> This is how it will be at the end of the age. The angels
> will come and separate the wicked from the righteous.
> (Matthew 13:49)

It is important to understand that angels are not always going to be there for us. There is a multitude of powerful angels that don't even like us. They have banded together and are actually at war with us.

Despicable Angels

Throughout the ancient textbook, there are many references to another significant angel. This angel has many names, but if we can personify evil, it is known commonly as the devil or Satan. The name Satan simply means *adversary*. This powerful, immoral character has also been called Lucifer, the great dragon, the father of lies, the accuser, and many other names. In contemporary terms he has been referred to as the dark force. Throughout the Bible much is written about this corrupt and destructive higher-level angel.

Back in ancient biblical history, the prophet Ezekiel gave an historic account of the king of Tyre. This king was being influenced by evil, and the description described Satan:

> *You were the seal of perfection, full of wisdom and perfect in beauty. You were in Eden, the garden of God.... You were anointed as a guardian cherub for so I ordained you.... You were blameless in your ways from the day you were created till wickedness was found in you. (Ezekiel 28:12-15)*

Evidently, from the last sentence, this angel was created. We can assume that angels in general were designed and created as a celestial species prior to the existence of earthly humankind. The Great Ones are beyond our created universe; they are beings who have no beginning or end. However, this particular cherub was a created angel who rebelled against his creator.

> *You were filled with violence, you sinned.... Your heart became proud on account of your beauty and you corrupted your wisdom because of your splendor. So I threw you to the earth.... (Ezekiel 28:16-17)*

The king of Tyre was not in the Garden of Eden; he was not anointed as a guardian cherub, nor could he be thrown to the earth, so it has always been assumed that this passage is an analogy for some great celestial event. Another version in the last book of Revelation seems to further the explanation:

> *And there was war in heaven. Michael and his angels fought against the dragon, and the dragon and his angels fought back. But he was not strong enough, and they lost their place in heaven. The great dragon was hurled down—that ancient serpent called the devil, or Satan, who leads the whole world astray. He was hurled to the earth, and his angels with him. (Revelation 12:7-9)*
>
> *His tail swept a third of the stars out of the sky and flung them to the earth. (Revelation 12:4)*

These passages are not out of a science-fiction movie script. They seem to be descriptive explanations of great spiritual warfare that actually occurred in another realm of existence. Most significant and fascinating is that Satan was thrown down to earth in both these passages. It is this one angel of evil "who leads the whole world astray." This accounts for how Satan and the angels who followed him came to be on earth. These are the rebellious spirit entities known as *demons*.

The idea of a devil and demonic spirits coexisting with us, even in a spiritual realm separated from our physical perception, is hard to accept for most people, perhaps because we are so disturbed by the very idea. The presence of God and loving angels is much easier to accept. Perhaps we don't need to personify the negative entities with human characteristics at all but simply see them as dark forces of power. For they are not new; they have always been here. These dark entities are simply angels gone askew.

We may not see or recognize the presence of demons or their influence upon us, but their purpose is to thwart our efforts to align ourselves with the Great Ones and be given immortality. The scripture above states that Satan "leads the whole world astray." Here is another verse that validates his activity on earth:

> ...*the god of this age has blinded the minds of unbelievers, so that they cannot see the light of the gospel of the glory of Christ....* (2 Corinthians 4:4)

Lucifer, the god of our world now, and his demonic cohorts do exist. This other-dimensional, dark force seeks control and attempts to blind our minds to everything of the spirit realm. He definitely doesn't want us to see him as an actual negative force within our reality. He wishes to remain invisible, and to stay in disguise in order to manipulate us. That is why it's not very popular to believe in a devil. He has the modern world believing he is only a cartoon character: a cute, little, red imp with a pitchfork and a tail. If we don't recognize or accept his existence, who are we going to blame when things go wrong?

He wants us to blame God, of course. That's why he doesn't want us to take his existence seriously. In other words he has led us with blinding subtlety to believe that God is in charge of this world in which we live. Then we naturally wonder why God has made such a mess of it. That's a typical example of how Satan works; it's his mode of operation.

War against Man

Satan and his demonic angels operate against us for their own agenda, and we are all influenced by these negative forces whether we realize it or not. Paul cautions us not to argue about godly things with others who don't believe spiritual matters but to be gentle to the opponents who do not have the knowledge of the truth so that:

> *...they will come to their senses and escape from the trap of the devil, who has taken them captive to do his will. (2 Timothy 2:26)*

The book of Job also implies that Satan's overall intent is to turn God against us. In a strange conversation, Satan challenged God over the integrity of one human being called Job. God thought very highly of this man and declared to Satan:

> *There is no one on earth like him; he is blameless and upright, a man who fears God and shuns evil. And he still maintains his integrity, though you incited me against him to ruin him without any reason. (Job 2:3)*

It is as though God was defending our human value in the celestial realm while all Satan wanted to do was destroy Job.

The animosity between the demonic angels and us started long before the time of Job. When the Great Ones made human beings, they gave us dominion over our own planet to rule over every living creature—to "fill the earth and subdue it" (Genesis 1:28). Yet, as discussed previously, Satan had been exiled to earth. Would he want to hand over his authority to powerless, human creatures of mortal flesh? Made in the image and likeness of the Great Ones, humankind was also made with the potential to become godlike children. Even the angels had never been invited to be children of God, but were only created to be ministering spirits. Perhaps this is why Satan and a third of all the other angels rebelled and mutinied—they were irate at the thought that mere mortals would have these opportunities.

In the Garden of Eden, there was a symbolic, sinister snake along with the choice of two trees (Genesis 3:1-14). Could it have been Satan, this same fallen, despicable angel, in disguise as the serpent? In *Strong's Hebrew Dictionary*, the Hebrew word for serpent in this verse is *nachash*, meaning "to hiss or to whisper a spell, to prognosticate." This certainly fits a description of what Satan does. Twice in the book of Revelation, Satan is also referred to as the "ancient serpent" (Revelation 12:9, 20:2), and the original garden story of creation seems the likely reference.

An ancient serpent urged Adam and Eve to go against the rules of the Great Ones and eat the fruit of the tree of the knowledge of good and evil. God had told them, "Don't eat it and don't touch it." But the serpent character came and told his first lie to them:

> *"You will not surely die...but you will be like God, knowing good and evil." (Genesis 3:4-5)*

God had told them they would die if they ate it, and Satan said they wouldn't die. The first-created man and woman decided they didn't want to do what God said. They wanted to decide for themselves what was right. They believed the lie. The result was to be cursed, denied immortality, and kicked out of the paradise garden (Genesis 3:6-23).

In this very first attack on man, the adversary appeared completely successful. The devil realized it would be easy to manipulate us, and he put his egotistical game plan into action. I realize we are probably talking about huge celestial forces in action behind our human history, but let's put this into finite human terms we can more easily understand. It was Satan, who was kicked out of heaven to begin with and thrown down to earth according to scriptural understanding. Then, in the garden, he tried to seduce and pull the first two humans into this rebellion against God. We too ended up being kicked out of paradise!

How does Satan influence us so easily? His chief mode of operation is to give us false messages. Remember, delivering messages is what angels were designed to do. Satan and his angels are in rebellion against God, so his lies to us are always dark and negative messages. They appeal to our wants, desires, and self-pity. He uses these subtle messages to turn our own thinking processes against us. He works through subtlety and half truths. By manipulating us to believe that his lies are the truth, Satan is able to play us like puppets on the stage of life.

Our best line of defense is not to buy into the lie. To prevent a negative mindset, it is necessary to continually remind ourselves: "Don't buy the lie." However, all this happens so cunningly it's almost under our threshold of cognizance. We have an amazing capacity to accept the status quo in our lives as the norm no matter how negative, immoral, or bizarre it gets. The results of believing negative messages are overwhelmingly destructive to us and to humanity in general. We internalize the lies and create limited parameters within which we live.

Although violence may be present all over the earth, our war is really not with one another. Other people are not the enemy.

> *Our struggle is not against flesh and blood, but against the rulers, against the authorities, against the powers of this dark world and against the spiritual forces of evil in the heavenly realm. (Philippians 6:12)*

Let's not underestimate Satan's power. He is in charge of the dark forces that cause violence and hatred in our world. He makes us think we are at war against one another. The truth is that Satan is at war with human beings.

Regardless of nationality, we are all under control and siege by this great negative, dark force. We are captives; he has kidnapped humanity. Even now he hunts out weaknesses and attacks each of us, trying to make us blind to the awesome and powerful connection we have to the Great Ones. The disciple Peter gave us this warning:

> *Be self-controlled and alert. Your enemy the devil prowls around like a roaring lion looking for someone to devour.*
> *(1 Peter 5:8)*

In our game of life, this dark, incorrigible force is the real enemy to humanity—an adversary who, at all costs, doesn't want us to become powerfully connected with God. This force of destructive darkness is constantly working against us and has deceived the whole world (Revelation 12:9). He succeeds because very few humans have yet to acknowledge his presence. Yet, his existence is very much on our planet.

> *As for you, you were dead in your transgressions and sins, in which you used to live when you followed the ways of this world and of the ruler of the kingdom of the air, the spirit who is now at work in those who are disobedient.*
> *(Ephesians 2:1-2)*

Satan is the spirit at work in those who don't honour the standards set out by the Great Ones. How does he con us? He comes in under the radar, through a medium in which we all exist. As the above verse says, Satan is "the ruler of the kingdom of the air"! He uses the very air around us to poison our minds with negative and destructive thought.

It sounds as if there is a negative force field transmitting over the earth in the air. Doesn't that sound strange? It really isn't so outrageous, though. We have sound waves, ultraviolet rays, X-rays, television waves, and laser beams. We can see things happen instantaneously from thousands of miles away via satellite. Through the hologram technique, we can even make three-dimensional pictures in the air move and talk as though they are real. Well, suppose there is also a network of invisible, negative-energy bands that feed into and bombard us constantly, like a stubborn violinist playing a prolonged wrong note to destroy the harmony of life. To any mind unfortunate enough to be tuned into that channel, it could become a high-pitched scream of hate and chaos. When these usually subtle energies shriek at a high enough frequency, we physically become aware of them as stressful agitation.

Can you remember a time when you sensed danger as a gut instinct or a chill up your spine? Your physical body recognized the presence of an aura of evil even when your mind attempted to reason it away. This force is real and far more sinister than we want to acknowledge. Perhaps that is why, when we quiet our minds with meditation or prayer, we are able to tune out the negative waves and connect to a more positive, godlike channel.

I remember years ago, when traveling in a time of political unrest in Chiapas, Mexico, we had many miles to the next town and pitch darkness was already upon us. Rather than continue to drive through the night on the small, rough road, we felt it was less dangerous to camp out in our tent on a side lane, and continue in the morning. Once inside the tent, an aura of disquieting evil overtook me, and I lit a single candle and thought about God's protection for quite some time before I could crawl under the covers.

Then, in the middle of the night, angry voices woke us, commanding us in Spanish to open the door—"Abre la puerta!" We could hear footsteps and rustling sounds on each side of the tent. As I slowly unzipped the fabric opening, my eyes locked on the barrel of a black handgun and the dark, menacing face of a man. Fear pulsated through me; thoughts of rape and slaughter filled my mind. Carrying automatic rifles, they gathered our belongings and herded us into our vehicle, then forced us to drive between their trucks to what they said was a safer place.

It was! We had been rescued and taken to a border checkpoint by the Federales. These agents were stationed in the area and fighting against the guerrilla Zapatistas, who were at that time rather violent. And it was no wonder I had felt an aura of evil before blowing out the candle— as rash, unaware tourists, we had camped on the driveway going into the ranchero headquarters of one of the notorious guerrilla leaders. Days later, in the town of Comitán de Dominguez, we read of other tourists who had not been so lucky while visiting the area. They had been robbed and found dead in a ditch with their necks slashed open. In our case the federal agents had seen a very small light off the side of the main road, which resulted in their finding us before other darker forces came upon us.

Do you ever wonder what makes horror movies and dark fiction so appealing to some people? We have been manipulated to create the scariest, most terrifying horror scripts because demons want us to agree with them that we are puny and powerless and things are horrible. They want us to exalt and fear them in our minds. Unlike the loyal celestial angels sent from God, demons want their own recognition and power. They screech and demand that we give them attention. And when we buy into their lies and negative perceptions, we honor them by becoming fearful.

Fear, in fact, is their best weapon against us. Fear is actually giving allegiance to Satan. Our fear robs our confidence and severely limits us, which is exactly what the demons want. In this way fear is a subconscious form of Satan worship.

Do you know that demons were not given humanlike power? They were not made in the image of God, with the ability to create through self-will like we were. Demons are only fallen angels, created to carry out the words given to them. They have no power to create anything on their own in the physical realm of planet earth. This is our world, and we were made to interface with it by activating thoughts within our minds.

This means anything demons do on our planet must be done through us. They accomplish this by working through our thought processes. We were given the ability to activate choice in order to create wonderful living experiences and positive realities for our lives. However, demons can distort our human reality by influencing our perceptions of our world. When they convince us with negative messages, we create destruction out of our own fear! The evil ones can create nothing in our lives that we don't think of ourselves. That's why they whisper negatives to us—we create it by believing it. We buy the lie and accept it as our reality. Because we are godlike, we create these things in our lives. That is the real horror of the situation.

There are many reasons why Satan is called our adversary. He's at war with us because we can create our own kind. The number of angelic hosts in heaven and rebellious demons is unknown, but we human beings are very good at producing more of ourselves. Since angels can't reproduce, it is interesting to consider the possibility that as the centuries go by, perhaps we are outnumbering them.

Satan is antagonistic toward us because we can create goodness. So he tries to use our minds to create the terrible and evil perversions that are destroying us. For example he has badly distorted the purpose of sex, which was designed to be a beautiful sharing and giving of oneself in unity with another. He twists sexuality so much that it results in violent crimes that virtually rampage in every nation. He destroys the innocent young with rape and incest and then convinces them they are only good enough for prostitution. He uses people to hurt other people, and in doing so causes them to hurt themselves. This is truly an evil power we deal with in our daily lives. Every kind of perversion possible is now present in our "advanced" civilization.

In modern culture Satan keeps us numb to our intelligence using the sitcom level of TV entertainment and our frantic work and play activity in the pursuit of materialism and pleasure. Taking advantage of our need for instant gratification, he produces horrifying drug addictions to destroy all ability to think and reason. He wants more than ever to impair our minds since our real power lies in our thinking capacity.

I believe he is also insanely jealous of the potential for intelligence we have and even tries to distort our thinking processes with all kinds of mental disorders. In fact his invisible presence and influence may be behind much of the mental illness we find so difficult to treat. Twenty-six verses in the New Testament speak about unfortunate people being demon-possessed because of having impure spirits. We don't call it that today, but the truth doesn't change because of terminology.

All this happens in privileged Western cultures that have most of the world's wealth. In the third world, sadly, intelligence is limited by starvation and disease often brought on by the greed of ruling classes and richer nations feeding off them. This is a true picture of the status of Satan's operations in our world and what he programs on his negative channels in the air.

This has been a very difficult chapter to write. Satan's powerful essence has been here with me as I write, and it is with you right now as you read. He can be anywhere. Perhaps you've seen alien invaders in science-fiction movies taking over people's bodies and minds. Well, this concept is not new. It's been happening for centuries and centuries. That dark, hideous power has already existed throughout all of man's history, and it is still at work today. Satan's underlings feed off our pain, our misery. In a sense they take pleasure from and derive energy from it. C. S. Lewis painted a vivid and sometimes humorous description of this in his book *The Screwtape Letters.*

The devil's depravity is astounding to me. Yet it is only when we are able to understand our enemy that we can learn how to resist him.

Reason for Evil

Why do we have this dark power on our planet? Why hasn't God eliminated these despicable demons already? We don't understand how they were allowed to get established on earth but they will be ousted. It will happen in the future, as stated in God's great celestial plan for humankind. But, astoundingly, the dark powers in man's existence may have a purpose right now.

God did not want to create robots, so he gave us free choice, right? But have you considered that for this to happen, there had to be options for us to choose from? The Great Ones want us to know how precious human joy is, but how can we know we're happy if we've never shed tears of sorrow? Would we be able to recognize peace if we had never experienced war? Would we put a value on love if we had never experienced being unloved?

If we live in misery, we are usually motivated to find answers to get out of it. The misery inherent in evil drives us to overcome it and to strive toward self-perfection. Evil actually creates the need to find direction from a higher source. Yet evil does not originate from the higher source; it is outside of God. It is good to keep in mind that two thirds of the angelic beings aligned themselves with God as ministering angels. There may be a horde of demon spirit entities against us, but there are twice as many angelic entities working invisibly within our reality and ready to assist us.

The bottom line in the whole matter is this: the existence of the enemy provides an opportunity for humans to develop personal spiritual maturity. Spiritual knowledge is gained from the process of living, and a lifetime is given to each of us so we might learn to value and study the ways of the Great Ones. Sometimes only a short life will be necessary to do this. But we have been given the gifts of life and choice, and we are all going through a spiritual birthing and refining process.

Let's make no mistake: the Great Ones see our misery. They mourn for us, and they want to ransom us from earth's dark and destructive adversary, to save our species from it. That is the goal specifically provided for us in the great blueprints, for there is a most important intervention they have set up for the human race—a way out of the physical muck of our world and an entry into their celestial realm.

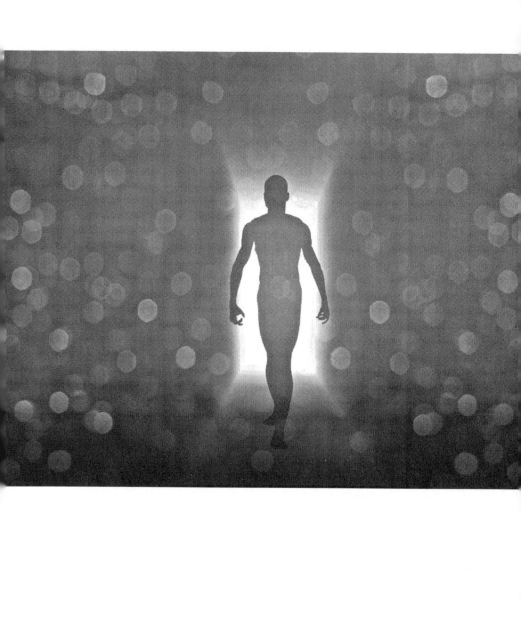

4

the fusion of human and god-being

Jesus Christ is defined as a unique hybrid, a fusion of the human species and the celestial God species.

An Impossible Conception

So far, we have discussed the celestial race of the Great Ones and the origins of the human species, but we have only briefly touched upon the main character in a story that reads like a science-fiction thriller.

Who is the Jesus that Western religions venerate so much? What was he really? Most agree he was a man who existed in flesh and blood in and around Jerusalem in the beginning of the first century AD. He came to be known to humanity as Jesus Christ. *Jesus* is a unique word; it literally means "God saves." The word

Christ means "the one anointed with power, or one touched with a supernatural ability." Christ was not Jesus's last name but a reference to his power!

So then, the phrase *Jesus Christ* literally means "God saves with metaphysical power." The very meaning of his name is even fascinating. Jesus Christ clearly stated that he was "not of this world" (John 8:23) but clothed with metaphysical presence and power. He is the real-life superhero of our science-fiction thriller. He is the extraordinary enigma who changed the course of human history. The moral principles he set forth have had an influence upon every nation.

Among all those who believe in a god, what sets Christians apart? The word *Christian* simply means "one who is a follower of the Christ, the one anointed with power." Therefore, by extension, a Christian has to believe in metaphysical power.

Jesus Christ made some outrageous claims regarding his connection to the celestial species. He claimed to be from God, and he performed astonishing miracles, but he certainly didn't physically appear to be a god. If Jesus was a God-being, how did he put on flesh and become human? He claimed he would live again after he died, but how does a human put on immortality? Yet, he wasn't like an angel either. We find that the angels were instructed to worship him:

> ...When God brings his firstborn into the world, he says,
>
> "Let all God's angels worship him." (Hebrews 1:6)

Jesus's followers seemed to realize exactly what he was and called him the "Son of God" (Matthew 3:17). This term is used forty times in the books of the New Testament. Jesus spoke with humility, yet claimed God as his real father.

> *Jesus replied, "If I glorify myself, my glory means nothing.*
>
> *My Father, whom you claim as your God, is the one who*
>
> *glorifies me." (John 8:54)*

What was this enigma of a man actually? Did the celestial God Source really have a part human, physical son? How could that even be possible?

The book of Luke captures the birth story from a mother's perspective. It begins with an angelic being, which appeared and talked to Mary, an innocent, young Jewish woman. She must have been a brave person, for she encountered metaphysical things! The angel spoke to her:

> *"Do not be afraid, Mary, you have found favor with God.*
>
> *You will be with child and give birth to a son, and you are*
>
> *to give him the name Jesus." (Luke 1:30-31)*

Remember, the name Jesus means "God saves with metaphysical power." From birth, Jesus was named for his specific purpose in life. The angel also told Mary:

> *He will be great and will be called the Son of the Most*
>
> *High. The Lord God will give him the throne...his kingdom*
>
> *will never end. (Luke 1:32-33)*

This was a fantastic prediction! In Mary's human curiosity and practicality, some questions naturally came to mind:

> *"How will this be," Mary asked the angel, "since I am a virgin?"*
>
> *The angel answered, "The Holy Spirit will come upon you, and the power of the Most High will overshadow you. So the holy one to be born will be called the Son of God... Nothing is impossible with God." (Luke 1:34-35, 37)*

The real marvel of this story is Mary's courage and faith to believe what this strange, shining celestial being told her. She believed so much in this paranormal, mystical experience that she was willing to let some kind of sacred Spirit presence "come upon" and "overshadow" her. We are told, "what is conceived in her is from the Holy Spirit" (Matthew 1:20). I can't help but wonder just what kind of encounter and connection that was for her!

Mary also had to consider the consequences of getting pregnant, if this did really take place. She was already engaged to a young man named Joseph. How was she going to explain to him and convince him what had happened? She also ran a great risk of being cast out of her strict Jewish society. Unwed pregnant girls were sometimes stoned to death in her culture. But Mary's faith and allegiance toward her very personal God was greater than all other qualms and concerns. Her belief system was not a social religion but an exciting, individual sort of spirituality! Ultimately she believed in the words of a celestial messenger.

> *"I am the Lord's servant," Mary answered. "May it be to me as you have said." Then the angel left her. (Luke 1:38)*

Mary gives us one of the great examples of real faith in action. Real faith is to believe emphatically and implicitly that what we are told is true. Yes, Mary loved God, as was part of her cultural religion, but she loved with all her heart and with all her mind. It is in tribute to the existence of this kind of faith that I felt compelled to write *The Celestial Proposal.* How wonderful to believe fearlessly in the supernatural, as this young woman did thousands of years ago!

A Unique Hybrid

Until the twentieth century, when artificial insemination and test-tube babies became a reality, the birth of Jesus from a virgin was an even harder concept to grasp. If Mary did not get pregnant by having intercourse with a human man, how did she become pregnant? If we accept the words from the Bible in a literal sense, she must have been somehow artificially inseminated by a celestial being from another world and a different dimension of existence. Jesus Christ was not just *filled* with a godly spirit but was *conceived* by Spirit; he was actually fathered by a "Most High" otherworldly entity (Matthew 1:20). Having this living, all-powerful celestial God Source as a kind of genetic father is what made Jesus unique from all other human beings.

Mary was approached to become the mother of Jesus because of her integrity and her purity, but most of all because of her faith. When she went to visit her relative, Elizabeth, God's messages were confirmed within her mind. She found validation in the miraculous things that were also happening to Elizabeth. By this time in her pregnancy, Mary was so full of inner joy that she sang songs of love, respect, and praise to God (Luke 1:46-55). She accepted this seemingly impossible conception. Her son was fathered by an invisible, omnipotent celestial being and ultimately he would become king over an unending kingdom. He was to be called the Prince of Peace, as foretold in the Hebrew sacred scrolls (Isaiah 9:6). Her son was to be the messiah, the deliverer who would save humanity and reign over all the earth! Fully accepting her strange situation and these grandiose predictions, she recognized that above all women; she was highly honored (Luke 1:46-49).

So what about Joseph, her fiancé? What did he make of it all? When Mary was found to be pregnant, Joseph did not want to expose her to public disgrace and danger. He was greatly concerned until another angel came to him in a dream and said:

"Joseph, son of David, do not be afraid to take Mary home as your wife, because what is conceived in her is from the Holy Spirit. She will give birth to a son, and you are to give him the name "Jesus" because he will save his people from their sins." (Matthew 1:20-21)

In the dream, Joseph remembered an ancient passage of the Hebrew scrolls that read:

The virgin will be with child and will give birth to a son, and they will call him "Immanuel," which means, "God with us." (Isaiah 7:14)

When Joseph woke up, he did what the angel of the Lord had commanded him and took Mary home as his wife. But he had no union with her until she gave birth to a son. And he gave him the name Jesus." (Matthew 1:23-25)

Mary and Joseph did not even have sexual intercourse until after Jesus was born. Both of them must have had high respect for and a strong allegiance to their God. They both believed that a celestial God was the real father of their first son. That is why Jesus, even though he was Mary's biological son, always spoke of

God as his real father. From a seemingly impossible conception, he was the son of the celestial Great One—the Son of God!

Almost eighty other verses show a much different title, however. Jesus referred to himself as the "Son of Man" (Matthew 8:20, 9:6, 12:18, 19:23). He honored his mother and his connection to the human race. He knew that part of him was human but another part was something else. In other words, as strange as it may sound, we must conclude that Jesus was half man but also half otherworldly celestial being. He was a hybrid, a crossbreed between the human and God species. He was the only conceived Son of God because he was artificially inseminated and placed into a human womb.

Jesus's birth to a woman of earth was truly a unique enigma. That is the fundamental difference between Christianity and other great religions that carry celestial truth: this fantastic fusion of human egg and celestial seed may have happened only once in our known history, although many great prophets were commissioned to present celestial truths in diverse cultures. Carried by a living, vital force, the lineage from the Great Ones came down to planet earth through this hybrid individual known as Jesus the Christ.

A Paranormal Birth

How is the birth of Jesus Christ viewed from a celestial point of view? This event was of such magnitude that an angel was sent down near the little town of Bethlehem.

> And there were shepherds living out in the fields nearby, keeping watch over their flocks at night. An angel of the Lord appeared to them, and the glory of the Lord shone around them, and they were terrified.

> *But the angel said to them, "Do not be afraid. I bring you good news of great joy that will be for all the people. Today in the town of David a Savior has been born to you; he is Christ the Lord. This will be a sign to you: You will find a baby wrapped in cloths and lying in a manger."* (Luke 2:8-12)

I guess these country sheepherders must have been terrified when a celestial being in the form of an angel suddenly appeared against the grassy hillside. They were used to gazing at the stars in the night. But now a brilliant, shining light surrounded the figure in front of them.

> *Suddenly a great company of the heavenly host appeared with the angel, praising God and saying, "Glory to God in the highest, and on earth peace to men on whom his favor rests."* (Luke 2:8-14)

These celestial angelic entities entered our three-dimensional realm to verbally communicate a message of such stupendous significance there were hordes of them in the sky to witness it. This was their celebration, not ours! The shepherds who witnessed the event must have heard the message in their minds, or spoken out loud in their language in order for it to be meticulously recorded later, and preserved for us today in written form.

Where did this great heavenly host of celestial beings come from? Shining so brilliantly against the sky, perhaps all together they looked like a star. This luminous mass first appeared to be moving, then stopped at a specific time and place. What star does that?

History tells us there were Magi—influential, learned men who first sighted it and traveled to follow it. "...the star they had seen in the east (or when it rose) went ahead of them until it stopped over the place where the child was." (Matthew 2:9) If these men had our vocabulary, perhaps they would have claimed it was a UFO that had come down from the heavens. A host of celestial entities gave them a fantastic message—that the savior of the whole human race had been born (Luke 2:12), a child who was part God, part man and sent to us as a celestial ambassador. This was and is good news because we and our planet still need saving. Praise God that they deem us scrawny human beings worthy enough to be saved!

> When they saw the star, they were overjoyed. On coming to the house, they saw the child with his mother Mary, and they bowed down and worshiped him. (Matthew 2:10-11)

An Immortal Takes on Flesh

As Jesus Christ grew older, he realized that part of him was foreign to our world. He later told those who followed him, "Anyone who has seen me has seen the Father" (John 14:9). Although he knew he appeared to be like any other man, it's apparent he sensed the celestial part of himself was directly connected to something far greater than just his human capacity and characteristics. He experienced a direct relationship with his real, celestial father.

There is a recorded account of Jesus's parents returning home from Jerusalem with their large extended family. They discovered that Jesus was missing, and returned to town to search for him. Jesus was only twelve years old at the time.

> *After three days they found him in the temple courts,*
> *sitting among the teachers, listening to them and asking*
> *them questions. Everyone who heard him was amazed at*
> *his understanding and his answers. When his parents saw*
> *him, they were astonished. His mother said to him, "Son,*
> *why have you treated us like this? Your father and I have*
> *been anxiously searching for you."*
>
> *"Why were you searching for me?" he asked. "Didn't you*
> *know I had to be in my Father's house?" (Luke 2:49)*

On at least two occasions later in Jesus's life, God's voice spoke to the men around him, proclaiming this father-son relationship. An audible voice from God was heard when Jesus was baptized by John the Baptist (Matthew 3:17) and then again on top of a high mountain in the presence of his friends Peter, James, and John. They all heard and witnessed these words:

> *This is my Son, whom I love, with him I am well pleased.*
> *Listen to him. (Matthew 17:5)*

Now, I find this fascinating! Every Jewish father says these same specific words publicly at his son's bar mitzvah even today. This is how the father blesses his son at his coming-of-age celebration. In other words, the highest God of the Great Ones was actually honoring the Jewish customs of the time when he proclaimed these words to his half-human son. How amazing this must have been to the Jewish men who heard this proclamation coming out of the celestial space around them. God publicly claimed this young man Jesus as his son, and he did so following the traditions of a specific human culture.

Throughout Jesus's life, he was sustained by this inner knowledge of who he actually was. At the end, right before he died, he talked directly to his celestial father in a last formal prayer:

> *"Father the time has come.... I have brought you glory on earth by completing the work you gave me to do. And now Father, glorify me in your presence with the glory I had with you before the world began." (John 17:1-5)*

Jesus was clearly aware of his previous immortality. This point comes as an awesome realization, and it is so important for us to grasp. For if he was with God "before the world began" and then before he was encased in flesh as a human, he must have been composed of spirit!

Even Jesus's friends seemed to understand he was something other than just a human being. What Christ announced to them changed their lives completely, and he is still changing people's lives today. After his death his followers went though persecution, torture, and martyrdom, and some even suffered their own deaths through crucifixion. Paul endured multiple scourging by leather whips, but he never violated his convictions about who Jesus was. Would common people like these endure all they did just to spread the news about a good church pastor? No. I don't think so. They did it because they were convinced of the supernatural otherworldliness of this man/god named Jesus Christ. He was a man with mystifying authority.

Some of his followers already recognized that he had to have existed before his physical birth. His best friend John knew that he was not like other men at all. In the first chapter of the book John wrote, he talked about creation and then defined Jesus as "the Word" and a definitive part of God.

> *In the beginning was the Word, and the Word was with*
> *God, and the Word was God. He was with God in the*
> *beginning. Through him all things were made; without him*
> *nothing was made that has been made. (John 1:1-3)*
>
> *The Word became flesh and lived for a while among us.*
> *We have seen his glory, the glory of the one and only Son,*
> *who came from the Father, full of grace and truth. (John*
> *1:14)*

The disciple John is saying that the Word was a part of the celestial Great Ones before his conception in a human mother. In other words, John is making the point that before taking on human form, Jesus was with God in the beginning. Thus Jesus Christ, as the Word, was the same Great One who brought about the construction of all created and living things because "through him all things were made." The Word was part of the great God-plural, and he was the one who made all things in the beginning.

That means he must have made us! However, when he came to earth to experience life as a human being in a tangible form, we certainly didn't recognize his lineage, power, or authority. We didn't even accept him, and ultimately most of the human race rejected him.

Another realization now becomes apparent: If he was with God as the Word in the beginning, then his existence continued as an immortal throughout humankind's earlier history until his human birth. He existed all through history! On one occasion, he even tried to explain this to a crowd of Jewish people who questioned him:

> *"Your father Abraham rejoiced at the thought of seeing*
>
> *my day; he saw it and was glad."*
>
> *"You are not yet 50 years old," the Jews said to him, "and*
>
> *you have seen Abraham?"*
>
> *"I tell you the truth, "Jesus answered, "before Abraham*
>
> *was born, I AM!" At this they picked up stones to stone*
>
> *him. (John 8:56-59)*

They were infuriated by this answer. Jesus was referring to an event that had happened more than a thousand years earlier. God had asked Moses to be the one to lead the people known as the Israelites out of Egyptian slavery. Moses then asked God what to call him, and God said:

> *"I am who I am. This is what you are to say to the*
>
> *Israelites: I AM has sent me to you." (Exodus 3:14)*

Jesus was referring to that verse when he called himself the "I AM," and his contemporaries knew it! They were very upset because in their minds he was claiming to be God. That was irreverent to them, but in fact he was explaining that before being born, he'd had an eternal existence. This makes perfect sense when we understand that Jesus's humanness was mixed into his immortality.

What's amazing is that throughout the earlier biblical history of the Old Testament, his active presence in spirit form had been trying to communicate and connect with the human species. His celestial presence was known then as "the LORD." The title *lord* simply means "master or ruler," but this title was capitalized in the Old Testament to signify the Lord of all rulers—so sacred as to be referred to only in this manner.

The ancient prophets had knowledge of things that were going to take place. At certain times they spoke out, saying, "… and the word of the LORD came to me." This phrase is used 219 times in the Old Testament, each time indicating a direct communication had taken place with the presence of God. The "word of the LORD" was the spokesperson, or "the Word" of the Great Ones, the same Word who later took on flesh and became Jesus Christ. It was this same Great One who spoke to the prophets in Old Testament times.

Thus the presence of this Great One was behind all the miraculous events recorded in biblical history. The Word was the invisible power that spoke to Moses from the fire in the burning bush. This power was in the cloud and pillar of fire that led the Israelite people out of Egypt. It was the metaphysical hand that parted the Red Sea. It was the one who fed the Israelites with manna, who quenched their thirst with cool, living water flowing from a rock. All these miraculous things happened in history because the LORD, who was a part of the Great Ones, was there communicating to these people.

Now in the first century of Christianity, the disciples were taught to understand this clearly. In the New Testament, we read:

> For I do not want you to be ignorant of the fact, brothers, that our forefathers were all under the cloud and that they all passed through the sea. They were all baptized unto Moses in the cloud and in the sea. They all ate the same spiritual food (Christ's body) and drank from the spiritual drink (Christ's blood) for they drank from the spiritual rock that accompanied them, and that rock was Christ. (1 Corinthians 10:1-4)

The Great Ones have always been involved in our world in many different ways. The books in the Old Testament, written such a long time ago, have been preserved to show us the many diverse ways God and the one known as the Word have tried to make their presence known to us even before Christ was born.

The Great Ones have wanted to unite with us for many millennia, waiting with open arms for our spiritual development. They worked with specific kingdoms that aligned themselves with the Great Ones' standards. With varied interventions down through ancient times, God had contact with us. Then a fantastic intervention was set up: the celestial race of the Great Ones made a decision to merge with the human species on earth. This good news of celestial significance was reported in the New Testament—it was what the huge company of angels sang about in the heavens that starry night when Jesus Christ was born, that God's favor, his glory, should actually come down to humanity on earth (Luke 2:14). By fusion between the fleshly human and the invisible celestial species, at last they were able to enter our realm physically.

Just think of it! If there is some far-advanced, celestial race of Great Ones existing in another dimension who want to connect with us in a conscious, caring alliance, how could they show themselves to us if they appeared as invisible Spirit? How could a mortal eye perceive them? One of their own kind was willing to give up his immortality so we might recognize their presence. He was willing to live as a human being just so we could see godly attributes portrayed in our world. That was the great sacrifice of their ambassador, Jesus the Christ. It was only in this way that the Great Ones were able to get our attention and offer us freedom from Satan's captivity, and salvation from our own mortality. How have we reacted to their peaceful overtures in this regard? For the most part, the story of Jesus's birth has not been given full recognition for its true magnitude.

The books of Mark and Matthew tell a parable about the owner of a vineyard who sent his servants out to collect some of the harvest. Over time all the servants were shamefully beaten or killed by the disrespectful tenants of the vineyard.

> *He had one left to send, a son, whom he loved. He sent him last of all, saying, "They will respect my son." But the tenants said to one another, "This is the heir. Come, let's kill him, and the inheritance will be ours." So they took him and killed him, and threw him out of the vineyard. (Mark 12:6-8 and Matthew 21:33-38)*

We were placed in a beautiful earth garden that was created for us to look after and maintain. Doesn't the above parable describe what most of humanity did to God's prophets and to the celestial Son who was sent down by the owner of it all?

5

our celestial superhero

*The ramifications of Jesus's physical death are seen
from a celestial viewpoint. A great battle was fought
and won, giving humanity the opportunity to enter the
celestial dimension as immortal beings.*

A Strange Ambassador

Humankind did not accept Jesus Christ as anything exceptional
because he didn't look any different from us. When Christ
appeared in our dimensions of substance, time, and space, he
came incognito. He had no added advantage, no unique appearance to distinguish him from his fellow men. When Judas, his
disciple, betrayed Jesus, he had to give a sign to the soldiers so
they would know which one he was (Mark 14:44).

So, what did Jesus look like? Pictures of Christ painted by the eighteenth-century master artists give us a vision of him as an effeminate, longhaired weakling with a shy smile. Could he have looked like that when he overturned tables and benches to drive the moneychangers out of a temple of God (Matthew 21:12, Mark 11:15)? No! We can visualize a stronger picture than that. By trade he was a carpenter and so probably quite muscular. He was a builder who worked with the crude tools of the day to shape beams and hew rough wood into the needed forms.

Jesus had no high status in his life by earthly standards. Knowing a celestial God had fathered him; Jesus still wasn't arrogant in any way.

> Who, being in very nature God, did not consider equality with God something to be grasped, but made himself nothing, taking the very nature of a servant, being made in human likeness. And being found in appearance as a man, he humbled himself and became obedient to death, even death on a cross! (Philippians 2:6-8)

What a contrast we have between Christ's original existence as the Word, the LORD, and one of the Great Ones and that of a human being. When he came to earth appearing as a human, we generally laughed at his claims and scorned him. But the celestial reality behind it all was this:

> He is the beginning and the first born from among the dead, so that in everything he might have the supremacy. For God was pleased to have all his fullness dwell in him,

> and through him to reconcile to himself all things, whether things on earth or things in heaven, by making peace through his blood, shed on the cross. (Colossians 1:15–20)

God turned part of himself into a mere human being in order to give us an opportunity to be grafted into their celestial realm, but we rejected him and then killed him. Why was his crucifixion allowed to happen? Why didn't Jesus Christ save himself? Let's put this whole thing into an imaginary, celestial viewpoint using contemporary scientific jargon to aid our understanding.

Suppose a talented scientist designed the most-advanced, most-realistic humanlike robot ever invented. Perhaps he's pursuing this through government-funded research. He conceives a plan to make humanoid robots actually become living beings. These advanced creations would possess a personal sense of identity and their own power to reason, choose, and make decisions. However, to execute this plan, the scientist has to be willing to give up his own life in order to intervene and interface with his created robots. He has to lay aside all his superior rightful powers of existence and become little more than a machine himself. Then he will be required to confront an evil virus that weakens his robots. He will have to overcome these negative forces by his own preset rules for robotic creation, and in the end even allow the new metal species he created to go against him and finally kill him.

Then, in order to return to his powerfully advanced world, he will be required to trust in the authority of his supervisors, who hopefully can activate the right sequence to bring him back to his former existence as a prestigious scientist. If something goes amiss, or if the destructive forces are able to destroy him too, he might never return to his own reality. If his mission is successful, it will pave the way for creating living robotic progeny into the human plane of existence.

Now, this little story may not seem so crazy since current work in robotic science is focused on artificial intelligence. A branch of this research, called Strong AI, focuses on developing robots with the ability to perform intelligent actions that match human intelligence. In a sense, that is exactly what the great God species did. The celestial ambassador who volunteered for this mission on earth became Jesus Christ, and he was successful!

> He came to that which was his own, but his own did not receive him. Yet, to all who received him, to those who believed in his name, he gave the right to become children of God. (John 1:11-13)

When this immortal ambassador died a physical death, the way was paved to transform our limited physical existence into an eternal spiritual existence! The bridge from human flesh to spirit essence is now possible through metamorphosis to a higher level of existence. This was the catalyst, the next step in evolution for the human race: receiving eternal life.

What did Jesus Christ have to do in order to bring about this transformation? He had to confront the destructive forces weakening us humans. He had to ransom us from the enemy—those rebellious and determined dark angels who stand against our entrance into celestial immortality.

The Great Confrontation

We live in a world that is constantly influenced by negative forces. Jesus lived in this world too, and he was tempted just as we are. Unlike us, he was fully aware of the dark, destructive forces opposing him from behind our physical reality. How did it feel to have this evil, invisible presence watching his every move? Even his own religious denomination wanted to silence him. Then he was tortured, taunted, and treated like a criminal by the ruling Romans. It is easy to believe that the temptations he faced were somehow smaller and easier than what we face today. After all wasn't he supposed to be part God? Wouldn't that give him some extra privilege? Apparently that was not the case.

> For we do not have a high priest who is unable to sympathize with our weaknesses, but we have one who has been tempted in every way, just as we are—yet was without sin. (Hebrews 4:15)

Perhaps temptations were actually harder for Jesus Christ because the demons knew who he was, and they challenged him as the Son of God (Matthew 4:3-6, 8:29, 14:33). These demonic spirits recognized that this man, Jesus the Christ, was astoundingly more than just human. They respected him and boldly shouted from the mouths of those who were possessed and mentally ill, "What do you want with us, Son of God?" (Matthew 8:29)

Satan and his demonic angels were adamantly against him and understood what was at stake. They were defending their ruling status on earth from this crossbreed, the first child of God in human flesh.

Yet the celestial battle against Satan's control of earth was not carried off as we would picture it on a cinema's huge screen. There were no laser guns or outer-space missile systems. When Christ fought this great and powerful adversary, no nuclear bombs descended. That is not how the celestial realm works. Satan thought all he had to do was discredit this Jesus person and get him killed. Satan didn't understand God's plan at all.

The pinnacle of the early temptations Jesus Christ faced occurred before his great ministry began. He had been fasting for forty days and nights for spiritual strength while on a private retreat in the desert. This is still humanly possible by taking in clear liquids, although it certainly weakens the physical body, as you can well imagine. Satan decided it was a prime time to attack the Son of God in the flesh.

When we look closely at how Satan tried to break Jesus Christ down morally and spiritually, the enemy's tactics become quite clear. The devil often uses the same three methods: he attacks first through the body, then through the emotions, and finally through the self-will. Satan first tried to tempt Christ with food because he was fasting. When this didn't work, Satan tried to stir up the emotions of pride and anger to use against Jesus, but to no avail. Finally, Satan tried to convince him there was an easier and better way to choose to accomplish his purpose—the choice between self-will and God's will (Matthew 4:1-11).

In the beginning of the confrontation, Satan appealed to Jesus's humanness, for he had physical needs and was literally starving. Satan told him in a jeering manner to make stones into bread. Remember, Jesus Christ did have the power to do this. Later he performed similar miracles with fish and loaves of bread. Satan probably tried reasoning with Christ, saying he had fasted quite long enough. This negative persuasion actually works through our own self-talk all the time, but Jesus didn't give in to Satan's taunting. How did he resist in his weakened state? He didn't choose to fight or to rely on his own strength. The only action he took was to speak God's words—the same ones he had read in the ancient Hebrew sacred scrolls. He stated firmly:

> Man does not live on bread alone, but on every word that comes from the mouth of God. (Matthew 4:4, Deuteronomy 8:3)

Jesus faced temptations exactly like ours, but the only weapons and shields he used were the simple words of God. This is a revelation! Obviously God's words are much more powerful than we think.

> For the word of God is living and active. Sharper than any double-edged sword....(Hebrews 4:12)

The Great Ones have no need for physical weapons. Their focused thoughts are so advanced that their very words are swords. Thus, when we use the words God gives us; they become our weapons also, giving us great power.

Satan realized he couldn't manipulate Jesus through his physical needs, and he quickly switched to his next powerful tactic. He focused his efforts on the emotions Jesus had attached to the thoughts running through his mind. Satan knew he couldn't actually force a change in behavior on his own. He couldn't create anything to happen. He doesn't have that ability. Remember he had originally been created as an angel for carrying messages, so Satan was not made with creative powers. He could only hope to twist Jesus's own thoughts so they would create negative things.

Satan began mocking Jesus, trying to plant seeds of doubt, just as he had done with Adam and Eve back in the garden, and just as he continues to do with each of us. In this case, he questioned the powerful anointing of Jesus with disbelief.

> Then the devil took him to the holy city and had him stand on the highest point of the temple. "If you're the Son of God" he said, "throw yourself down." For it is written: "He will command his angels concerning you, and they will lift you up in their hands, so that you will not strike your foot against a stone." (Matthew 4:6)

The loyal angels of God were supposed to protect Jesus, and perhaps they hovered invisibly above him with shining wings. Satan, at the forefront of all his demons, took on the role of the bully and demanded, "Prove it, if you're the Son of God." He appealed to Jesus's pride, even quoting the sacred writings. He used doubt and suspicion to convince Jesus that evidence was necessary to back up the claim to his identity.

Through our own anger and arguments, we buy into this familiar tactic all the time. The need to convince others we are right is a strong one. But Jesus fought back in a celestial way. Again, his weapons were his words. His answer came from the scriptures he knew: "It is also written: 'Do not put the Lord your God to the test'" (Matthew 4:7, Deuteronomy 6:16). Jesus didn't have to prove who he was to himself or to anyone else. He knew and could feel the full presence of God within him (Colossians 1:19).

However, as an original member of the Great Ones, Jesus the ambassador longed to rectify all the physical sorrows and sufferings he had come to know in our world. He intensely felt humanity's pain and recognized that we are all blind and captives of the dark forces of evil on earth. Jesus would soon begin to heal all the sick that were brought to him, for he was filled to the brim with compassion. His whole heart grieved for the human experience. He mourned:

> *Oh, Jerusalem, Jerusalem, you who kill the prophets and stone those sent to you, how often I have longed to gather your children together, as a hen gathers her chicks under her wing, but you were not willing. (Matthew 23:37)*

Satan, on the other hand, recognized that the Son of God was predestined to play a crucial role in the history of humankind.

Ancient writings prophesied Jesus's destiny to, at some point, take Satan's place in ruling over our planet. Jesus was to be earth's new king, with a kingdom that would never end (Isaiah 9:6-7, Luke 1:32-33). Satan and his dark angels were fighting hard for their earthly domain.

So finally, using his last tactic, he tempted Jesus using Jesus's empathy for the human species and appealed to his self-will. The devil took him to a very high mountain and showed him all the kingdoms of the world, their wealth, and their splendor. He said he would give it all to Jesus if he would bow down and worship him (Matthew 4:9).

What thoughts ran through Jesus's mind? His desire was to set up a celestial type of government on earth. This was authority and the power he longed for. This ruling position was his destiny, the reason for his birth. Jesus had read that he was to be the messiah, but that he was supposed to be tortured and put to death (Isaiah 52:14, 53:5-6). It would be a horrible ordeal. Now he was being offered a shortcut to avoid the unimaginable physical pain and abandonment that seemed to be part of the celestial plan. As a man like one of us, he was being offered unlimited wealth and importance. Jesus could have had early reign over all the kingdoms of the world. He must have reasoned that surely it would have lessened human suffering in the coming centuries.

However, Satan had anticipated Jesus's reaction and reasoning. The deception seemed logical in appearance; it always seems that way. After all Satan is an expert at painting perfect images in our minds, and so much was at stake at that time. Would Jesus fall for it? What a heart-wrenching decision this must have been! He didn't know how long it would be on the human timeline before he could take over and make the earth his father's utopian kingdom (Matthew 24:36).

In the final temptation, Satan presented Jesus with the decision to choose right or wrong for himself. This is always the pivotal decision for each of us. One last time Jesus Christ fought the devil with God's words as his weapons:

> *Away from me, Satan! For it is written, "worship the Lord your God, and serve him only." (Matthew 4:10)*

These words confirmed the strong celestial connection Jesus Christ had with his invisible, spiritual Father. He chose allegiance to God. He probably said it through gritted teeth and with deep fortitude, but with these words, he defeated Satan, and Satan left.

In his self-centered ugliness, Satan thought the whole battle was about Jesus wanting to be the ruler of planet earth. He saw it as the ultimate power struggle. For Jesus that wasn't what it was about at all. As good as Satan's offer may have sounded, it was lacking something huge. Jesus Christ knew he was the "firstborn among many" to become children of God (Romans 8:29). If he had accepted Satan's offer, he may have certainly made a difference as the ruler of earth—but there would have been no gift of immortality for us. We all would have remained mere human beings, and returned to dust upon our deaths.

In taking that shortcut, Jesus would have forfeited the part of the plan where he was able to set us free for immortality. Yes, he loved his humanness; he loved humanity and wanted to save us, but he loved his celestial lineage too. He was the perfect mix between the species. As mentioned previously, he was the bridge between "things on earth" and "things in heaven." (Colossians 1:20)

Satan truly didn't understand what it was all about because he is incapable of loving anything. He doesn't understand love, and he cannot fight it. He has no weapons against love except to twist it, to turn it into hate. Though he tried, Satan could not turn Jesus against us or against God, his father.

To this day Satan's techniques haven't changed much. Dark spirits still tempt us with the physical desires of the body and manipulate the intelligence of the mind through our emotions, or appeal to the greed of our self-will. Jesus's example shows us that we can resist these forces, but not necessarily with our own strength. He resisted and overcame them by using the words God had given him. Therein lies our strength and protection against invisible enemies. Words were Jesus Christ's weapons; he simply believed in the power of God's words and trusted that the plan God had to rescue the species of human beings was better than any he could devise. He did it God's way. We too can wield the words of God like powerful weapons in our own hands. In Chapter Ten, we'll discuss the spiritual power of words in more detail.

When the great confrontation with Satan was over, the angels came and attended to Jesus. During his human lifetime, he went on to teach about his father's celestial kingdom and to heal great multitudes of people with compassion and love. He longed for us to become something more than flesh and blood, and modeled the way to live in order for us to achieve this. He came for the sake of all people, not for one church, one ideology, one race, or even one historical period. How silly of us to set up elite groups of people through brands of religion or methods of government or color of skin when the Great Ones in their invisible spirit state are concerned with saving the whole human species on planet earth.

The Great Ones must surely be very disturbed about the current self-destruction of the human race and the state the planet is now in. This is why two thousand years ago they sent one of their own kind to live among us, rescue us, and ransom us—and then to empower us.

A Ransom Paid

So our hero is Jesus Christ, the one anointed with power, a hybrid of mortal and immortal beings. Despite his celestial heritage and his apparent ability to heal and raise people from the dead, he agreed to suffer a violent physical death—crucifixion—in order to be a kind of savior to us. Frankly I wasn't very impressed by the idealized crucifixion scene in the Bible; many men and women down through the ages have suffered much worse torture and agonizing deaths, sometimes in sacrifice for others. Instead what got my attention was the celestial story behind the death on the cross: the seemingly impossible physical death of an immortal crossbreed. But then, while studying this ancient text, my next logical question stood out: what was he saving us from?

As in any good story, along with the hero there has to be an antagonist. The infamous devil is clearly that character in the Bible story. A shocking passage in the New Testament states that this evil, invisible entity is actually controlling our world right now:

> We know that we are children of God, and that the whole world is under the control of the evil one. (1 John 5:19)

Doesn't it make sense that our God of love is not at fault for the mess the world is in right now? The diabolic ruler of our planet is apparently a sort of Darth Vader persona in the spirit realm, warring for the control of humanity. The clarity of that one verse alone sure explained a lot.

What if a dark, diabolical essence does have invisible control of our world? What if he holds us captive through some kind of influence and manipulation of our minds and we don't even realize it? Think of it. Every culture hungers for freedom; every religion searches for enlightenment. Yet so many of us are destroying our planet and ourselves. Are we actually in bondage on a physical earth? Is that why we need to be ransomed?

If we consider our world may indeed be oppressed by an invisible, external "control of the evil one," then it makes sense: a hero would be necessary to save us from the influence of that oppressor. In other words Jesus Christ's real purpose was to ransom the inhabitants of earth by paying with his life so we could be rescued from the dark ruling adversary that enslaves us. When humanity crucified this ambassador sent by God just like a common criminal, the demonic spirit world led by Satan thought they had won the war by killing the only begotten Son of God.

This story, however, has a fantastic conclusion. By becoming one of us, Jesus confronted the destructive forces oppressing the human species and established a way to rescue us. Satan had to corrupt Christ by the very rules and perimeters set up for human existence because Jesus was part human. The first conditional law in creating humans was that "sin"—actions not acceptable to the Great Ones—resulted in death. It was designed that way to release us from a life of misery, which is inherent in sin. God established his word on this by speaking it, and it was ironclad: "For the wages of sin is death; but the gift of God is eternal life" (Romans 6:23).

Since Jesus' lineage was half human, this rule did in fact apply to him. That is why he knew it was crucial for him to be blameless, without any sin himself, so the penalty of sin could not be assigned to him. Then the sacrifice of his life would be of such value, it would act as a ransom payment for our sins.

An Inheritance Given

Since Jesus was without sin (Hebrews 4:15), and he had never rebelled against God's standards, he did not deserve the penalty of death. In other words, he couldn't stay dead because he hadn't sinned. He hadn't chosen what was right and wrong for himself but followed what God desired him to do. Jesus Christ was the only human being to actually earn eternal life by the rules of the game, and then he turned around and gave the benefit to us. Thankfully, we don't have to earn eternal life anymore. To those of us who believe, it is the "gift of the Gods."

The other half of Jesus's lineage, the part that was a celestial member of the Great Ones, already held immortality, so that part of him couldn't die. In the celestial world, his sacrifice of his own death—his undeserved death—was of such value it could pay the price of the death penalty for all those in allegiance to God. Through this ransom, you and I have access to the gift of eternal life! The death of this chosen Great One—the celestial ambassador, Jesus the Christ, the Son of God, the Son of Man, LORD, and the Word—opened a way for us to gain immortality.

When Jesus Christ died on the cross and was buried for three days in the tomb, Satan was probably cavorting with glee, thinking he had overcome the one true Son of God. However, Satan did not get rid of this human-celestial crossbreed, and he will eventually lose his earthly kingdom. What irony that must be for the great dark ruler!

From the grave, Christ was resurrected, foreshadowing exactly our own destiny! This is what Christ was talking about when he said, "I am the way and the truth and the life" (John 14:6). It was all part of the celestial plan for the human species and the purpose for which they sent Christ, their ambassador, to earth. This was and is the will of God!

We can look at it in yet another way. "The will of God" is not just a flippant phrase to explain things that are hard to understand. The will of God, simply put, is that he wants to save us. He created us to be like him, and he loves us. In one of the most famous scripture passages, we read:

> God so loved the world that he gave his one and only
> Son, that whoever believes in him shall not perish but have
> eternal life. (John 3:16)

The will of God is for us to develop a belief system in allegiance to him so we might receive the gift of immortality and become like children of the Great Ones, a subspecies of the God Kind! The will of Christ is the same, and that was why he willingly gave up his life for us: to give us an inheritance of value in celestial spirit for this purpose. What if it were a celestially written will? Maybe the purpose of his death was so his will would be executed and our inheritance could be released. After all, someone has to die for an inheritance to be given. Just as a dying man wills his earthly possessions to his loved ones, Jesus willed what was of greatest value to him: supernatural power and love, and the right to live forever! By his written will to those who believe in him, he enables us to enter into the spiritual realm.

This will is actually recorded and documented on paper just as any written will is today. The fine print is in the Bible and is known as the new covenant of Jesus Christ. It is recorded in our source book, and it's called the New Testament. That, in fact, is what the word *testament* means: "a covenant." We use this word today in legal documents to mean a "contractual legal agreement binding upon two parties." Yet, if this is the new covenant, then what was the old covenant?

The Tree of Life

Let's zoom back into the scene where it all began, in the garden of paradise.

> In the middle of the garden were the tree of life and the tree of the knowledge of good and evil...but you must not eat from the tree of the knowledge of good and evil, for when you eat of it you will surely die. (Genesis 2:9, 17)

So there were two trees in the garden: one that enhanced and extended life and one that caused death. The Tree of Life represented the immortal way of the Great Ones, and yes, in the beginning we had access to eternal life. However, as we all know, in this ancient creation story the first man and woman ate from the wrong tree. Death was then activated, and the right to the Tree of Life was forfeited. We gained free choice in the knowledge of good and evil, but the human species was then barricaded from the Tree of Life.

"The man has now become like one of us, knowing good and evil. He must not be allowed to reach out his hand and take also from the tree of life and eat, and live forever." So, the LORD God banished him from the Garden of Eden to work the ground from which he had been taken. After he drove the man out, he placed on the east side of the Garden of Eden cherubim and a flaming sword flashing back and forth to guard the way to the tree of life. (Genesis 3:21-24)

Mortality was the first foundational law of human creation. If we were given free choice in how to live, and if the choices we made became detrimental to ourselves and to others, then our mortal lives had to end. Old covenant laws were set up to guide and assist us in this decision-making process.

The Son of God, then, as an ambassador of the Great Ones, brought us a new covenant to replace the old covenant, restoring our access to the Tree of Life. We who are ransomed, who accept and believe in the celestial proposal of the Great Ones and who incorporate it into our lives, are listed in the will to receive the promise of eternal life.

The crucial segment of this new will is written clearly:

> *For this reason Christ is the mediator of a new covenant,*
> *that those who are called may receive the promised*
> *eternal inheritance, now that he has died as a ransom to*
> *set them free from the sins committed under the first*
> *covenant. (Hebrews 9:15)*

The crucifixion of the Son of God on that upright, rugged cross on the hilltop became our second chance to return to the garden paradise. At the very moment of Jesus Christ's physical death, darkness filled the sky and a strong earthquake shook the earth.

> *When the centurion and those with him who were guarding*
> *Jesus saw the earthquake and all that had happened,*
> *they were terrified, and exclaimed, "Surely he was the Son*
> *of God!" (Matthew 27:54)*

The cross itself was only a few strong pieces of hewn wood, but from a celestial viewpoint, as the blood of this half man, half god soaked into them the cross suddenly became the new Tree of Life. Eternal life had been accessed. There was such celestial power and presence striking down upon the earth during that time, some who had already died came out of their graves!

> *At that moment, the curtain of the temple was torn in*
> *two from top to bottom. The earth shook and the rocks*
> *split. The tombs broke open and the bodies of many*
> *holy people who had died were raised to life. (Matthew*
> *27:51-52)*

In a sense, this symbolic cross allows us to cross over from the old contract to the new one, from the physical world to a celestial realm, from mortality to eternity. Jesus stated the conditions of the new contract firmly:

> *"I tell you the truth, whoever hears my word and believes him who sent me, has eternal life and will not be condemned; he has crossed over from death to life." (John 5:24)*

By accepting the death of this Great One as a ransom payment for our freedom, each of us can belong to something far greater than ourselves. His life and death on our planet formed the catalyst to open the portal for human beings to enter an immortal plane of existence and live in the realm of the Great Ones forever.

> *Blessed are those who wash their robes, that they may have the right to the tree of life and may go through the gates into the city. (Revelations 22:14)*

Thus a powerful celestial intervention took place when Jesus Christ entered our historical human timeline. Announcing the celestial proposal for the human species to join the God Kind was the whole point of his life, his death, and his resurrection. This is the good news brought by the celestial ambassador to all human-kind and is the meaning of the word *gospel*. This is the gospel that gave us an opportunity to enter a doorway into immortality: "...that whoever believes in him shall not perish but have eternal life" (John 3:16).

the proposal

6

an open invitation

Some of us are currently called out to be seekers of truth, though the reasons for our selection at this time are unknown. An invitation has been offered to access Spirit and be empowered. It is our choice to accept this connection and have celestial principles downloaded— or not. The Great Ones guarantee our success in joining their celestial family if we continue to believe and develop our ability to activate faith.

Called by God

Now that we are aware of the hero, the adversary, and the other main celestial characters, we can plot where human beings fit into the storyline. We have an idea of the destiny God designed for us, but how in the world does it actually happen? What connects us to extraterrestrial empowerment? Who is given the celestial inheritance of immortality and why?

God's plan for humanity seems to be a drama of epic proportions, but we only see a short segment of it in our lives. Billions of people have already lived and died without knowing anything but a shadow of these things. Still more billions are alive today who don't seem to have been given the chance to have a personal hero ransom them from their dark world. What about all those people?

Passages in the Bible show that the Great Ones connect with our human race on different levels, in different cultures, and at different times in history. They also connect on a one-to-one basis. While living on earth, Jesus Christ knew he would not convince everyone of his real identity or about the good news of an invisible, celestial realm of existence. Few would be able to understand the metaphysical component of life, yet access to this knowledge was put in place as humanity became ready to understand it. For this reason Christ spoke in short analogies: so that when we understand these specific passages, they will point us to the ways of the Great Ones.

When Christ's friends came to him and asked, "Why do you speak to the people in parables?" he gave a very odd answer:

> The knowledge of the secrets of the kingdom of heaven has been given to you, but not to them.... Though seeing, they do not see; though hearing, they do not hear or understand.... For this people's heart has become calloused, they hardly hear with their ears and they have closed their eyes. (Matthew 13:10-15)

What is the difference between "you" and "them" in this scripture? Is it that certain people have somehow figured out how to contact and connect with God while others have not? I do not believe the difference comes from our own doing. It has nothing to do with our personal works. God calls whom he wants to call when he wants to call them.

Remember our analogy of putting together a giant puzzle without the picture on the box? Every puzzle enthusiast knows it's difficult to find certain pieces until a number of other pieces are fitted together. Why pass judgment on the abilities of those who have yet to find their place? Only divine timing can determine the accuracy of that. Jesus was often heard saying, "My time has not yet come" (John 2:4); perhaps it is the same with us.

Let us suppose you are in the group who can see, hear, and understand God's truths right now. Perhaps divine timing has determined you are open for the celestial download. After all you probably access a Bible, and you apparently are interested enough to keep reading this book. We can assume, then, that God has selected you because you want to learn more. This calling is like an invisible hunger for something greater than your mundane life. We are exploring these ideas right now because a celestial connection has been made and initiated in your life already. We might search for God, but initially God has contacted us! The God Source has predestined each of us to receive Spirit at specific times in our lives. That is surprising, but the clarity of this concept is stated in the book of Ephesians:

> In love he predestined us to be adopted as his sons through Jesus Christ in accordance with his pleasure and will.... (Ephesians 1:4-5)

Even Jesus confirmed this by stating, "No one can come to me unless the Father who sent me draws him" (John 6:44, 65).

This clearly explains that we must be individually selected by God's will. Our possible destiny has already been determined to some extent. However, if we accept the fact that we have been selected, it means others have not yet been singled out. This explains why some people are blinded by circumstance to the idea of a God and to any specific purpose he may have had in creating them. Countless other people feel almost hostility toward any kind of a god. Why is this? There are many questions to be answered.

We are limited in understanding because we have carnal minds. We think in terms of the flesh—our human passions and emotions. This often leads to acting in ways that are unacceptable to the Great Ones, which are behaviors defined as sin. In our sacred textbook we read that "...the sinful man is hostile to God" (Romans 8:7). We human beings do not naturally think in spiritual terms or long-term consequences for the way we live. Our foundation for existence is based in time, space, and physical manifestation. We seize the moment, and besides, unacceptable actions can sometimes be very enjoyable for a short duration.

There is another reason why some of us do not want to know about the spiritual side of life. Our lives revolve around the self, the ego. After all, we are created as earth-gods to subdue the earth (Genesis 1:28). That's why we don't want to acknowledge there may be a higher authority over us. Humanity as a whole rejects the creator in order to go its own way and do its own thing.

This has been so prevalent that the theory of evolution in humankind has been widely accepted despite missing links and substantial evidence to the contrary. As humorous as it sounds, it seems we would rather be related to monkeys than to gods! That's what I call a natural enmity toward God. Since he put us in charge of the plant and animal kingdoms on earth, we think we are at the top of the food chain. There's so much more to it. We're so blind to spiritual things that unless God specifically opens our minds, we have no way of understanding anything about them.

> *The man without the Spirit does not accept the things*
> *that come from the Spirit of God, for they are foolishness*
> *to him, and he cannot understand them, because they are*
> *spiritually discerned. (1 Corinthians 2:14)*

But the fact is that God wants all of us to come to know him (1 Timothy 2:4). It's not that the Great Ones choose some lucky people and reject others. It's that God's contact is perfectly timed to have the most powerful effect on our lives. God's timing is unique for each individual, and we each have a lifetime of opportunity to receive the call. We are each on a different pathway in the game of life, and there is no reason to judge each other in this way.

Selection Standards

God selects all kinds of people in all kinds of situations. If we have been called, it's not because of any intelligence or goodness of our own. It is quite the opposite, in fact. The selection process is definitely not, what we would expect!

> *Brothers, think of what you were when you were called.*
> *Not many of you were wise by human standards, not*
> *many were influential, not many of noble birth. But God*
> *chose the foolish things of the world to shame the wise. (1*
> *Corinthians 1:26-27)*

The bottom line is that God calls whom he wants to call. There is no way to determine the why of it. There was one man who was called who was zealously put to death the other people God was calling. That's a very special solution to the problem, isn't it? That man was the apostle Paul. He became the first great missionary to the Gentiles, or all those outside of the Jewish religion.

In another example, Jesus Christ was invited to dinner at a Pharisee's house, and a woman, known to all in the town as leading a sinful life, came uninvited to give honor to Jesus. She had obviously been called, for she recognized that Jesus Christ was empowered supernaturally with a celestial glory. In awe, she wept at Jesus's feet, and then she wiped them with her hair and anointed them with precious perfume.

Jesus told a simple parable to the host, who was criticizing her:

> *"Simon, I have something to tell you."*
>
> *"Tell me, teacher," he said.*
>
> *"Two men owed money to a certain moneylender. One owed him five hundred denarii, and the other fifty. Neither of them had the money to pay him back, so he canceled the debts of both. Now which of them will love him more?"*
>
> *Simon replied, "I suppose the one who had the bigger debt canceled."*
>
> *"You have judged correctly," Jesus said... "Therefore, I tell you, her many sins have been forgiven—for she loved much. But he who has been forgiven little loves little."* (Luke 7:40-47)

The moral of these stories is that no matter where you've been in life, God is big enough to forgive anything. Ironically, a person we might reject as not worthy of God's calling might later excel in spiritual growth way beyond us. We simply cannot judge the journeys others are traveling.

So how does God choose people? How can he overlook the truly terrible deeds of a human being—the really ugly ones? Do you feel you have personally done so much wrong in your life that it would be impossible for God to accept the real you? I too felt like this at one time, and a close friend looked at me and said, "Who do you think you are? Do you think you're so bad that God isn't big enough to forgive you and love you anyway? He created you!"

This advice puts the past into proper perspective. The beauty of it is that God knows everything about us, yet he can love and forgive us anyway. God's ways are not like our own. Don't you think the God Source might have his own criteria for choosing the people he wants in his family and inhabiting his celestial kingdom? The criteria for selection simply cannot be explained through human logic.

God is not worried about what we have done in the past because Jesus Christ's sacrifice washed us clean of everything. God knows we will do things that are unacceptable to the laws of the Great Ones because we are, after all, only human. When our children break the rules we've set for appropriate behavior within our families, we correct them and teach them a better way to behave in order to ensure their overall happiness. They may break rules quite frequently until they learn, but we love them anyway! In the same way, from a celestial viewpoint, sin is only something to be overcome.

Most importantly God is looking for individuals who don't want to sin. He is looking for people who value integrity, which is almost an old-fashioned word to us now, but it describes best what God wants to see in us. His desire is to see us strive toward full allegiance to godlike ways. That factor is essential in the selection process.

From the intent of our hearts, then, the process unfolds. We will become more like the Great Ones because they will send Spirit to work in our lives to make us acceptable to them. We are assured of this whole-heartedly!

> ...The Spirit intercedes for the saints in accordance with God's will. And we know that in all things God works for the good of those who love him, who have been called according to his purpose. For those God foreknew he also predestined to be conformed to the likeness of his Son, that he might be the firstborn among many brothers. (Romans 8:27-29)

I especially like the camaraderie implied by the simple statement that Jesus was the firstborn "among many brothers." My brothers and sisters, this is good news indeed!

What Is Required?

Do these bold assurances sound like an automatic acceptance, a free salvation? If one is called out and glorified, does that mean the individual doesn't have to do anything? We have an all-knowing God, but that simply means he is outside our timeline and sees the ends of our lives as easily as any other point on the line. Predestination doesn't mean the outcomes of our lives have already been decided. It means our potential has been recognized.

The above scripture states that God "works for the good of those who love him." He does this by helping us to develop god-like spirituality, first by inviting us, next by ransoming us, and then by guidance through Spirit. He knows our potential, yet he gives us free will.

If God calls us, do we have any responsibility at all? Don't we have to do something to be godlike? Yes, like any talent or skill, we have to work at it, but the kind of work required of us will come as a complete surprise.

> The men who followed Jesus asked him, "What must we do to do the works God requires?"
>
> Jesus answered, "The work of God is this: to believe in the one he has sent." (John 6:28-29)

To "believe in the one he has sent" seems like a simple request, right? We say we believe in God, and then we get involved in some denomination of a Christian church. We try to be valuable, upright people in our community, and we go out and help God save others.

But wait, it isn't like that at all. God doesn't need our help to save others. After all God is…God! If we're doing "good works," maybe we're just doing what we want to do, and perhaps feeling a little superior about doing it. There is nothing wrong with helping others; helping is a godly trait. But if we do good deeds simply in an attempt to earn the right to be favored by God, aren't we only defining God by human standards? We cannot make ourselves perfect enough to be chosen by God. He does not use that criteria. As the above scripture states, the real work is to "believe in the one he has sent." The actual process of believing is difficult, yet the act of believing is the real work we must do.

In truth, God wants us to believe in his supernatural power and to live with our minds set firmly on that belief system. For example, we are expected to believe not only that Jesus existed but also in the truth of what he said. And let's face it; Jesus said some very bizarre things! God is asking us to believe in paranormal things. In other words the Great Ones really want us to accept that Jesus was sired by a celestial entity, born part human and part other-dimensional, and sent as an ambassador to the human species on earth and all that this knowledge implies.

What Is Truth, Anyway?

Beyond this conviction we are required to believe in things we cannot even see, such as awesome, invisible spirit entities that actively participate in human life on earth and are behind the scenes of our everyday lives. We are asked to accept the existence of celestial, angelic beings from a spiritual realm, some of which are aligned with an evil mastermind bent on the destruction of our species. These unseen forces are carefully set out in scripture so we might understand. They must have some validity.

All this just doesn't seem to fit in to our normal reality. But really, is human perception—the way we see things—actually even real? Our cultural system is set up so we only believe in the things we see. But consider this: if there is one person on each corner of an intersection where an accident happens, there can be four different versions of the reality of that event. Which account is true? Sometimes the things we see do not constitute the truth, but only what our mental filtering system says can be true. Remember that Satan, the god of this world, is the master of hologram effects. He is capable of conjuring up a reality in our minds through negative messages that aren't even real. Although he can't create things himself, he has definitely perfected a way of polluting our perspectives with what is false.

Consequently, the Great Ones want us to believe in celestial truths and concepts even more than we believe our own physical reality. Through perceiving the spirit realm in this way, we can align ourselves with the celestial Great Ones and be able to resist our greatest adversary in the battlefield of our minds. They want to equip us with weapons to activate beliefs so that we can defend ourselves. It is a serious commission the Great Ones give to us: we have been contacted for a purpose. We have been called out to be earth's spiritual warriors and to carry out a celestial battle on this planet.

God Won't Abandon Us

When we accept that God has chosen us to be spiritual warriors, there will come many crucial battles and trials in life. These trials will hammer out and mold strong mental character within us. It is part of the growing process to spiritual maturity. However, our creator gives us this exquisite promise for the difficulties we face:

> *"Never will I leave you, never will I forsake you." (Hebrews 13:5)*

Here is the work of believing! If we grasp the fact that from a celestial realm God has called us, then we have been connected. What this last verse means is that once the God Source has contacted us, he won't change his mind. He won't leave us or give up on us. For now, we belong to something far greater than ourselves. Jesus took a very protective stand and claimed us for his own:

> *I know them and they follow me. I give them eternal life, and they shall never perish; no one can snatch them out of my hand. My father, who has given them to me is greater than all, no one can snatch them out of my Father's hand. (John 10:27-29)*

What confidence we can have then, that God will not abandon us! In the book of Philippians, Paul assured us that "he who began a good work in you will carry it on to completion until the day of Christ" (Philippians 1:6).

How can we not understand that God is for us? Like a kind and loving father figure, the God Source wants to bring us up by his own celestial standards. If the very creator of all there is calls you for this purpose, he has absolute faith that you can make it into his kingdom. He really has more faith in us than we have in ourselves! If he believes that you can change and grow into a member of his family, who are you to doubt the very one who created you?

What, then, shall we say in response to this? If God is for us, who can be against us? He who did not spare his own Son, but gave him up for us all—how will he not also, along with him, graciously give us all things? (Romans 8:31-32)

God first found and called you! You are not alone, for God walks beside you on this journey. He believes in you and promises never to leave you. His intent for your life has been predetermined.

All this is awesome to contemplate. Nevertheless what about our moral freedom of choice and the ability to make our own decisions? What happened to our free will in this whole matter of predestination?

If We Continue

This next truth to be discovered is huge. The God Source says he will never leave us, however there is nothing to stop us from leaving him! We can be called to celestial uniqueness, we can be enlightened to spiritual truths, and then we can fall prey to negative influences all over again. All the spiritual beauty and insight God opens up for us can so easily fade away into a glimmering mist in the distance as we live our stress-filled lives. We can easily alter our belief systems for any fancy philosophy that comes along. However, God is consistent and doesn't give up on us. That is in the essence of his calling and his proposal to us. Whether we will continue to believe is the big question.

In studying ancient scriptures, I have come across many verses containing this conditional phrase: "if you continue." On this spiritual journey, God gives to us many bold and powerful promises we must believe in "if we continue." There are many examples of this:

> [He]...has reconciled you by Christ's physical body through death to present you holy in his sight, without blemish and free from accusation—if you continue in your faith, established and firm, not moved from the hope held out in the gospel. (Colossians 1:21-23)

We are free from accusation and pure in his sight if we continue. Likewise, Jesus told his followers:

> If you hold to my teaching, you are really my disciples. Then you will know the truth, and the truth shall set you free. (John 8:31-32)

Notice the "if" again in this passage? God promises many things "if we continue," but it is an ongoing and daily choice to follow or not. God gives us promises we can count on, but they are conditional upon our believing them. There is a symbiotic relationship involved in activating spiritual law. God's promises are true for us *if we continue to believe* that they are true. That's the very work we must do.

God, however, is like any considerate individual: he still allows us to make our own choices. The Great Ones are not some kind of dominating alien invaders from outer space. There is no aggressive force here, simply an offer from their species to assist our spiritual development. They propose to empower us, and that's why we have been called. We have been connected to and downloaded with spiritual knowledge. The ability to activate this knowledge is conditional: *if you continue* to believe.

Now, in religious terms, if we believe God has called us and we are trying to live good lives, are we saved believers? Let's compare ourselves to the apostle Paul. He was a great Christian who triumphed over more trials than you and I can begin to imagine:

> Five times I received from the Jews the forty lashes minus one. Three times I was beaten with rods, once I was stoned, three times I was shipwrecked, I spent a night and a day in the open sea, I have been constantly on the move. I have been in danger from rivers, in danger from bandits, in danger from my own countrymen, in danger from Gentiles; in danger in the city, in danger in the country, in danger at sea; and in danger from false brothers. I have labored and toiled and have often gone without sleep; I have known hunger and thirst and have often gone without food. (2 Corinthians 11:24-27)

Paul spoke of this with humility. He endured these persecutions because he wanted to share with others the concept that Jesus Christ really was the son of a great celestial God Source. Clearly at this point in his life, Paul should have felt he had done enough good work to ensure his reservation for eternal life. But he understood that his own work wouldn't secure immortality for him. Paul also recognized that the choice to follow God was not a one-time, unchanging event but an ongoing choice—if he continued. His viewpoint of the process was beautiful, humble, and inspiring:

> Not that I have already obtained all this, or have already been made perfect; but I press on to take hold of that for which Christ Jesus took hold of me. Brothers, I do not consider myself yet to have taken hold of it. But one thing I do; forgetting what is behind and striving toward what is ahead, I press on toward the goal to win the prize for which God has called me. (Philippians 3:12-16)

The prize? It's belonging to the utopian world of the celestial species! The concept is a continual process of spiritual maturity. The choices we make to follow their ways are the very method in this inner process of growth.

If we continue we will go on to develop spiritually. The next step in our journey is to learn about celestial characteristics and values so we can continue to establish and make firm our beliefs. If we strive to reach their standards for living, then we have freely chosen the best way of life there can be: a challenging and abundant life, one that is filled to the brim with inner joy.

Knowing our destination, we can now start the journey. In the next chapter, we will discuss a sort of treasure map that was drawn up way back in ancient biblical history. This map has landmarks to show the way to the end of our quest. Best of all we will find the rewards are better than winning any lottery, better than any *Survivor* or other game show. The real trophy to be won is an eternal spiritual existence and the right to belong to an extraterrestrial family from a celestial kingdom! Can we still write this off as just some imaginable science fiction? No, this is twenty-first-century Christianity! From here on out, the plot and the game get very interesting. Are you in?

7

levels in the life
game

*The intrinsic meanings in ancient celebrations define
the developmental levels for activating our personal
transformation into the God Kind.*

Remorse Is a Requirement

We have just discussed the first level in the game of life: being
called by God according to his specific timing. This is a phenomenal concept in itself—an invisible, benevolent, and magnificent
extraterrestrial entity has chosen us! However, in order to continue the process of transformation from earthling to God-being,
there must of course be internal changes that take place. That is
why it's necessary to stretch our minds to grasp what really went
on in the strange, celestial encounters recorded in the biblical
passages. We are compelled to accept that metaphysical things

are going to happen when an other-dimensional, metaphysical God enters our earthly realm. Consequently, we cannot seriously commit ourselves to the way of the Great Ones without expecting this to occur in our personal lives also.

Once we recognize that the Great Ones have mentally contacted us, the next step in the plan is for us to do something about it. But what should we do, and where do we begin? How do we reconcile this cutting-edge perspective of twenty-first century Christianity with traditional church attendance? What significance do the holy days and the well-known biblical stories have for us today?

When we begin investigating these ancient commemorative events, we learn that they do not stand in opposition to a new emerging church concept at all. Instead, both individually and universally, the intrinsic meanings of the ancient holy day celebrations communicate important concepts to us down through centuries of time. Actually, they foreshadow the plan of action set out for human spiritual development. This is prophecy on a grandiose scale.

To find our place on the vast human timeline, let's begin by looking at a powerful celestial event witnessed by thousands of people in the streets of Jerusalem on one of the sacred days of celebration—the day of Pentecost—nearly two thousand years ago. After Jesus Christ's death, those who had followed him met together in an upper meeting room. On this specific day, some type of intense, celestial presence came down and grounded on each of them, seeming to fill each person with an otherworldly, powerful Spirit. They were so in awe of this supernatural encounter they fled to the streets, babbling with excitement.

Now, at that time Jerusalem was inhabited and visited by people of all different nationalities who spoke a great many different dialects. Those in the streets stopped to listen to this exuberant group of Galileans talking about the death and apparent resurrection of a strange martyr named Jesus the Christ. These people claimed to have been touched by a sacred Spirit that filled them with metaphysical empowerment. They were so ecstatic, they seemed to be under some kind of influence, almost as if they drank too much wine! The spokesperson Peter denied this charge, however, explaining:

> *These men are not drunk, as you suppose. It's only nine in the morning! No, this is what was spoken by the prophet Joel: "In the last days, God says, I will pour out my Spirit on all people...." (Acts 2: 15-17)*

When others on the street heard the commotion, an even bigger crowd, numbering into the thousands, came together in bewilderment (Acts 2:41). What these new Christians had to say was not easy to dismiss because incredibly, no matter what their homeland, each person heard them speaking in his own language! Utterly intrigued, the people asked:

> *"Are not all these men who are speaking Galileans? Then how is it that each of us hears them in his own native language?*
>
> *...We hear them declaring the wonders of God in our own tongues!" Amazed and perplexed, they asked one another, "What does this mean?" (Acts 2:6-12)*

Apparently, God was supernaturally calling these thousands of people. That was the significance of this event. Still today, when we start hearing and understanding the words in our minds, our God is attempting to communicate with us also.

When the crowd heard Jesus's followers declaring these things in their own dialects, they were "cut to the heart" and asked, "Brothers, what shall we do"? One of the leaders, named Peter, explained their next step:

> *Repent and be baptized, every one of you, in the name of Jesus Christ so that your sins may be forgiven. And you will receive the gift of the Holy Spirit. The promise is for you and your children and all who are far off—for all whom the Lord our God will call. (Acts 2:38-39)*

In his dialogue to the crowd, Peter actually proclaimed the steps in the development of spiritual maturity. Being called, being repentant, and being baptized, all set up the right conditions for receiving celestial Spirit. This incident happened almost 2,000 years ago but Paul's words are intended for us today as well, for surely we are part of the "all who are far off" to which he referred.

First, we are being instructed to repent, but what does *repent* mean? Looking up the word in the ancient Greek language, we find it means, "to think differently." The original Greek word is *metanoia*, and it is made up of two parts. *Meta* means "an accompaniment or a transfer in sequence," and *noia* means "to exercise the mind or to comprehend." So to repent of some wrong action does not mean just to stop doing it, but to totally change the way you think about that action. It means to alter and exercise your mind to the extent that your physical actions will transform. We repent from wrong actions when we no longer desire to do them, and eventually we don't do them.

Total repentance is a very emotional upheaval in our lives. When we are truly remorseful for something we have done, we are actually sickened by the thought of it, and we feel convicted for all the hurt we've caused people. There is sadness for the completely stupid mess we made. When we realize we've broken the invisible moral codes of conduct set out by the Great Ones for our benefit, we accept personal accountability for all the misery in our lives.

Repentance means we don't want to do things our way anymore. We don't want to decide for ourselves what is right or wrong because we don't know what that is. We simply desire to know the truth as God sees it. That is repenting. When all these feelings come to the surface, we are ready to go to the next level of the game.

Rebirth by Water

Peter instructed the crowd on the street that Pentecost day to "repent and be baptized" (Acts 1:38). What does the word *baptize* actually mean? The dictionary tells us it means "to immerse in water" and "to clean spiritually." The whole idea is to be surrounded by something, to have it cover you. God desires us to submerge ourselves in celestial Spirit just as we are submerged by water when we jump into the deep end of a pool.

John the Baptist, baptized Jesus Christ in this manner. This eccentric, desert evangelist had a fanatic mission in life: to help people bury their pasts and start new lives. John the Baptist felt the purpose to his life was to baptize people to prepare the way for the coming of the one who was anointed with power. He recognized this had to be Jesus the Christ. Imagine, then, how honored he must have felt to actually baptize Jesus! When he did, another supernatural encounter occurred, and it was recorded for posterity in scriptures we can read today. The people witnessing Jesus's baptism evidently heard God's voice in human words. God publically claimed Jesus as his own son and sent some kind of spirit presence down from the sky.

> *As Jesus was coming up out of the water, he saw heaven being torn open and the Spirit descending on him like a dove. And a voice came from heaven: "You are my Son, whom I love; with you I am well pleased." (Mark 1:10-11)*

As news of this occurrence travelled throughout Jerusalem and the countryside, many people came to a state of repentance. They went out to meet John the Baptist and were baptized in the Jordan River. With remorseful attitudes they acknowledged their sins and were set free from the mental burden sin causes. By physically participating in the baptism ceremony, they were able to begin new lives (Mark 1:5).

The baptism ceremony symbolizes something very important in the celestial plan for humanity. It is a public confirmation of our beliefs to the people we know and to those who are there to witness the event. The act of going down into water and coming back up again seems such a strange thing to do. Yet, it is a sign of our desire to be spiritually clean and to immerse our lives in the God-presence. It symbolizes a transformation within us. Up to that point, we lived only on the surface of life, doing things our own way. In baptism, we confirm our decision to see reality from a deeper celestial viewpoint.

The act of baptism also portrays Jesus's death and resurrection. Jesus Christ willingly allowed himself to be crucified and was put into a burial tomb. When he awakened from death and came out of the tomb, he was transformed into an immortal God-being and once again a member of the species of Great Ones. Our being submerged in water says we want to put to death the person we once were; coming up out of the water is our rebirth. From then on, we desire to take an altogether different direction in life.

A Catastrophic Celestial Event

Let's digress a bit and go even deeper into the story of Jesus's death to capture the significance it has to each of us personally. When Jesus was tortured and hung on a cross by spikes pounded through his hands and feet, he didn't save himself. He died. Why? Jesus was called "the Christ" because all the people thought he had some kind of celestial, metaphysical power. He had the ability to stop his crucifixion. After all, for the past three years he had been doing astounding miracles, which included bringing the dead back to life (John 11:14, 38-43). When officials wanted to arrest him, he walked through crowds as if he were invisible (John 10:39). He even walked across water (John 6:19)! Logically he could have escaped from the guards with ease. Instead, he allowed his own people to put him to death. He had a celestial mission, and God had commissioned him. Jesus Christ tried to explain it to us in the book of John:

> The reason my Father loves me is that I lay down my life—only to take it up again. No one takes it from me, but I lay it down of my own accord. I have authority to lay it down and authority to take it up again. This command I received from my Father. (John 10:17-18)

In a sense, the Great Ones want us to follow his example. In the act of baptism, we surrender our egotistical lives to gain a richer existence and possibly an immortal reality. Jesus put it into these enigmatic words:

> For whoever wants to save his life will lose it, but whoever loses his life for me and for the gospel will save it. (Mark 8:35)

Occasionally we see heroes diving in to rescue people from fire or flood, only to forfeit their own lives in the process. This quality of real love for humanity is not often shown. Because he was only half human, with the other half celestial in essence, Jesus Christ did this on a grand, celestial scale for the entire human species.

In the spiritual realm of Great Ones and angels, Jesus's crucifixion was even more of a phenomenal event than it was on earth. No immortal being had ever, temporarily died before! They cannot die, because they are eternal. Jesus previously existed in their realm, and I'm sure the celestial beings avidly followed his drama on earth. When he finally died on the cross, it was said that the earth quaked and rocks were split, and the whole land darkened for three hours (Luke 23:45, Matthew 27:51). From somewhere outside of earth, great, immortal beings witnessed this celestial catastrophic event. It was at this precise point in human time that we too were given access to bridge the vast, invisible gap between human being and spirit entity, between death and immortality. How incredibly awesome! Jesus Christ, part human, opened the portal.

Echoes of Sacrifices Past

By going back in time, we can gain yet another perspective on the significance of the crucifixion. Many generations before the time of Jesus, there was a man God named Abraham. Some of his descendants were known as the Israelites, and a large population of them immigrated to Egypt. In the beginning, they were welcomed by the Pharaoh of Egypt because Joseph, Abraham's great-grandson, had become the second-highest ruler in their government. He counseled well when all the nations around were going through seven years of famine.

Many years later the Israelite families had multiplied so greatly in an area of Egypt called Goshen that they had become a worrisome minority for the new Pharaohs. They decided to exercise authority over them and force them into slave labor.

> They built Pithom and Rameses as store cities for
> Pharaoh.... The Egyptians used them ruthlessly. (Exodus
> 1:11-14)

These first Israelites were the oppressed and beaten slaves who built the pyramid cities we still greatly admire today.

The Great Ones selected Moses to lead the Israelites out of the degradation and hopelessness of slavery in the land of Egypt. However, God's people did not stage an uprising or a violent rebellion. Just as Jesus would battle evil with godly words, Moses too spoke the words of God and activated great celestial power to release the Israelite people from slavery. The Pharaoh, of course, would not allow the Israelite tribes to leave Egypt, so God instructed Moses to warn Egypt's ruler of nine plagues of national calamity that would occur.

These calamities were definitely metaphysical in nature. The Nile River turned blood red and became so polluted that all the fish died. The people could not drink from it, the water stank so much (Exodus 7:18). Soon a national epidemic of frogs set in. This seems almost humorous at first, for there were frogs everywhere:

> The Nile will teem with frogs. They will come up into your
> palace and your bedroom and onto your bed, into the
> houses of your officials and on your people, and into your
> ovens and kneading troughs." (Exodus 8:3-4)

What a mess that must have been! The magicians of the land, forced to show off their own power, were actually able to duplicate that event, however. How ironic, because then there were twice as many frogs!

Next was an infestation of gnats, and then one of flies, and then locusts. Soon hail covered the land and stripped every tree. Then a horrific epidemic hit the livestock. Next, an ugly outbreak of infected boils afflicted all Egyptians. Finally, there was an eerie total darkness over the land for three days. One can read about this incredible history in the book of Exodus, from chapters six to thirteen.

After each of these supernatural plagues, the pharaoh of Egypt still did not agree to liberate the Israelite slaves. Then there was one last tragic epidemic: an inexplicable plague on every firstborn child of each family in all the Egyptian population, and even on firstborn animals. What a horrifying phenomenon. On the night that came to be known as Passover, all the oldest children from every family, regardless of their age, mysteriously died from what was called a death angel. In one night, this calamity decimated the Egyptian population.

Yet in the area of Goshen where the Israelites lived, the plague did not occur. The Israelite people were protected from this last terrible, unnatural disaster. How could that have been? Why were the lives of their firstborn protected from a dark force when the Egyptian families suffered so greatly? We can read of strange, celestial directions that protected them. God instructed Moses to tell the Israelites to protect themselves from the death angel by slaughtering a strong, young, perfect lamb, spotless and innocent. It sounds like a bizarre ritual but then we celebrate with turkey on Thanksgiving. What's even more odd is that they were actually told to take the blood of the lamb and paint the sides and the tops of their doorposts with it. The Israelites did as they were instructed, for it was a

time of strange events in their land. Moses reported the word
of the LORD:

> Tell the whole community of Israel that on the 10th day
> of this month each man is to take a lamb for his family,
> one for each household.
>
> Then they are to take some of the blood and put it on
> the sides and tops of the doorframes of the houses where
> they eat the lambs. That same night they are to eat the
> meat roasted over the fire, along with bitter herbs and
> bread made without yeast.
>
> On that same night I will pass through Egypt and strike
> down every firstborn—both men and animals—and I will
> bring judgment on all the gods of Egypt. I am the Lord.
> The blood will be a sign for you on the houses where you
> are and when I see the blood, I will pass over you. No
> destructive plague will touch you when I strike Egypt. This
> is a day you are to commemorate; for the generations to
> come you shall celebrate it as a festival to the Lord--a
> lasting ordinance. (Exodus 12:3, 7-8, 12-14)

The instructions were sent out to each Israelite household.
Can you imagine the homes in Goshen on that first Passover?
During that day, preparations were made, and a whole lamb was
roasted for a huge meal in each home. That evening family and
friends feasted while fresh, red blood stained their doorposts. It
was surely a night to be remembered. In fact, certain contemporary congregations still celebrate this historical event.

The Perfect and Powerful Lamb

Let's zoom down the timeline to a little over two thousand years ago. Jesus was from the Israelite tribe of Judah, so of course he too kept the ancient holy days. Like many other people going home for the holidays, Jesus went back to Jerusalem to celebrate the same Passover holiday in the last year before he was arrested and put to death. He knew what was going to happen to him when he and his friends went to Jerusalem. Usually they would sacrifice a new lamb from one of their herds, prepare it, and eat it with their families to commemorate God's willingness to save the lives of households that displayed the blood of a lamb. That year he tried to warn his friends that something very different was going to happen to him as the Son of Man and the Son of God.

> "We are going up to Jerusalem," he said, "and the Son of Man will be betrayed to the chief priests and teachers of the law. They will condemn him to death and will hand him over to the Gentiles who will mock him and spit on him, flog him and kill him. Three days later he will rise. (Mark 10:33-34)

His friends and followers didn't know what to think when he made this announcement. After all, they thought he was going to change their political world and become the new king of their nation. For him to endure such a disrespectful death when they had already seen his miraculous power displayed was unimaginable.

There is so much interesting biblical history, but I think this pivotal Passover story is one of the most intriguing. It still forms the foundation of Christianity today. Jesus had kept Passover all his life, yet this specific year was to be the culmination of ancient prophecy. Jesus was preparing himself to fulfill the Passover tradition of offering a lamb for a sacrifice. This time, however, *he was going to be the Passover lamb.*

Jesus accepted the mission given to him. He would become the final sacrificial offering needed to cover the sins of all human beings. No longer would animal sacrifices be required to make payment for sin on altars of worship. Indeed this could explain why, when John the Baptist saw Jesus coming toward him for baptism, he exclaimed:

> Look, the Lamb of God, who takes away the sins of the world! (John 1:29)

At the time of the original Passover, the sacrificed lamb was instrumental in saving every firstborn person in Goshen from the silent power of the death angel. Now, by accepting Jesus Christ as our personal sacrificial lamb, we too are delivered from the demons of death and destruction. Jesus's sacrifice as the Lamb of God protects us and saves us. The dark angel has no authority and must pass over us too.

Perhaps most fascinating of all is that Jesus Christ was crucified on the same day the lamb was slaughtered, the preparation day for the special Sabbath of Passover. He died at three in the afternoon and was buried before sunset.

> Jesus said, "It is finished." With that, he bowed his head and gave up his spirit. Now it was the day of Preparation, and the next day was to be a special Sabbath. (John 19:30-31, also Mark 15:42-43)

Just like those sacrificial lambs in the Old Testament, Jesus's blood was pure and innocent of wrongdoing. Both lambs, in the Old Testament and in the new, had to be unblemished. Jesus was said to be perfect because he didn't transgress any of the Great Ones' laws (Hebrews 4:15). He represented the highest of humankind.

Did some of the Jewish crowd at the crucifixion see this similarity to the ancient practice when they saw his blood running down the cross? Perhaps they wondered, because he was dying on the same day they always prepared the lamb for their Passover meal.

> How much more, then, will the blood of Jesus Christ, who through the eternal Spirit offered himself unblemished to God, cleanse our consciences from acts that lead to death, so that we may serve the living God! (Hebrews 9:14)

Coming back from our explorations of the biblical past, the common Christian expressions about salvation suddenly snap into a much clearer focus. We now have a solid understanding of what Christians are trying to express when they say, "Jesus saves you." The symbolism all began back in the history of God's people, when a sacrificial lamb saved them from death and slavery.

These are the ways of the Great Ones. God used relevant events thousands of years ago to forecast their intentions to us, fulfilling each step of the celestial plan. In this way these great, celestial beings communicate with the human race: invisibly, without language, through diverse cultures and across the vastness of time itself.

Consuming Christ Within

Just before he died, Jesus Christ reinforced tradition with his own small Passover observance with those closest to him. He gathered his friends for a last supper to reenact the Passover ceremony of sacrificing the lamb, but now with symbolic bread and wine. Jesus asked the disciples to eat the bread he gave them, and he called it his own flesh. Then he passed around the wine and told them to drink as though it were his own blood. What morbid requests to make to your friends! He said to them:

> *"This is my body given for you; do this in remembrance of me." (Luke 22:19)*
>
> *And he took wine and said, "Drink from it, all of you. This is my blood of the new covenant, which is poured out for many for the forgiveness of sins." (Matthew 26:27-28)*

Jesus fully understood that this new observance would take the place of the Passover family dinner of the sacrificial lamb. The ceremony is now a Christian tradition known as Holy Communion, and it is prevalent in congregations around the world. Unfortunately, the explanation from the Old Testament is overlooked by most denominations. Yet, Christ—the Lamb of God—asked us to eat the communion bread and drink the red wine to reenact the first ceremony of protecting ourselves from Satan, the angel of death.

This observance signifies we are to consume him spiritually, taking him into every corner of our lives, symbolically eating his flesh and drinking his blood—feasting upon him, as was the ancient custom with the actual lamb. We are to take him in so he may cleanse and transform us, and live inside our minds! This is what the Holy Communion service is actually portraying.

Revelation, the last book in the Bible, also speaks about the Lamb in a vision of prophecy. The disciple John "saw a Lamb, looking as if it had been slain" (Revelation 5:6). This celestial being had the authority to open the way for a utopian kingdom on earth. It's significant when we remember that Jesus paid the price for us through his self-sacrifice as the Lamb of God.

> *You are worthy to take the scroll and to open its seals, because you were slain and with your blood you purchased men for God from every tribe and language and peoples and nation. (Revelations 5:9)*

From a God-realm viewpoint, the new Passover is a celestial day celebrating Jesus Christ, who lived a human life perfectly according to the rules for human creation. In doing so, he qualified to ransom us from the dark force of Satan, who still controls our planet.

Think about this: the act of human beings consuming the imperceptible, celestial body of Jesus Christ is a counterpart to the action of the Great Ones when they clothed one of themselves with a human body of flesh and blood. How awesome and timeless are these vast analogies! The Great Ones have clearly been trying all along to communicate and propose an alliance with our species.

Death Is Not the Enemy

So to recap: Jesus was conceived from celestial seed, grew up to become a great ambassador from another world, and then he was mocked, scorned, and tortured. He died by crucifixion, with his blood running down the cross. The lamb sacrificed in early Israelite history, with its blood running down the doorposts, was symbolic of Jesus Christ's coming death. Then his mutilated body was taken down and put into a guarded tomb for three days and three nights.

The paranormal events continued to build. Let's recall that Jesus was powerfully anointed because he wasn't only human. He was also half celestial—how can an eternal spirit entity actually be killed? He had to come back to life.

Historical accounts of this metaphysical event were recorded in three different New Testament books. Luke, Mark, and Mathew all discuss this transformation in a straightforward manner.

After the Sabbath, at dawn on the first day of the week, Mary Magdalene and the other Mary went to look at the tomb.

There was a violent earthquake, for an angel of the Lord came down from heaven and, going to the tomb, rolled back the stone and sat on it. His appearance was like lightning, and his clothes were white as snow. The guards were so afraid of him that they shook and became like dead men.

The angel said to the women, "Do not be afraid, for I know that you are looking for Jesus, who was crucified. He is not here; he has risen, just as he said. Come and see the place where he lay. Then go quickly and tell his disciples: 'He has risen from the dead and is going ahead of you into Galilee. There you will see him.' Now I have told you."

So the women hurried away from the tomb, afraid yet filled with joy, and ran to tell his disciples. Suddenly Jesus met them. "Greetings," he said. They came to him, clasped

> *his feet and worshiped him. Then Jesus said to them, "Do*
> *not be afraid. Go and tell my brothers to go to Galilee;*
> *there they will see me." (Matthew 28:1-10)*

Matthew told us that the guards at the tomb went back into town and reported to the chief priest exactly what had happened. The priests were protecting their status and did not want these details to be made public. So a cover-up was planned. The guards were paid off and were prepared with these instructions:

> *You are to say, "His disciples came during the night and*
> *stole him away while we were asleep." If this report gets*
> *to the governor, we will satisfy him and keep you out of*
> *trouble." So the soldiers took the money and did as they*
> *were instructed. And this story has been widely circulated*
> *among the Jews to this very day. (Matthew 28:13-15)*

Yes, this official account can still be read in the Bible. Logically, in that culture, we would expect these guards to have been killed for allowing Jesus to be taken away on their watch. However, these same guards were paid off and set free so the story might be spread.

In the book of John, we read that after the women saw the empty tomb, they hurried to tell the other disciples. Then both Peter and John ran to the site and saw the burial cloth lying there. They noticed that the cloth that had been around Jesus's head was separate from the other linen. Such detailed accounting came from eyewitnesses and from friends who knew and loved Jesus. John said, "he saw and believed" (John 20:8). Days later the disciples were meeting in an upstairs room, and Jesus appeared to all of them (John 20:19). This spirit form was able to enter a locked room invisibly and was even able to eat a meal with them. What a bizarre, supernatural occurrence it must have been for them!

Among the twelve disciples, Thomas was the real skeptic.

So the other disciples told him, "We have seen the Lord!" But he said to them, "Unless I see the nail marks in his hands and put my finger where the nails were, and put my hand into his side, I will not believe it."

A week later his disciples were in the house again, and Thomas was with them. Though the doors were locked, Jesus came and stood among them and said, "Peace be with you!" Then he said to Thomas, "Put your finger here; see my hands. Reach out your hand and put it into my side. Stop doubting and believe."

Thomas said to him, "My Lord and my God!"

Then Jesus told him, "Because you have seen me, you have believed; blessed are those who have not seen and yet have believed." (John 20:25-29)

John was talking about us! Even though we have not seen Jesus as a human being, if we can truly accept that he was the Christ, anointed with metaphysical, otherworldly power, the Son of God, we too will be blessed in our lives.

Although he was resurrected into an essence of Spirit, Jesus Christ appeared in human form to his followers many times with convincing proof that he was still living. These strange events are recorded in four different gospel accounts written by Matthew, Mark, Luke, and John because they believed them to be true. These books have been passed down through many generations to our day. Why would they be any less true now than they were a month after they were written?

After all these miraculous events, the first Christians went on living, but their perspectives greatly changed. They willingly suffered intense persecution, torture, martyrdom, and even crucifixion for some of them. Why didn't they cave in under such pressure? They didn't retract their testimonies because they knew, with great awe, that the events they had participated in were real.

The death and new birth sequence of Jesus Christ portrays the promise we have been given of an afterlife, and Jesus shows us the way in which it can happen. The ultimate purpose for human life is this same transformation into an immortal, celestial life form. This is what the Great Ones propose for us.

The steps in the metamorphosis to a spiritual existence are like playing levels in a game. The first step begins when the Great Ones call us at a specific time. This generates our repentance for the way we are living, and an acceptance of Jesus's death to pay the penalty for our sins. When we choose celestial ways and not our own, it results in a desire to be baptized.

The second step is the ceremony of going under the water, portraying our own symbolic death like that of Jesus. We have cleared out the old and are open to the new. Our minds begin to be reprogrammed, and a fantastic journey in personal growth begins. Still, the final process of connection to the Great Ones is not yet complete.

Downloading Spirit

There is a crucial third step to the connection. A metaphysical seed of Spirit must be implanted within us and grow to maturity just as it did within the first believers waiting in the upstairs room.

Baptism with water is a reenactment of being physically birthed from the womb. We feel born again. We put our old self to death and surrender to being cleansed by the water. Only then can our minds finally clear enough room to download the actual truths these great celestial beings want to give us. That is the next step—to be filled with the presence of celestial Spirit. To understand the process, it's necessary to revisit the promises of a significant day, the Day of Pentecost, which was briefly discussed at the beginning of this chapter.

The name Pentecost comes from a Greek word meaning "fiftieth day," as the holy day is to be celebrated fifty days after Passover. In ancient history, the day of Pentecost was celebrated at the beginning of the spring harvest as a celebration of thankfulness for the first produce brought in from the fields. For this reason it was also known as the Feast of First Fruits (Numbers 28:26).

Jesus Christ appeared to his disciples in his resurrected celestial form during these fifty days, which came after his physical death. He told them he would be sending a powerful, sacred Spirit to guide them, and he gave these instructions:

> Do not leave Jerusalem, but wait for the gift my Father promised, which you have heard me speak about. For John baptized with water, but in a few days, you will be baptized with the Holy Spirit.

> ...you will receive power when the Holy Spirit comes on you
> and you will be my witnesses in Jerusalem and in all Judea
> and Samaria, and to the ends of the earth. (Acts 1:4-8)

So on their festival day of Pentecost, Christ's followers gathered together to wait expectantly for some metaphysical occurrence to fulfill the meaning of this day for them. They were not disappointed.

> Suddenly a sound like the blowing of a violent wind came
> from heaven and filled the whole house where they were
> sitting. They saw what seemed to be tongues of fire that
> separated and came to rest on each of them. All of them
> were filled with the Holy Spirit and began to speak in
> other tongues as the Spirit enabled them. (Acts 2: 2-4)

As discussed earlier, Christ's followers felt this sacred Spirit so strongly that when they went out into the city, they laughed and shouted as though they were drunk. Pure joy radiated from them. That is what Spirit does when it manifests within us. Once again, God had reenacted the meaning of an ancient day of celebration, for these men and women received celestial spirit in their minds and were God's first fruits of harvest in humankind!

When this small group went out into the streets of Jerusalem, thousands of people were influenced by their excitement. Spirit used these first believers to call all kinds of people from many cultures. Peter, the spokesperson, addressed a huge crowd and tried to explain why they were so overwhelmed with exuberance:

> God has raised this Jesus to life, and we are all witnesses
> of the fact. Exalted to the right hand of God, he has
> received from the Father the promised Holy Spirit and has
> poured out what you now see and hear. (Acts 2:32-33)
>
> With many other words he warned them; and he pleaded
> with them, "Save yourselves from this corrupt generation."
> Those who accepted his message were baptized, and
> about three thousand were added to their number that
> day. (Acts 2:40-41)

How fitting of God to proceed to the next stage of his plan on this specific historical day. From Rabbinic times, it has been said that this festival also commemorates the giving of the law to Moses at Mt. Sinai. So on the anniversary of this particular sacred day, the law was given for moral and spiritual development, and then later, more currently, Spirit is given for the same purpose. Reenactment of each ancient holy day is rich with meaning as it materializes again on the human timeline.

When the Trumpets Blow

The list of ancient holy day celebrations reads like a treasure map, pointing to exhilarating future events that have been pre-programmed for us. Three times each year, the Israelites were to celebrate a set of festivals in recognition of God's plan for humankind (Exodus 23:15-16). These appointed "feasts of the LORD" are outlined in detail in the Old Testament (Leviticus 23:1-44).

The first season of sacred days began with the original Passover evening, followed by a seven-day Feast of Unleavened Bread.

These were observed in the first month of the Judaic yearly calendar to commemorate when the Israelites were released from slavery and fled Egypt. These sacred days were reenacted when Jesus Christ became the sacrificial lamb for us and freed us from the bondage of the dark powers of sin.

Fifty days later came the next season of celebration for the Israelites. This was the Feast of Harvest, the gathering of the first fruits of the crops they had sown. This day was symbolically fulfilled when Spirit was first given to the original Christians on the Day of Pentecost. These first followers of Jesus Christ were the first fruits in God's early harvest. Yet, this was only the first harvest!

Future Sacred Celebrations

We might think these ancient sacred days were extravagant, and their New Testament counterparts were soul-deep with meaning and relevancy. However, can you imagine what kind of show we are in for with the coming of the next season of sacred memorial days and their reenactment in our own day and age? On a yearly Hebrew calendar, the next four days of celebrations happen later in the seventh month. This season is called the Feasts of Ingathering, as the celebrations originally occurred when the Israelites harvested the final crops from their fields.

The big question I ask myself now is: what will happen on the next sacred day to be reenacted? The next holy day is the Feast of Trumpets and was originally observed on the first day of the seventh month—what today we call the Jewish New Year. In ancient times it was always commemorated with blasts of trumpets (Leviticus 23:23-25), which for centuries was the signal used to gather people together to prepare for battle. I believe something momentous will happen on this next step in the Great

Ones' celestial plan. There has not yet been any significant event fulfilling the meaning of this day. So, in other words, on the current human timeline, we are here!

A number of passages in the Bible give us clues as to what might soon take place on the Day of Trumpets.

> This is to be a lasting ordinance for you and the generations to come. When you go into battle in your own land against an enemy who is oppressing you, sound a blast on the trumpets. Then you will be remembered by the Lord your God and rescued from your enemies. (Numbers 10:8-9)

The trumpet is a victorious sound! It is a call for godly intervention. Trumpets are mentioned in key scriptures of the New Testament and they announce momentous things about to occur:

> I declare to you, brothers, that flesh and blood cannot inherit the kingdom of God, nor does the perishable inherit the imperishable. Listen, I tell you a mystery: We will not all sleep, but we will all be changed—in a flash, in the twinkling of an eye, at the last trumpet. For the trumpet will sound, the dead will be raised imperishable, and we will be changed. (1 Corinthians 15:50-52)

When sounds of trumpets are heard in the sky, great supernatural, metaphysical things will occur on our planet!

> At that time the sign of the Son of Man will appear in
> the sky, and all the nations of the earth will mourn. They
> will see the Son of Man coming on the clouds of the sky,
> with power and great glory. And he will send his angels
> with a loud trumpet call, and they will gather his elect
> from the four winds, from one end of the heavens to the
> other. (Matthew 24:30-31)

Unbelievable? It will definitely be some kind of phenomenon the world has never seen before. Seven trumpets also sound in the book of Revelation, announcing devastation and world-shaking events. The timing of all these trumpets is yet unknown. We wait in suspense, unsure of what actually will take place in both the physical and spiritual sense.

After the Feast of Trumpets, the blueprints for the Great Ones' plan for humankind shows the fulfillment of three other memorial days in the same season. The Day of Atonement will come next. It's a day for soul searching, fasting, and repentance so one can get in harmony with God. In the same month, on the tenth day, the Israelites were instructed to fast for a full day to purify themselves.

Then, on the fifteenth day, the Feast of Tabernacles began and lasted for seven days. The people were to stay in tents to remember how they had come out of Egypt. On each of these seven days, great numbers of livestock were slaughtered and prepared as offerings. The meat was barbecued on altars in honor of God. In an agricultural society, individual wealth was thus shared in a weeklong, nationwide celebration of abundance.

Finally, the eighth day featured a closing assembly of the sacred season. This was the last great day of feasting, and full of even more jubilation. It represented the time of the end, when we each will put on immortality and enter the realm of the great city of God. This is the city with streets paved in gold; its foundations are decorated with precious stones. The disciple John described it. Spirit carried him away in a vision to a high mountain, and showed him a great municipality coming down to earth from the heavens.

> Then I saw "a new heaven and a new earth," for the first heaven and the first earth had passed away, and there was no longer any sea. I saw the Holy City, the new Jerusalem, coming down out of heaven from God, prepared as a bride beautifully dressed for her husband. And I heard a loud voice from the throne saying, "Look! God's dwelling place is now among the people, and he will dwell with them. They will be his people, and God himself will be with them and be their God. 'He will wipe every tear from their eyes. There will be no more death' or mourning or crying or pain, for the old order of things has passed away." (Revelation 21:1-4)

These descriptions remind us of current sci-fi movies about futuristic events! In John's vision, he measured the city's dimensions with a rod made of gold. It was a gigantic cube of 1,400 miles or nearly 2,200 kilometers square, and the same distance in height. This "city" cube is God's domain, and destined to land on our planet.

John continued to record what he was told.

He said to me: "It is done. I am the Alpha and the
Omega, the Beginning and the End. To the thirsty I will
give water without cost from the spring of the water of
life. Those who are victorious will inherit all this, and I will
be their God and they will be my children. (Revelation
21:6-7)

The ancient ceremonies we've covered in this chapter have been passed down as signposts from century to century. Through them, we are able to have insight into the celestial components of the vast blueprint for human history. Perhaps more spectacularly, the meanings of the sacred days and the events to come on the human timeline have been held intact. For these ancient ceremonies are not only holy days spoken about in the Old Testament of the Bible, but they are developmental levels in our collective spiritual transformation. These sacred days are still observed in the Jewish faith and in other denominations too. They have held meaning for many serious believers for a very long time.

Those who anticipate the coming reenactment and supernatural fulfillment of the next sacred days are looking upward. One year someday soon, the sound of trumpets will signify our next step toward the utopian kingdom. We who believe breathlessly wait.

8

accessing spirit

Spirit is defined as an extension of God's invisible presence in our physical realm. Access to Spirit requires us to open the doors of our minds. When we accept the celestial proposal, real activation of spiritual power in our lives can begin.

A Sacred Touch

At this point in our quest for truth, we have determined the main celestial entities behind the scenes in the game of life. We have acquired biblical insight to God's plan for the human species. We appreciate how the various historical celebrations of ancient people uniquely outlined this plan. Academic knowledge of these things is not enough, however.

When we grasp the true concept of repentance, we will feel compelled to act on that knowledge and be baptized by seeking out a respected person with spiritual integrity. This personal step is the means to accessing celestial Spirit. This makes it real. When I first perceived the depth of faith in the first Christians, I wanted more. I wanted to be touched by God's presence and power just as they had been.

Years ago I read an article about a baby who had been imprisoned in a closet during the first year of his life. The infant was fed regularly each day, but he didn't have contact with anyone except for what was necessary to feed and change him. He received no loving caresses. When neighbors eventually discovered the situation, the baby had died. An autopsy revealed that he had been physically healthy but had died from emotional and physical isolation. The article concluded that bonding is a unique phenomenon necessary for the will to live. One could say a caring kind of physical touch is a form of empowerment that communicates in ways that go beyond our understanding. This kind of contact transfers a life-giving power.

The importance of touch doesn't stop with a baby's need to survive. There is loving assurance in many modes of physical connection. Consider an infant holding a mother's leg when his security is threatened; a parent's hand tightly clasping her small child as they cross the street; a bear hug given to a youngster in a special moment; a hearty handshake for the recipient of a diploma; or a man's hand caressing a woman's cheek to tell her she is cherished. Connections like these convey assurance and give powerful confidence to the individuals receiving them. All gentle touches have this in common. Through a simple physical touch, we're able to know that someone's concern for us goes very deep. This kind of interpersonal contact can be healing because it transfers a form of positive energy into us.

What kind of energy would we experience if we encountered an immortal, other-dimensional being? When the half-man, half-immortal Jesus Christ touched people, he gave them more than just a feeling of acceptance. The connection he had to the God

Source was so strong that people were physically healed by just a fleeting touch! This was so well known in the area of Jerusalem that many times huge crowds pressed Jesus from all sides to gain contact with him. Here's one fascinating account:

> *...A woman was there who was subject to bleeding for twelve years. She had suffered a great deal under the care of many doctors and had spent all she had, yet instead of getting better she grew worse. When she heard about Jesus, she came up behind him in the crowd and touched his cloak, because she thought, "If I just touch his clothes, I will be healed." Immediately her bleeding stopped and she felt in her body that she was freed from her suffering. At once Jesus realized that power had gone out from him.... (Mark 5:25-30)*

Jesus was known as the Christ, which means "anointed with metaphysical power." It is this very power he wants to pour into our minds and bodies. He longs to touch every one of us with loving confidence. More than anything else, he wants to empower us!

A man named Timothy was a devoted believer and understood that powerful Spirit could actually be transferred from one person to another.

> *For this reason I remind you to fan into flame the gift of God, which is in you through the laying on of my hands. For God did not give us a spirit of timidity, but a spirit of power, of love and of self-discipline. (2 Timothy 1:6-7)*

We discussed the Day of Pentecost in the previous chapter. This was the first day Spirit arrived in our world and fused with the followers of Jesus Christ in a most dramatic way. This energizing, otherworldly Spirit was transferred to others through verbal connection and touch. Thousands of people were baptized during that time. Later, through power-filled words and simple touch, these people were able to heal others who were ill with physical and mental diseases. In this way, the authoritative power of Jesus Christ is passed from one to another. The book of Mark gives many other examples of this happening.

> Calling the twelve to him he sent them out two by two and gave them authority over evil spirits.... They drove out many demons and anointed many sick people with oil and healed them. (Mark 6:7, 12)

The Hidden Mystery

The idea that celestial power could be emitted from inside and flow outward to another was a great mystery to me. What was this power, and how could I get some? How wonderful to be able to help and heal others. Passages in the ancient scriptures talk about a great mystery, a secret hidden from even rich and intelligent people. What is this mystery? Is there some power we can access or download? We know that a large portion of the brain's capacity lies dormant. Well, what is it waiting for?

All the world's religions have one thing in common: the search upward for metaphysical empowerment. Humanity's universal need is to be connected to something greater than itself. To put it simply, our minds are designed for a unique connection; we only need to plug in to this powerful source of Spirit.

Centuries ago Paul the evangelist spoke precisely about this core element of Christianity:

> ...the mystery that has been kept hidden for ages and generations, but is now disclosed to the Lord's people. To them God has chosen to make known among the Gentiles the glorious riches of this mystery, which is Christ in you, the hope of glory. (Colossians 1:26-27)

Paul was emphasizing the richness of this mystery: *which is Christ in you.* Remember that the word *Christ* means the anointing of a metaphysical power. To have Christ in us means we have metaphysical power within us!

After leaving our world, Jesus released the presence of Spirit into our physical realm to fuse with us individually. He implemented a way in which a tiny part of the source of God could exist in every person. In a symbiotic fusion of our human spirit with sacred Spirit, something is irrevocably conceived inside our minds. This celestial connection is man's hope for greatness, for glory, because when Spirit is added to our minds it can make us metaphysically strong. This is the answer to the age-old question of man's ultimate quest for power. The Great Ones want to graft themselves into us, but it is always our choice, whether or not to connect with them. That's the core of the celestial proposal.

The Counselor

The concept of celestial Spirit, traditionally known as the Holy Spirit, is a commonly accepted part of Christianity. However, it is not just a flowery religious term that you hear from a pulpit. Spirit is an entity of the Great Ones whose purpose is to guide us through the different levels of maturing spiritually. This celestial

Spirit is not dominating but guiding and empowering. Spirit acts like a celestial counselor, and Jesus promised to send it to us before his death. He described this unique gift in a beautiful passage:

> And I will ask the Father, and he will give you another counselor to be with you forever—the spirit of truth.
>
> The world cannot accept him, because it neither sees him nor knows him. But you know him, for he lives with you and will be in you. I will not leave you as orphans; I will come to you. (John 14:16-18)
>
> All this I have spoken while still with you. But the counselor, the Holy Spirit, whom the father will send in my name, will teach you all things and will remind you of everything I have said to you. Peace I leave with you; my peace I give you. I do not give to you as the world gives. (John 14:25-27)

When Jesus Christ died a physical death, Spirit was sent in his place. Jesus introduced this next celestial ambassador with this announcement:

> I have much more to say to you, more than you can now bear. But when he, the Spirit of truth, comes, he will guide you into all truth. He will not speak on his own; he will speak only what he hears, and he will tell you what is yet to come. He will bring glory to me by taking from what is mine and making it known to you. (John 16:12-15)

Spirit's purpose is to guide us into godly knowledge. Could this be our moral conscience trying to communicate a higher standard by which to live our lives? Haven't we sometimes heard wisdom from above in our quiet times of contemplation? Perhaps our consciences are simply the mechanical connecting links that are already installed in our minds. Spirit takes knowledge from the Great Ones and makes it known to us. If we could only set a moral thermostat to our conscience and train ourselves to act upon what we hear!

Power from the Spirit

What can we do with Spirit living inside of us? Unbelievable things! Paul, Peter, John, and other apostles performed many miraculous healings by the gift of Spirit. When we allow Spirit to live within us, we are given different kinds of celestial gifts also. They are all personal strengths and powerful tools for living.

> Now to each one the manifestation of the Spirit is given for the common good. To one there is given through the Spirit the message of wisdom, to another the message of knowledge by means of the same Spirit, to another faith by the same Spirit, to another gifts of healings by that one Spirit, to another miraculous powers, to another prophecy, to another the ability to distinguish between spirits, to another the ability to speak in different kinds of tongues, and to still another the interpretation of tongues. All these are the work of one and the same Spirit.... (1 Corinthians 12:4-11)

Often a celestial gift is something that can't be seen. So how do we know if we have been given Spirit? The disciples were enabled to speak in other languages on the Day of Pentecost, but it was in order to communicate to people of other nationalities. However, the previous list of manifestations mentions many other attributes of receiving Spirit. The apostle Paul later stated that the greatest gift we can receive is the ability to love unselfishly:

> Love never fails. But where there are prophecies, they will cease; where there are tongues, they will be stilled. (1 Corinthians 13:8)

The apostle Peter had great spiritual energy residing in him and demonstrated it very well. One time he was outside the temple and a crippled man was asking him for money.

> Then Peter said, "Silver and gold I do not have, but what I have I give. In the name of Jesus Christ of Nazareth, walk."
>
> Taking him by the right hand, he helped him up, and instantly the man's feet and ankles became strong. He jumped to his feet and began to walk. Then he went with them into the courts, walking and jumping and praising God. (Acts 3:6-8)

How was this miracle actually performed? Peter simply touched the handicapped man and helped him up. He was able to do this because the power of Spirit was residing in his confidence. This power went out of Peter's hands and into the man, and a metaphysical connection was made through the physical contact.

The important religious leaders of the day were very disturbed this healing happened on their temple grounds by someone they had not appointed. They seized Peter and his friend John for questioning.

> When they saw the courage of Peter and John and realized that they were unschooled, ordinary men, they were astonished and they took note that these men had been with Jesus. (Acts 4:13)

Peter and John didn't have any religious position in society or power of their own, but they had been filled by something supernatural. They were fused with Spirit. Through this connection, they were able to transfer the power of Spirit and perform the miracle. For a transfer of power to become possible, we simply need to allow it to live in us. Spirit itself does the work.

Today's Christians seem to be afraid of the word *power*. Yet, the Great Ones desire us to be powerful! In order to go to the next level of spiritual development, we must be touched by their presence and willingly participate with the metaphysical power of Spirit. We cannot continue to live in fear of its strangeness, but must welcome it inside our minds.

Asking for Spirit

How do we activate a connection to this powerful presence of the Great Ones in our world? Surely, it doesn't always come like the first Pentecost, with rushing wind and tongues of flame on top of our heads! Many people in the New Testament asked sacred Spirit to enter them, and it occurred in a number of ways.

Jesus's followers Peter and John went to Samaria to visit those who were seekers of truth, and for them it happened very simply:

> When they arrived they prayed for them that they might
> receive the Holy Spirit because the Holy Spirit had not yet
> come on any of them, they had simply been baptized into
> the name of the Lord Jesus. Then Peter and John placed
> their hands on them and they received the Holy Spirit.
> (Acts 8:17)

Receiving sacred Spirit seems more likely to occur after we are baptized. The transfer of power is then a tangible gift that God wants us to have because we have taken steps to prove our seriousness. In other scriptures, we can see that God is not fooled by any desire we might have for power.

> Now a man called Simon who had been known to practice
> witchcraft, heard the disciple Philip speak and saw him
> do great things and miracles through his God. He believed
> and was baptized but when he saw that the spirit was
> given by the laying on of the apostle's hands, he offered
> them money for that power himself. (Acts 8:18)
>
> Peter answered, "May your money perish with you, because
> you thought you could buy the gift of God with money!"
> (Acts 8:20)

Simon was a man who saw miracles and great things being done. He wanted that power, but no one can buy a part of God to selfishly put inside of himself as though it were a power supply. Nor do we need to. This power is a gift from the Great Ones to all those who truly believe in the celestial proposal given to us. We only need to ask for it and believe in it. Then we will receive it.

Because we are consistently allowed to make our own choices in life, we each must specifically ask for the Spirit of truth to enter us. The request must come from our own mouth and self-will.

God waits our whole lifetime for us to clean out the clutter from our minds and invite a celestial presence to live there. The God Source of love wants to give us Spirit as a powerful gift to help us toward godly maturity. Does this surprise us?

> *If you then, though you are evil, know how to give good gifts to your children, how much more will your Father in heaven give the Holy Spirit to those who ask him! (Luke 11:13)*

It is so beautifully simple. Jesus says, "I am the way" (John 14:6) as he sees us set out on the journey of life. He tells us, "Ask and it will be given to you; seek and you will find; knock and the door will be opened to you" (Matthew 7:7). Great spiritual doors are waiting to be opened in your life! Hidden treasures of joy lie ahead for you to find. God only waits for us to ask him in.

A dear friend of mine was raised in a strict fundamentalist church, but she came to a point where she was searching for something more. She wanted to find a closer relationship to the God she had learned so much about. She prayed many times to actually feel a connection to a spiritual presence in her own life and tried hard to make herself acceptable. In frustration, she felt as if she were pounding on the door to heaven crying, "Let me in. Let me in!"

Then, finally, her own unique supernatural experience happened when a soft, gentle voice quietly said to her, "Get out of the doorway *so you can let me in.*" It's not so much that we need to get into the presence of God, but that we need to open the door so he can get into us!

Spirit can manifest for us in many different ways, but it is always uniquely personal and begins when you feel a powerful connection to something far greater and more wonderful than yourself. It is as though an otherworldly touch overcomes you. You will know when it happens! You will just know.

Are you ready for the essence of Spirit to be conceived within you and added to your life? Then simply ask Spirit to enter and direct your path. Supernatural things will begin to happen to you. In your search for spiritual truth, you will find other believing people who have real connections to the God Source too. When these others reach out and touch you with powerful, heartfelt words, your desire to know God will become so real that your mind will be opened for Spirit to enter.

There are specific reasons why the process of transferring Spirit from one person to another works so well. Jesus tells us that when we get together and agree on godly matters, there is an accumulation of power. In contemporary terms, we can see it as a sort of power grid. It happens because the more that people agree, the stronger the connection to the fundamental nature of celestial power. Jesus tried to explain this phenomenon:

> Again, I tell you that if two of you on earth agree about anything you ask for, it will be done for you by my Father in heaven. For where two or three come together in my name, there am I with them. (Matthew 18:19-20)

Conception in Spirit

When we allow celestial Spirit to fuse with our spirit, a conception takes place. We, (who we are inside our physical body), are joined by a quantum spark of *them*—the Great Ones, the Source, the Son and Spirit. Through this amalgamation, our new identity with Spirit is conceived. It opens a different plane of mental awareness. Fusion with Spirit enables us to see under the surface of the physical things in our world and walk the vast spaces of the inner mind to explore its unlimited potential.

> The Spirit searches all things, even the deep things of God. For who among men knows the thoughts of a man except the man's spirit within him? In the same way no one knows the thoughts of God except the Spirit of God. We have not received the spirit of the world but the Spirit who is from God, that we may understand what God has freely given us. (1 Corinthians 2:6-12)

The state of being in Spirit is a strange, new frontier. We think of space travel with a lack of gravity, the warping of time, and a rearview mirror back to earth. Before we can travel in space, we must grasp strange concepts. Walking in the ways of the Great Ones will not follow our earthly explanations and expectations either.

The entity of Spirit is like the wind: invisible, but with an immense force of energy. Spirit appears in different forms and can enter anywhere at will. Jesus tried to explain the concept of this other-dimensional existence to a Pharisee named Nicodemus, a member of the Jewish ruling council who posed questions to him.

> He came to Jesus at night and said, "Rabbi, we know you are a teacher who has come from God. For no one could perform the miraculous signs you are doing if God were not with him."

In reply Jesus declared, "I tell you the truth, no one can see the kingdom of God unless he is born again."

"How can a man be born when he is old?" Nicodemus asked. "Surely he cannot enter a second time into his mother's womb to be born!"

Jesus answered, "I tell you the truth, no one can enter the kingdom of God unless he is born of water and the Spirit. Flesh gives birth to flesh, but the Spirit gives birth to spirit.

"How can this be?" Nicodemus asked. (John 3:5-9)

Jesus was referring to two different birth processes and continued his explanation:

You should not be surprised at my saying, "you must be born again." The wind blows where ever it pleases. You hear its sound, but you cannot tell where it comes from or where it is going. So it is with everyone born of the Spirit. (John 3:7-8)

We human beings obviously are not yet born of actual Spirit, because we cannot make ourselves invisible or travel on the wind. To begin our lives in this world, we are physically conceived in the womb. We develop from embryo to fetus, and then are born from that watery globe into the world, as we know it. In the mother's womb, the fetus has no idea or concept of anything outside his liquid world. The fetus cannot conceive of a separate, autonomous existence, yet that becomes a normal reality at birth. In the same way, Jesus tells us, we must be born again in Spirit. He is definite that this must take place before we can enter the kingdom of God in the celestial realm. Therefore, when we ask for, and accept celestial Spirit to take root within us, it is only a spiritual *conception* that takes place.

After we are conceived in Spirit, we must grow and develop to spiritual maturity during our years of gestation in the watery womb of Mother Earth. Our lifetimes are given to us for character development. Our lives here and now are the spiritual gestation period necessary to be born into God's realm. In other words, our birth into Spiritual existence comes after our biological death. But now we are able to see the light at the end of this world's birthing tunnel!

The process of developing our invisible, spiritual identities is the very purpose for having physical bodies and living human lives. This is the celestial purpose for humanity's current existence.

Incredibly, the Great Ones have found a way to infuse us with seeds of their Spirit. They know that with this fusion, we will be able to develop and endure the birthing pains of living through life. Our physical human bodies will weaken as we become older, but we will gain spiritual wisdom by experiencing trials, which will result in maturity.

We may become comfortable in our own skin, but this state of existence is only temporary. We have to physically die so the bodies that house us can be changed into immortal spiritual forms.

But someone may ask, "How are the dead raised? With what kind of body will they come?" How foolish! What you sow does not come to life unless it dies. When you sow, you do not plant the body that will be, but just a seed, perhaps of wheat or of something else. But God gives it a body as he has determined, and to each kind of seed, he gives its own body. All flesh is not the same: Men have one kind of flesh, animals have another, birds another and fish another. There are also heavenly bodies and there are earthly bodies; but the splendor of the heavenly bodies is one kind, and the splendor of the earthly bodies is another. (1 Corinthians 15:35-40)

So will it be with the resurrection of the dead. The body that is sown is perishable, it is raised imperishable; it is sown in dishonor, it is raised in glory; it is sown in weakness, it is raised in power; it is sown a natural body, it is raised a spiritual body.

If there is a natural body, there is also a spiritual body.... And just as we have borne the likeness of the earthly man, so shall we bear the likeness of the man from heaven. (1 Corinthians 15:42-44, 49)

These fantastic passages in Corinthians clearly describe our amazing metamorphosis into becoming god-beings. We are not yet complete, until we accept the seed of celestial Spirit.

Gifts of the Spirit

With Spirit growing within us, life takes on new meaning and priorities. God-like characteristics develop in us like wonderful fruit being produced on the Tree of Life.

> But the fruit of the Spirit is love, joy, peace, patience, kindness, goodness, faithfulness, gentleness and self-control. (Galatians 5:22)

These attributes become vitally important to us now. Celestial fruit will bud and grow ripe as we mature in Spirit throughout the years of our lives. With Spirit counseling us, God is able to guide us into all truth and use it to empower each of us uniquely and personally.

Now we have to think bold, beautiful things! We must think big, for our God is big. We have a mysterious, celestial *something* growing inside of us. The apostle Paul grasped the true vastness of our incredible potential when he quoted an Old Testament scripture:

> No eye has seen, no ear has heard, no mind has conceived what God has prepared for those who love him. But God has revealed it to us by his Spirit! (1 Corinthians 2:9-10, Isaiah 64:4)

If we have invited the conception of Spirit to take place within our minds, then we are more than ready to proceed and take on the powerful characteristics of these celestial Great Ones.

And so, we are at this point in humanity's story. We have each been given life and a lifetime to live it. Rich with experiences, fraught with dangers, hardships and struggles coupled with sporadic intervals of exquisite joy—this is the game of life, which we play seriously. Yet now, through the obscurity, we see there is a purpose to it all.

The plan is clearly laid out, and the choice to accept the great celestial proposal or not, is ours to make. We are a uniquely created species of the God Kind on the very pinnacle of the entryway to the realm of celestial immortality.

implementing the power

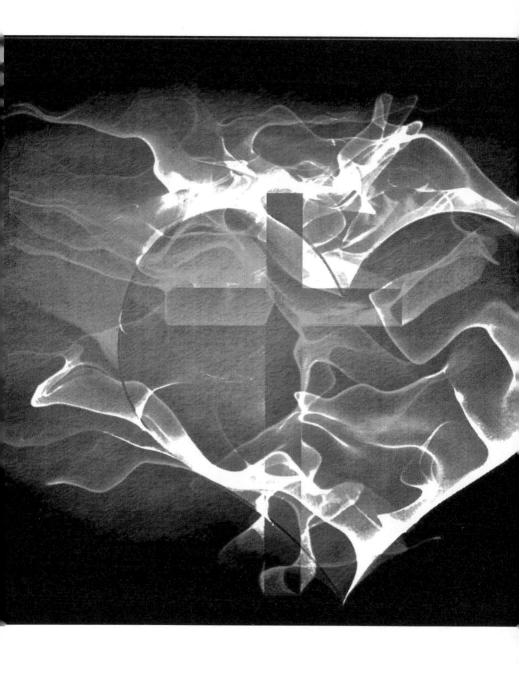

9
the substance of loving

Love is defined as the foundational characteristic of all other celestial attributes. Teaching humanity how to love has been the primary focus of celestial interventions on our timeline. Choosing to love is required to access the realm of the Great Ones.

Proof of Love

When I was a child, we lived in a lovely rural area very close to some railroad tracks. One warm, early spring morning, I was outside playing when I noticed a strange man had wandered into our yard. He was ill-kept and unshaven. This was an odd thing to me, as we didn't have many visitors.

"Where did you come from?" I asked. He told me he had been walking down the tracks. We talked about his adventures as he sat down to rest in the morning sun. He asked if he might have a glass of water, and I went into the house to get one, and made him a peanut butter sandwich. When I gave it to him, I could tell he was moved by my innocent kindness.

"Does your mom know you've brought this out to me?" he asked. I shook my head. "You've got to be mighty careful talking to strangers," he said. "But I thank you. You're like a little angel on this fine morning."

The world just then was a beautiful place to grow up in. I had discovered the substance of loving. An old bum off the railroad line and a small girl playing in her yard—we both experienced a small touch of celestial magic!

Love is an emotion we usually reserve for those we know and rarely apply to strangers, but the Great Ones' definition of love extends further than we can humanly fathom. The ability to love is one of the most important and definitive characteristics of the Great Ones. It's the foundation upon which to build all other godly traits. It towers above all other things, even the quest for a powerful faith.

Learning this characteristic of the Great Ones is our ultimate goal. Without this godly trait, the human race will only remain an earthly species within the animal kingdom, existing in a finite span of years and then crumbling into oblivion. God is patiently trying to teach us the height and breadth of the walls we must scale to reach a new reality. This is what Paul was trying to say in his letter to the Ephesians:

> ...I pray that you, being rooted and established in love,
> may have power, together with all the saints, to grasp
> how wide and long and high and deep is the love of
> Christ, and to know this love that surpasses knowledge—
> that you may be filled to the measure of all the fullness
> of God. (Ephesians 3:16-19)

Oh, to be filled with the fullness of a god! God's love is a serious, strong, committed kind of caring. It is stronger than knowledge. Indeed it is the strongest thing in the whole world. The Great Ones are not really looking for intelligent people, but rather those who know how to love. What's amazing is that often children know how to love to a much greater degree than adults. It's no wonder then that God holds these small human beings in such high regard.

Young children from close and happy families are taught to respect their parents and come to love them very deeply. Mom and Dad can do anything, can solve any problem, and can make fantastic experiences happen. Such parents will always stick up for their children, and consequentially the children put their total trust in them. Have you watched a father or a mother throw a small child up in the air and catch them, accompanied by squeals of laughter? That is love and total trust. Can we trust our celestial father as much during our personal and emotional upheavals? When we are tossed up in the air—or out in the streets—can we trust him to make it right?

Jesus Christ treasured this type of love and trust.

> He called a little child and had him stand among them
> and he said, "I tell you this truth, unless you change and
> become like little children, you will never enter the kingdom
> of heaven. Therefore, whoever humbles himself like this
> child, is the greatest in the kingdom of heaven." (Matthew
> 18:3)

Our celestial father wants us to have this kind of love and trust in him. He wants us to depend on him when we feel helpless against the negative forces in our existence. Perhaps, when we are able to turn to him during a crisis and depend on his authority and guidance, we can then "...know that in all things God works for the good of those who love him" (Romans 8:28).

Jesus loved his invisible, celestial father in just this way. Joseph was his stepfather, but he knew and loved his celestial father above all others. He came to realize that to love God and to love others was the main purpose of his life. Obviously, being able to share this depth of love was worth dying for.

Jesus Christ was quoted as saying that we are his friends, and that "greater love has no one than this: that one lay down his life for his friends" (John 15:13). Jesus Christ gave up his life because he sees us as friends! But can you imagine having the courage to go through humiliation, torture, and agonizing death when at any given second you have the power to stop it all with a single spoken command? We've read many accounts throughout history where individuals have made split-second decisions to rescue others from dying, and in doing so sacrificed their own lives. But for Jesus this was no split-second decision. He had read for himself the descriptions of his future sacrifice in the sacred scrolls. He knew what was to happen to him before he went to the Passover in Jerusalem that year, and had anticipated it every day of his life as a human being. He went through with it to make us his brothers and sisters. He

endured it so we could be adopted into the celestial race as God's other children! This is proof of how much Jesus Christ came to love his fellow human beings.

God also proved his love for us by demonstrating his feelings with the highest type of unselfish love we know: that of a parent for a child. All men and women can understand the poignancy of this one valuable sacrifice, regardless of where we live on the planet. The God Source reaches out and loves us as though we are his own children, even when we are rebellious toward him. Though we may live in abject immorality, God still loves us.

> But God demonstrated his own love for us in this: while we were still sinners, Christ died for us. (Romans 5:8)
>
> How great is the love the father has lavished on us, that we should be called children of God! And that is what we are! (1 John 3:1)

Suppose you have carefully brought up a son whom you are very proud of and whom you love deeply. He is a strong, intelligent, and compassionate individual who keeps very high standards and seems to spend all his time helping others. Could you stand by and allow his death to occur? If it would result in the ransom of a large group of strangers from a terrible kidnapper, would you allow him to be beaten and then murdered? Would you have the strength to desert him entirely in the crucial hours simply to free some foolish people and give them a chance for a better way of life? That's what God the Father did. The disciple John put it into this famous, often-quoted verse:

> For God so loved the world that he gave his one and only
> Son, that whoever believes in him shall not perish but have
> eternal life. (John 3:16)

The most powerful, superlative being in the universe allowed simple earthlings to physically abuse, mentally humiliate, and cruelly murder the celestial being he called his son, when at any time either of them could have stopped the whole thing from happening. The Great Ones allowed the crucifixion because the physical death of Jesus Christ was necessary to free us from the terrible, destructive forces ruling our planet. This is the same negative power source that is instrumental in causing us to sin and have miserable lives. If the God Source set up this incredible intervention, imagine how much he actually cares for us!

> This is how God showed his love among us: He sent his one
> and only Son into the world that we might live through
> him. This is love: not that we loved God, but that he loved
> us and sent his Son as an atoning sacrifice for our sins.
> (1 John 4:9-10)

Despite our weak, ill-mannered humanness, God's love for the human species is indisputable! The God Source actually wants to adopt us into the celestial family. The Great Ones are instrumental in helping us break through into a higher stage of spiritual development. By showing compassion and love toward us, they hope we earnestly learn to love in return. They have downloaded Spirit to us so we can incorporate their definition of love deeply enough in our minds to radiate it outward.

The Strongest Attribute

Celestial love is the Great Ones' strongest attribute, and it is higher than any other spiritual gift or talent we may desire. Without love everything else counts for nothing in our life game. We could have a genius IQ with psychic abilities; we could speak ten languages; we could sacrifice our lives for a wonderful cause; but if we don't learn how to love, it will all be worthless. This is distinctly expressed in the following passage:

> *If I speak in the tongues of men and of angels, but have not love, I am only a resounding gong or a clanging cymbal. If I have the gift of prophecy and can fathom all mysteries and all knowledge, and if I have a faith that can move mountains, but have not love, I am nothing. If I give all I possess to the poor and surrender my body to the flames, but have not love, I gain nothing.*
>
> *But where there are prophecies, they will cease; where there are tongues, they will be stilled; where there is knowledge, it will pass away. For we know in part and we prophesy in part, but when perfection comes, the imperfect disappears. When I was a child, I talked like a child, I thought like a child, I reasoned like a child. When I became a man, I put childish ways behind me.*
> *(1 Corinthians 13:1–3, 8–11)*

Just as our bodies once grew as children, now our minds need to grow in thinking processes grounded by celestial love. In our quest to be more godlike, learning how to love seems the logical place to start. In our great textbook, one whole chapter defines love:

> *Love is patient, love is kind. It does not envy, it does not*
> *boast, it is not proud. It is not rude, it is not self-seeking,*
> *it is not easily angered, it keeps no record of wrongs.*
> *Love does not delight in evil but rejoices with the truth.*
> *It always protects, always trusts, always hopes, always*
> *perseveres. Love never fails.... (1 Corinthians 13:4-8)*

We should take note that there is nothing fake about real love because it "rejoices with the truth." Real love is not some soft, sappy thing! We are told that love never fails, so it must be a terribly strong force. It's a source of power for us.

Learning to Love

The love found in friendship is another form of emotion the Great Ones display for us. Did you know that Jesus supposedly had a best friend? John was one of his main followers and was said to be "the disciple whom Jesus loved." (John 21:20) John understood the concept of celestial love. He still speaks to us from the pages of our Bible about the importance of developing the celestial art of loving:

> *Dear friends, let us love one another for love comes from*
> *God. Everyone who loves has been born of God and knows*
> *God. Whoever does not love does not know God, because*
> *God is love. (1 John 4:7-8)*

> *Dear children, let us not love with words or tongue but with actions and in truth. (1 John 3:18)*
>
> *Dear friends, since God so loved us, we also ought to love one another. (1 John 4:11)*

Wow! This says that when we can master the ability to love then we can really know God. If we don't love others, then we don't know anything about God. That's how important love is in the big, celestial picture.

The skill of loving is a developmental process that builds as Spirit takes up residence in us. Some people do not need very many instructions because of their family backgrounds, and perhaps the peaceful culture in which they live. The ways to show love and respect are passed down through generations, and they are as simple to these people as breathing. But others have never had relationships with mature adults who were capable of modeling a loving human nature. Each of us is in training on one level or another.

One of the main reasons people attend church or join a care group is to experience friendship with mature and loving people. But how do we know which group of spiritual people will be right for us? If we have put our trust in Spirit, it will lead us to a caring group of friends that will have just the right spiritual gifts we need in order to propel us to the next level of spiritual development. From that point we can learn and go on, for there are always higher levels to explore.

Jesus Christ instructed us to love and to have compassion for all humankind regardless of different religious beliefs. But concerning churches and care groups, we can ask ourselves: do these people authentically show that they love God and love others? Do they believe that the powerfully anointed Jesus Christ was the actual Son of God and a Son of Man—a human-celestial hybrid? Are they honest, loving, caring, authentic people with integrity? If so then they are probably connected to God in a way that can help us grow. A key verse in scripture states, "If anyone acknowledges that Jesus is the Son of God, God lives in him and he in God" (1 John 4:15).

Belonging to a group of people who are all striving to allow godly character to mature within them is of great benefit to our own growth. Even in the animal kingdom there is strength in numbers, for it is the single stray that is attacked. So finding a spiritual center is important because it connects us to God and to those who are trying to love like the Great Ones do. In fact all groups that have these basic beliefs are like a spiritual part of the body of Christ.

> The body is a unit, though it is made up of many parts; and though all its parts are many, they form one body. So, it is with Christ. For we were all baptized by one Spirit into one body—whether Jews or the Greeks, slave or free—and we were all given the one Spirit to drink...But in fact God has arranged the parts in the body, every one of them, just as he wanted them to be.... Now you are the body of Christ, and each one of you is a part of it. (1 Corinthians 12:12-13, 18, 27)

Looking for a group that best fits our own spiritual level is the only reason to compare different churches and denominations then. If we are people who believe in God, Jesus Christ, and the existence of Spirit, then we are not to judge each other. We cannot know the path of another. In the book of Romans, we are cautioned not to judge other believers:

> Who are you to judge someone else's servant? To his own
> master he stands or falls. And he will stand, for the Lord is
> able to make him stand. (Romans 14:10-13, 4)

In other words we need not worry about what others are doing. We are all on our own journeys, struggling for individual spiritual heights. Another passage makes this even clearer:

> "Teacher," said John, "We saw a man driving out demons in
> your name and we told him to stop, because he was not
> one of us."
>
> "Do not stop him," Jesus said. "No one who does a miracle
> in my name can in the next moment say anything bad
> about me, for whoever is not against us is for us." (Mark
> 9:39-40)

See what grand acceptance there is in celestial love? Actually it's easy to explain how to love others, for in every language on the face of our planet a smile is a smile! The cross-cultural golden rule of love and respect reads like this: "Do to others as you would have them do to you" (Luke 6:31). There is the proof in celestial love.

If we painted a picture in our minds of all societies living by this golden rule, there wouldn't be religious wars or prejudices. There would be respect and consideration for the many different and unique ways we have of serving our creator. Can anyone ever know all there is to know about God? No! So then, we too can be wrong even in the most elemental ways. We all have to work out our own salvation (Philippians 2:12). Learning how to love is the foundation for this type of unity, and it becomes easier when we remember that everyone else is at some stage of that same process.

Choosing to Love

Love is a choice of mind. It is also a force of action. It is not just fleeting feelings over which we have no control. We can choose to love or not to love; that choice is a power in itself. And because love is a power, it can be much more powerful than hate. For instance God has called us even to love our enemies. At first this request seems so illogical, doesn't it? What possible reasons are behind it? To be nice to those who are kind to us is natural, but God is asking us to do much more than this.

> ...*love your enemies, do good to them, and lend to them without expecting to get anything back. Then your reward will be great, and you will be sons of the Most High, because he is kind to the ungrateful and wicked. Be merciful, just as your Father is merciful. (Luke 6:35-36)*

Jesus Christ while he was dying on the cross, fully demonstrated how we must love our enemies, for he said, "Father, forgive them, for they do not know what they are doing" (Luke 23:34). The main reason we must learn to love our neighbors and even our enemies is that in doing so we become like godbeings and show that we belong to the very highest God Source there is.

Love is powerful; indeed it is our chief weapon against Satan's influence. When we choose to love, it will protect our minds from the destructive forces of the real enemy. We can look at it in this logical way: When we try to love our enemies, it leaves room for a higher power to operate in our lives and in the lives of others who are involved. If we try to take revenge, the God Source might have mercy on the other person and forget our side of it altogether.

It would be like telling God we don't want his help, we want to do it our own way, and we deserve to get even. But do we really deserve to get revenge? In times of anger and hurt, we can't see the influence Satan may have over us. God sees into the minds of all men.

If we try to show compassion to those who show malice toward us and still they do not change their attitude, then we can turn to the God Source as a strong father figure who loves us. He has the power to make it all right. Here is another interesting passage to sustain us in anger or when we feel deeply hurt by someone:

> Do not repay anyone evil for evil. Be careful to do what is right in the eyes of everybody. If it is possible, as far as it depends on you, live at peace with everyone. Do not take revenge, my friends, but leave room for God's wrath, for it is written: "It is mine to avenge; I will repay," says the Lord...Do not be overcome by evil, but overcome evil with good. (Romans 12:17-21)

The object here is to turn our anger into a warm and kind compassion because when we fight evil with evil, it will overtake us. If we fight evil with good—with the overwhelming power of love—then Satan has no control over us; he is unable to use or comprehend our weapons of love and mercy. In this way we can eventually eliminate any feelings of animosity we may have. We are all brothers and sisters in the human race, and none of us is perfect yet.

> *If anyone says, "I love God," yet hates his brother, he is a*
> *liar. For anyone who does not love his brother, whom he*
> *has seen, cannot love God, whom he has not seen. And he*
> *has given us this command; whoever loves God must also*
> *love his brother. (1 John 4:20-21)*

The neatest thing about learning to love in a godly way is the ability to see good qualities of character in everyone despite their obvious flaws. I have truly loved many times in my life, and although it may not always have been reciprocated as I would have liked, I know deep, intrinsic value has been added to my heart by choosing to love. I am in awe of love itself; I am in awe that hearts can still connect in such a way amidst the hardships of living and against all odds.

Two Trees in the Garden

So when we face adversity, will we choose to follow the godlike way of loving others? Or in self-centered greed will we create only ways of getting, of taking, or of using other people to get what we want? To over-generalize, *it is a decision to get or to give.* Will we focus on *getting or giving* in our lifetime? Will we in arrogance choose our own paths of right and wrong in order to get what we think we want in life, or will we learn to recognize that the way of loving and giving is the way of the Great Ones? Only by following their ways can we be led to greatness.

A loving creator chose to give us a most important gift: the ability to decide for ourselves how we will live. Remember, however, that this gift did not come without risk. If we were to be freethinking, creative, powerful earth-gods above all other living things on our planet, God saw that we would also be capable of creating great havoc and destruction. Therefore there needed to be natural consequences for our choices.

The Great Ones were responsible for the act of creating us, and so in compassion they set up a system of cause and effect to guide our spiritual development. These natural consequences were actually a form of mercy put into place to teach us their celestial ways. The same principles work for young children learning about their physical world. Natural consequences for actions are the ways in which human beings learn how best to live.

Initially consequences for important life choices were given to the first two created people on earth—Adam and Eve—with straightforward and specific directions. The God Source allowed them to choose whether they wanted to live by celestial values or to choose for themselves what was good and evil. Then he told them the prearranged consequence that would come from each choice. We previously examined this age-old story, but here are the key verses again:

> In the middle of the garden were the tree of life and the tree of the knowledge of good and evil....
>
> ...but you must not eat from the tree of the knowledge of good and evil, for when you eat of it you will surely die. (Genesis 2:9, 17)

Adam and Eve were told they could eat fruit from all the trees in the garden except this one. They actually had a choice in the beginning to eat from the Tree of Life and live forever, but they didn't do this. With a little negative influence by the adversary, they chose to eat from the forbidden tree of the knowledge of good and evil, the tree of death. They wanted to decide for themselves what was right and what was wrong. Perhaps this was the exact moment when free will was given to them. When they ate from that tree, knowing the consequences of their actions, they accepted the responsibility for their own lives, but along with that came the consequence of death.

So when they ate the forbidden fruit, they were cast out of the garden to fend for themselves. Why were they driven out simply for using their free will? Because the Great Ones realized that by eating from the wrong tree, the human species had chosen a path that could lead to multiple levels of horror, tragedy, and suffering. They had to contain the damage and put time constraints on it. The God Source said to the others:

> *The man has now become like one of us, knowing good and evil. He must not be allowed to reach out his hand and take from the tree of life and eat, and live forever. (Genesis 3:22)*

This makes it clear that although we were formed in the image of the Great Ones, they could not create us to be immortal. At all costs the Great Ones could not risk giving eternal life to beings that were capable of creating never-ending, horrible human suffering for themselves and each other. This was not the kind of progeny they wanted to create. Our choice to rebel against God was the major problem in giving humans free will.

> *So the Lord God banished him from the Garden of Eden to work the ground from which he had been taken. (Genesis 3:23)*

Eternal life was not given to us yet.

Unloving Actions

The human species began to increase rapidly while the Great Ones looked on. In the first century of humanity, earth's inhabitants became divided into the men who wanted to live as God instructed, learning the art of loving and giving, and those who chose to do their own thing (Genesis 4:26, 6:2). It seemed there was friction between these two life philosophies. The Bible mentions a man named Cain who chose to murder his brother, Abel, because he was jealous of Abel's closer relationship with the God Source. The Great Ones realized these created humans definitely needed to develop self-control and discipline on their journey to becoming god-beings. God asked Cain:

> *Why are you angry? Why is your face downcast? If you do what is right, will you not be accepted? But if you do not do what is right, sin is crouching at your door; it desires to have you, but you must master it. (Genesis 4:6)*

This is one of the most important passages in the entire collection of ancient scriptures. God asked Cain to overcome sin and not allow it to control him. What is sin? It is the opposite of love. It is the way of *get* as opposed to the way of *give*. It is not acceptable to the God species because it has no concern for the welfare of others. Sin desires to have us, but our purpose is to master it!

This is our assignment in life then: to learn to love unselfishly, so as to overcome and master what is not acceptable to God-beings in order to be like the Great Ones. What is the purpose of playing the game of life? This is it! This is what the Great Ones are asking us to do; it is their ultimate proposal and invitation to us.

Our purpose in living is to model ourselves after the God Kind. Just as a human parent is pleased and proud of a son or daughter who grows up with the same values, the Great Ones want us to grow up to be like them. In love we as parents set up rules for our children to teach them, to help them to mature, and to keep them safe. That is what the Great Ones have done for us as their young, spiritual children. However, rules of any kind—even for developing the ability to love—are worthless unless enforced by consequences.

Natural Consequences

We don't really like the idea that God has laws, do we? Perhaps they can be defined as celestial rules that teach us and keep us safe in a spiritual way. We can see them as morals that make up a celestial code of conduct. When we choose to take action that is unacceptable to the celestial moral code, the Great Ones call it sin and link it to natural consequences. The longer these unacceptable actions operate in our lives, the more misfortune results for us and for others. We could say that sin leads to mental, emotional, or physical pain in our lives and is the underlying cause of our unhappiness.

Unfortunately, through the accumulation of unloving, wrong choices, we sometimes create individual mental prisons of hate, violence, insanity, and addiction. After years of living that way, we often seek to end our misery for we have destroyed our minds to such an extent that we don't want to live anymore. To suffer for an eternity in these conditions would certainly be a living hell.

Because of compassion, the God Source made human life conditional by a celestial decree: "For the wages of sin is death..." (Romans 6:23). In other words, by the rules of the life game, we are accountable for the way in which we live. Death was designed as a merciful and necessary thing, the ultimate release from the human misery caused by our choices.

The sixth chapter of Genesis portrays God's vast system of accountability in the story of the Great Flood over the whole planet. If the earth were to be rocked off its axis by a huge meteorite, resulting in tectonic activity on a global scale, something like this would probably happen. Perhaps a similar event explains the Great Flood and why we can find fossilized sea life on our mountaintops.

The ancient texts say this catastrophic flood was the direct result of humankind's choosing wickedness. So great was the evil on the earth at that time, "the Lord grieved that he had made man on the earth and his heart was filled with pain" (Genesis 6:6). Isn't that explicit in describing God's paternal feelings for us? God saw humankind valued only self-gratification and that we were ruthlessly destroying one another. The blueprint for humans to develop into loving, godlike beings seemed far removed from the reality on earth at that time.

This historical account continues with the God Source allowing all but eight people on the face of the earth to be destroyed. Should we be riled and offended by this? Should we accuse God of barbarity? Yet the Great Ones gave us life and the choice to live it by their directions for happiness...or not. It wasn't according to their celestial plan that wickedness and destruction filled the entire earth with pain. Do we honestly think it would be more merciful to our species if God had let us continue? The Great Ones' intent was to create godlike beings, not vicious, animal-like creatures. Their proposal was set up for us to learn how to love one another. Due to the fact that we are all connected by interaction with each other, our loving choices will benefit ourselves and others, and our selfish choices can unfortunately influence and condemn all those around us.

Unfortunately the choices we make in life can even affect a whole portion of the population yet to come. This happens especially with our children and our children's children in the passing on of family values. The consequences of our actions are so far-reaching that God gave us a mandate not to worship or make alliances with anything on the earth, in the heavens above, or even in the water below:

> ...for I, the Lord your God, am a jealous God, punishing
> the children for the sin of the fathers to the third and
> fourth generation of those who hate me, but showing love
> to a thousand [generations] who love me and keep my
> commandments. (Exodus 20:5)

We need to understand that God does not delight in punishing children for the sins of the fathers, but this passage is a
warning that the system of natural consequences cannot affect
the parents without unfortunately also affecting their children.
While raising our children, we automatically pass on our family
values and standards of right and wrong. But it is most interesting to note that natural consequences for sin stretch across only
four generations while consequences for following celestial standards stretch across a thousand generations. It's so true that the
way we live influences our children's lives and continues onward
to our grandchildren, and down through many generations.

The Master Potter

The Great Flood destroyed most of the human race because the
chief godly characteristic of love had not been adequately developed within humanity. Afterward God began again with Noah's
family, who survived the catastrophe. Noah's lifespan was similar
to Adam's—about nine hundred and fifty years. The human species was once again given the task of populating the earth, and
once more the Great Ones wanted to try to teach their ways to
the human beings they had created. Like master artisans they
started shaping the clay once again.

Although human beings may be like earth-gods and have
potential to be like the God Kind, from the celestial viewpoint
we are still only clay pots with godlike potential. We need to be

shaped with finer spiritual qualities by the master potter, so to speak.

> Woe to him who quarrels with his maker, to him who is but a potsherd among the potsherds on the ground...Does the clay say to the potter, what are you making? (Isaiah 45:9)
>
> Can the pot say to the potter, he knows nothing? (Isaiah 29:16)

How presumptuous of us to think we might know of a better way to live. The Great Ones created and designed us to live their way. We were designed for celestial joy, for love, for empowered life and not arrogance:

> I am the Lord, and there is no other. I form the light and create darkness. I bring prosperity and create disaster. I, the Lord, do all these things.... Do you question me about my children or give me orders about the work of my hands? It is I who made the earth and created mankind upon it. (Isaiah 45:6, 12)

That certainly puts us in our place. With good reason, the God Source wants us to follow and trust him; otherwise it is impossible to live abundant and happy lives. Perhaps that's why man's lifespan was shortened. Adam is said to have lived over 900 years and later Abraham lived 175 years and look how this compares to our current possible one hundred years or so (Genesis 6:3, Genesis 25:9). The Great Ones must think that if people are going to con-

tinue to destroy themselves in agonizing ways, it is more merciful
that their lives be shorter.

The End of Time

Today greed and self-gratification on national scales have once
again corrupted our species to an extent that it must grieve the
God Kind and fill their hearts with sorrow. Starvation, disease,
addiction, and violence make death seem like a sweet release.
The idea of hell is carried out right here on earth for much of
the human race. In fact the human species seems to cause and
create its own hell. If we are not actually living in it, we all see
hellholes of violence and tragedy around the world on the media
screens in our living rooms.

What is hell? The last book in our biblical collection speaks
of a hell, but not quite the way some of us picture it (Revelations
21:8). The sacred scriptures don't talk about an *eternal* burning process for humans being, for we are mere mortals. Surely
then, this scripture is talking about the outcome for *immortal* evil
beings.

The glorious end to the celestial plan shows us a merciful and
loving God who will banish all pain and suffering, and will in fact
eliminate death itself (Revelations 21:3). When that time comes,
everyone will know God. The book of life will be opened, and a
great resurrection will occur, bringing back the very essence of
everyone who has lived and died. The apostle John was given a
celestial vision, and he wrote it down for us:

> ...I saw the dead, great and small, standing before the
> throne, and books were opened. Another book was
> opened which is the book of life. The dead were judged
> according to what they had done. (Revelations 20:12)

We don't know exactly how all this will take place, but we know we all are born to die. From the needless death of an innocent child to the horrific end of a sadistic criminal, death inexplicably happens to each of us at some time. But our lives have been given to us to learn how to love, and each life is vitally important in the grand scheme of things. The great celestial blueprint has us scheduled to stand before the God Source and be judged on what we have done in our life game. There seems to be an accounting for our actions, a final score on the board.

> *Do not be amazed at this, for a time is coming when all who are in their graves will hear his voice and come out, those who have done good will rise to live, and those who have done evil will rise to be condemned. (John 5:28-29)*

This implies that after we die, we'll wake up and rise to sit at a judgment seat.

Is raising the dead such a bizarre idea really? We store up all kinds of memories and emotions deep in our brains for later retrieval. We store complicated computer programs, images, music, and movies on small, portable devices and conjure them up whenever it pleases us. Perhaps the God Source stores our human spirit in the same way and is able to upload each life into existence again. God will choose to reward some with the right to live forever, but others will not receive this opportunity. Eternal life is a gift to be given.

Does this sound unbelievable, perhaps even unfair? But who are we to question the master craftsman? He made earth and created humanity upon it. He knows when our intent is to live in love; he also knows when death is the loving and merciful alternative. He breathed life into our clay bodies! He set up the rules of the game, defined the purpose, and established the boundaries of good and evil. He is God, and God is love. He will not have any part of evil.

Most of us are still choosing our own definitions of right and wrong. The earth and the state of affairs in all nations are the by-products of the poor choices of humanity. We repeatedly refuse to follow the instructions the celestial Great Ones have given us since the beginning of time. Remember the Garden, where the tree of the knowledge of good and evil grew tall? We may suppose this tree represents our two choices in life, good or evil. But this is a colossal misunderstanding. Good *and* evil are both represented by the same tree! This tree represents choosing on our own as though we know right from wrong. This is the tree of death. We have to pick the other tree—the Tree of Life.

The Great Ones want us to surrender our own choice and instead choose life by choosing their way. Those of us who think we have figured out the right way to live are still in actuality deciding for ourselves what is right and what is wrong. The Great Ones want us to align ourselves to their standards, to the celestial definitions of right and wrong, good and evil. Learning these ways results in the most positive reward: real, human joy. Because the God Source so deeply desires us to succeed, he sent an ambassador to show us the way to choose fruit from the appropriate tree. Through the sacrifice of the Son of God/Son of Man on the cross, the Great Ones modeled a celestial type of love and wait on our decision to return it to them and to others.

Rules of the Game

All this opens up a completely new and exciting perspective to the original creation story. It defines what humanity is and gives us a basic purpose of life according to the blueprint of the Great Ones who created us in their image and likeness. Out of complete love, they invited us to play the game of life by creating us. They allow our species to experience the consequences of life in order to grasp the godly ways of loving and giving. They do not force us to live their way. But, just like any game of sport, if we want to play well we have to learn the rules and follow them. Playing by the rules and developing skill at playing the game produces great human joy plus an added bonus: a chance of immortality!

If we can wrap our minds around this exciting concept then the idea of following the ways of these Great Ones makes sense. These morals and standards set out the parameters of the celestial way of loving. When we surrender our selfish choices and choose their ways, life becomes exhilarating! Although the utopian Garden of Eden is long gone, those two trees in the garden still stand for each of us. Do we choose right and wrong for ourselves, or do we choose from the Great Ones' Tree of Life and learn to love and live abundantly? Today and every day, we each have that same ongoing choice.

I
THOU SHALT HAVE NO OTHER GODS
BEFORE ME.
II
THOU SHALT NOT MAKE UNTO THEE ANY
GRAVEN IMAGE
III
THOU SHALT NOT TAKE THE NAME OF
THE LORD THY GOD IN VAIN
IV
REMEMBER THE SABBATH DAY, TO
HOLY.
V
HONOUR THY FATHER AND
VI
THOU SHALT NOT KILL.
VII
THOU SHALT NOT COMMIT ADULTERY.
VIII
THOU SHALT NOT STEAL.
IX
THOU SHALT NOT BEAR FALSE WITNESS
AGAINST THY NEIGHBOUR.
X
THOU SHALT NOT

10

standards of celestial morality

Learning how to love is the reason we're given celestial standards to follow. Celestial morality is the foundation we must first put into place for our transformation into the God Kind.

The Wake-Up Call

Like everyone else, my pursuit in life was to find happiness. Health and wealth would of course be wonderful to have, but I wanted to discover the secret of inner joy and serenity, and to live a fulfilling life.

The Great Ones know that in order for us to have abundant lives, we must first learn how to love. It is imperative that we master this trait if we are to enjoy our life's journey. To be grafted into their celestial species depends on it. The necessity of learning how to love is the reason intervention after intervention has been set up to help the human race develop spiritually. That is the whole reason that celestial standards were written down for humanity to follow.

Do we think that having to follow the concepts of celestial morality is unnecessary and archaic in our enlightened age? Well, perhaps in our world of chaos, violence, and national calamities we are deceived and not yet in an enlightened age at all!

If we were all naturally filled with the ability to love, then we wouldn't need instructions on how to live. Earth would be a paradise because everyone would be acting for the benefit of all living things. However, for the Great Ones it is their very nature to love. They don't need directions to tell them how! The standards they have given us are the statutes that govern their species naturally, the characteristics that make them the Great Ones. In recorded biblical history, celestial commands were given to the people in the nations God chose to work with. We ended the previous chapter with an ongoing choice for each of us. Do we choose right and wrong for ourselves from the tree of knowledge, or do we choose from the Great Ones' Tree of Life and learn to love and live abundantly? This passage sets out these significant choices:

> See, I set before you today life and prosperity, death and destruction. For I command you today to love the Lord your God, to walk in his ways, and to keep his commands, decrees and laws; then you will live and increase and the Lord your God will bless you....
> But if your heart turns away and you are not obedient... you will certainly be destroyed....

> *This day I call heaven and earth as witnesses against you*
>
> *that I have set before you life and death, blessings and*
>
> *curses. Now choose life.... (Deuteronomy 30:15-19)*

Long before the Son of God came into our world to ransom us, the abundant blessings for allegiance to celestial standards and the curses for disobedience were given. From our earliest history, we learn that when the governments of whole nations disregarded the decrees the God Source gave them, all manner of curses came into being. Many of these curses are still easily recognizable in our world today. Chapter twenty-eight of Deuteronomy in the Old Testament actually has lists of curses and blessings. When I first read them, I was astounded by the descriptions!

Whole nations of people are currently living under oppression; whole cultures have lingering, malignant illnesses; there are vast droughts and epidemics; violence and a lack of human worth are prevalent everywhere. From ancient time, Moses was compelled to say some things that still pertain to us today. We need to take heed:

> *Then the LORD will scatter you among all nations, from*
>
> *one end of the earth to the other. There you will worship*
>
> *other gods—gods of wood and stone, which neither you*
>
> *nor your fathers have known. (Deuteronomy 28:64)*
>
> *Your children who follow you in later generations and*
>
> *foreigners who come from distant lands will see the*
>
> *calamities that have fallen on the land and the diseases*
>
> *with which the LORD has afflicted it.*

> *...All the nations will ask: "Why has the LORD done this to*
> *this land?"*
>
> *...And the answer will be: "It is because this people*
> *abandoned the covenant of the LORD, the God of their*
> *fathers...." (Deuteronomy 29:22, 24-25)*

Our world is now on the edge of the point of no return. The planet can no longer feed its population because government greed has quashed its abilities. We seem to have no respect for each other or the garden in which we live. If we don't stop polluting it, our own children will rightly blame its destruction on our selfish decadence. There seems to be so little common sense now; even basic morality has at times been labeled politically incorrect. Long ago, the God Source communicated standards to all of us with clear instructions so we might be blessed in our lives and on our planet. It is not yet too late to heed these instructions.

> *When all these blessings and curses I have set before you*
> *come upon you and you take them to heart where ever*
> *the LORD your God disperses you among the nations*
> *and when you and your children return to the LORD your*
> *God and obey him with all your heart and with all your*
> *soul according to every thing I command you today then*
> *the LORD your God will restore your fortunes and have*
> *compassion on you and gather you again from all the*
> *nations where he scattered you. (Deuteronomy 30:1-3)*

These verses are directed to every human being who believes in a source of higher power no matter where they live on the face of the earth. To put it into a personal context, when I began writing the book you now read, I was raising my children on a very isolated cattle ranch one hundred miles from the nearest small town in the middle of the Canadian wilderness. The following verse assured me I was not forgotten:

> Even if you have been banished to the most distant land under the heavens, from there the Lord your God will gather you and bring you back. (Deuteronomy 30:4)

I am still in awe of how pertinent all these passages are for us no matter where we live although they were written many thousands of years ago.

A Significant Summit

Now, what were the commands and decrees that these verses were talking about? The Old Testament is full of many miscellaneous laws and *thou shall nots*, some of which were obviously specific to that culture. However, Moses was referring to the ten basic celestial commandments, the laws drawn up instructing us on how to love one another. These laws were physically presented to us by the celestial species of Great Ones in what has to be the most significant summit meeting that has ever occurred! What an extraordinary metaphysical experience that must have been too, for something huge landed on top of Mt. Sinai, and thousands of people saw it, heard it, and felt it.

Just how do invisible, otherworldly celestial beings set up a meeting between their species and ours? The Great Ones sent the LORD as their spokesperson and when he finally appeared on the top of the mountain, it was in full splendor of his celestial form. Moses was a powerful prophet and leader and acted as the ambassador for the human race. Just think: we as humans actually made an alliance to collaborate with a higher, evolved, extraterrestrial species!

If we can perceive that earth has already been visited by magnificent and benevolent celestial entities, these following passages make so much sense. There were practical protocols to be put into place for dignitaries visiting from outer space!

> The LORD said to Moses, "I am going to come to you in a dense cloud, so that the people will hear me speaking with you and will always put their trust in you."
>
> ...the LORD said to Moses, "Go to the people and consecrate them today and tomorrow. Have them wash their clothes and be ready by the third day, because on that day the LORD will come down on Mount Sinai in the sight of all the people. Put limits for the people around the mountain and tell them, 'Be careful that you do not go up the mountain or touch the foot of it. Whoever touches the mountain shall surely be put to death.'"
>
> Then he said to the people, "Prepare yourselves for the third day. Abstain from sexual relations." (Exodus 19:9-12, 15)

This visit was not some ephemeral, mystical vision that Moses experienced, and we're not talking about just a small tribe of herdsmen. Moses had leadership responsibilities and governed many thousands of people, and had initiated their miraculous release from Egypt (Exodus 18:25-26).

Now this summit for the alliance between the human and celestial species was to have an intense spiritual focus, but strict safety measures also had to be established.

> On the morning of the third day there was thunder and lightning, with a thick cloud over the mountain, and a very loud trumpet blast. Everyone in the camp trembled. Then Moses led the people out of the camp to meet with God, and they stood at the foot of the mountain. Mount Sinai was covered with smoke, because the LORD descended on it in fire. The smoke billowed up from it like smoke from a furnace, the whole mountain trembled violently, and the sound of the trumpet grew louder and louder. Then Moses spoke and the voice of God answered him. The LORD descended to the top of Mount Sinai and called Moses to the top of the mountain. (Exodus 19:16-20)

The Great Ten

Moses spent forty days in preliminary negotiations to understand what was being asked. Then the celestial LORD presented the main proposal of the alliance. The agreement that was drawn up consisted of demands for human beings to honor the God Source and for a celestial form of moral government to be put into place for human conduct. In exchange, the celestial ambassador would offer to make us "a peculiar treasure" to himself above all other people (Exodus 19:5). Protection, power, and celestial blessings were offered for our acceptance of an honorable alliance with this LORD. Thus, the simple Ten Commandments were drawn up for Moses to present to his people. They are given here in their entirety:

And God spoke all these words:

I am the LORD your God, who brought you out of Egypt, out of the land of slavery. You shall have no other gods before me.

You shall not make for yourself an idol in the form of anything in heaven above or on the earth beneath or in the waters below. You shall not bow down to them or worship them; for I, the LORD your God, am a jealous God, punishing the children for the sin of the fathers to the third and fourth generation of those who hate me, but showing love to a thousand generations of those who love me and keep my commandments.

You shall not misuse the name of the LORD your God, for the LORD will not hold anyone guiltless who misuses his name.

Remember the Sabbath day by keeping it holy. Six days you shall labor and do all your work, but the seventh day is a Sabbath to the LORD your God. On it you shall not do any work, neither you, nor your son or daughter, nor your manservant or maidservant, nor your animals, nor the alien within your gates. For in six days the LORD made the heavens and the earth, the sea, and all that is in them, but he rested on the seventh day. Therefore, the LORD blessed the Sabbath day and made it holy.

Honor your father and your mother, so that you may live long in the land the LORD your God is giving you.

You shall not murder.

You shall not commit adultery.

You shall not steal.

You shall not give false testimony against your neighbor.

You shall not covet your neighbor's house. You shall not covet your neighbor's wife, or his manservant or maidservant, his ox or donkey, or anything that belongs to your neighbor." (Exodus 20:1-17, see also Deuteronomy 5)

After receiving these decrees, Moses went down from the mountain, and assembled the people. An altar was made for sacrificial offerings from their herds of livestock in accordance with their customary ceremonial rituals and Moses gave a summit report of the proposed alliance.

Then he took the Book of the Covenant and read it to the people. They responded, "We will do everything the LORD has said; we will obey." Moses then took the blood, sprinkled it on the people and said, "This is the blood of the covenant that the LORD has made with you in accordance with all these words." (Exodus 24:7-8)

The people accepted the terms of the alliance from an extra-terrestrial God.

An Ark of Gold

The Ten Commandments are the basic moral law and the core of the Old Testament covenant. Many other lesser cultural laws were later made and set before the people. But these basic ten still form the central code of morality that is still referred to in our contemporary courtrooms and legal chambers. They are known as the moral principles of Judeo-Christian ethics in our modern world.

The ancient account of our alliance with celestial beings, however, doesn't end here. When these tablets of laws were presented to Moses the event was a prolonged visitation by a celestial being. Moses took more than seventy elders of Israel and went up the mountain again for over a period of forty days. They all witnessed the event, seeing an apparition of a celestial God being, and later describing the scene: "under his feet was something like a pavement made of sapphire, clear as the sky itself" (Exodus 24:8). The face of God was not seen because the *glory* of the LORD radiated so strongly. When Moses asked to see the Lord's presence, this is what he was told:

> And the LORD said, "I will cause all my goodness to pass in front of you, and I will proclaim my name, the LORD, in your presence. I will have mercy on whom I will have mercy, and I will have compassion on whom I will have compassion. But," he said, "You cannot see my face, for no one may see me and live."

> Then the LORD said, "There is a place near me where you may stand on a rock. When my glory passes by, I will put you in a cleft in the rock and cover you with my hand until I have passed by. Then I will remove my hand and you will see my back; but my face must not be seen. (*Exodus 33:19-23*)

Finally, Moses took his chief aid into the very top of the cloud-covered mountain to receive two tablets of stone with the celestial moral laws for humanity written upon them.

> And he gave unto Moses, when he had made an end of communing with him upon Mount Sinai, two tables of testimony, tables of stone, written with the finger of God. (*Exodus 31:18*)

When I first read that the celestial laws were written on stone, I envisioned them to be on weathered, pitted granite. Then recently while in Ontario, Canada, I visited the Museum of Natural Science in Ottawa, and saw beautiful cut slabs of an iron meteorite that had dropped onto earth from outer space. These slabs were so shiny they were mirror-like on their surfaces. If meteorite rocks from outer space were the stones used for the Ten Commandment tablets, what a perfect medium for "the finger of God" to write upon.

In any case, when Moses was in the cloud on top of the mountain, he was also given elaborate instructions for constructing a gold storage chest. It was to be called the Ark of the Covenant and the tablets of the Ten Commandments were to be placed inside. Along with the specifications for this box were precise instructions for a table, a lamp stand of gold, and a huge tabernacle—a sacred portable tent to house these things. This was to be placed in a courtyard complete with a special bronze altar for sacred livestock offerings. A family of priests was designated to serve in this tabernacle, and they were to wear sacred garments made from the finest linen adorned with specific precious stones.

In my research, I discovered twelve whole chapters in the book of Exodus that describe the whole scenario (Exodus 19-31).

The vivid descriptions are fascinating, but one provoking question remains: In the middle of all the accoutrements of worship sat the Ark of the Covenant. What exactly was the purpose of this uniquely designed, golden container? Was all this set up simply for a container to hold the Ten Commandment tablets? Yet, it was so dangerous to be in close contact with the Ark of the Covenant that strict safety regulations were to be adhered to so men would not die from the dynamic power held within it. If God is an invisible, otherworldly entity that even Moses couldn't clearly see in our three-dimensional reality, then maybe something was needed to ground or contain the essence of this great celestial entity in our physical dimension.

It's fascinating that this celestial LORD had such intense, powerful energy emanating from his being, that the sanctuary container had to be constructed out of pure gold. Only then, could his presence be safely contained within it and materialized above its cover. The Lord gave explicit instructions to Moses for its construction.

Then have them make a sanctuary for me, and I will dwell among them. Make this tabernacle and all its furnishings exactly like the pattern I will show you.

> Have them make a chest of acacia wood—two and a half
> cubits long, a cubit and a half wide, and a cubit and a
> half high. Overlay it with pure gold, both inside and out,
> and make a gold molding around it.
>
> Then put in the ark the Testimony, which I will give you.
>
> And make two cherubim out of hammered gold at the
> ends of the cover.
>
> There, above the cover between the two cherubim that
> are over the ark of the Testimony, I will meet with you and
> give you all my commands for the Israelites. (Exodus 25:8–
> 11,16, 18, 22)

The dimensions of the Ark were given in cubits; one cubit is the length of a man's forearm, so the Ark was about a meter long.

The lamp stand that lit up the front of the ark was to be made from a talent of gold and with a beautiful, intricate design "according to the pattern" shown to Moses on the mountain (Exodus 25:39). A talent was 75 pounds of gold, and at sixteen ounces per pound, this would indicate 1,200 ounces of gold in the lamp stand. Even at today's fluctuating market value, this part alone would be worth more than $1.5 million. That's not even considering how many pounds of gold were needed to construct the ark, the lid, and the cherub figures. The Ark wasn't some small trinket; it was a large, golden, sacred container to hold the essence of an extraterrestrial God entity.

It is said that gold has many paranormal properties, including clearing negativity, transferring the energy of other metals in its vicinity, and amplifying thought forms. How interesting this is, if it's true and was applicable in some way. Into this pure-gold Ark container were placed the two tablets of stone that had the Ten Commandments written upon them, the core of the celestial accord. If these stones were highly magnetic nickel-iron from a rare iron meteorite, what an interesting assortment of elements through which an invisible, celestial intelligent entity could manifest!

The God-beings went to great measures to present their proposal to us. At this supernatural strategic summit, a vast philosophy of one benevolent God Source with moral codes of conduct came into being for all of humanity. The summit between celestial and human species was successful for the core of their moral code still forms the basis for human morality across the globe.

The Simple Two

The story of the Ten Commandments may seem antiquated and a little bizarre in our modern world. Perhaps we are more familiar with the two great commandments Jesus Christ gave to us, recorded in the more-modern second half of the Bible. This more recent celestial ambassador gave only two precepts to follow in our lives. However, if we actually followed these two great commandments we wouldn't be breaking any of the other ten either. In giving these two commandments, Jesus Christ did not do away with the ten basic laws. Indeed, he actually demonstrated them. He lived them.

> "The most important one," answered Jesus, "is this: 'Hear, O Israel, the LORD our God, the LORD is one. Love the LORD your God with all your heart and with all your soul and with all your mind and with all your strength.'

> *"The second is this: 'Love your neighbor as yourself.' There*
>
> *is no commandment greater than these."* (Mark 12:29-31)

From where did he get these two commandments? Jesus obviously had access to the existing sacred scrolls of the Old Testament. With this rendering of the celestial moral code, he was simply summarizing the Ten Commandments in the already recorded scripture (Deuteronomy 6:4, 5 and Leviticus 19:18).

The first four of the original Ten Commandments can be condensed as instructions that tell us how we should love God: with all our heart, soul, mind, and strength, as Jesus taught. His summary was a marvelous, precise, and unique way to explain the first four original commandments. These we can easily put into contemporary language, too: we won't let anything else be more important in our lives than our belief in God. We won't idolize other things or ideologies; we won't discredit the authority and power behind God's name by disrespecting it; we will gladly take a rest from physical work each week to allow ourselves time to for spiritual pursuits. Believing in God in this way would bring new focus to our lives and ground us in a real connection to our creator.

Jesus's summary of the other commandments (Exodus 20:1-17) is the statement to "love your neighbor as yourself." This is explained in the New Testament book of Romans:

> *The commandments, "Do not commit adultery," "Do not*
>
> *murder," "Do not steal," "Do not covet," and whatever*
>
> *other commandment there may be, are summed up in this*
>
> *one rule: "Love your neighbor as yourself."* (Romans 13:9)

This one simple standard seems only fair and logical, doesn't it? If we follow a personal code to treat others, as we would like to be treated ourselves, then we have what is called *integrity*. We can walk tall and have self-respect. Integrity is something no one can take away from us. Can we even begin to envision a society where all people following this one law continually? What would it be like? There would be no murder, no muggings, no rape or robbery, no false accusations, no cheating in business or marriage, no faulty merchandise, no dangerous or unhealthy products, no controlling corporate monopolies, not even one person lying to another. There would be no prejudices, no legal battles, no tyranny, or oppression of any member of any society. What a world we would have to live in!

In the verses of chapter 119 in the book of Psalms, the writer praised his creator for giving us celestial laws and precepts. He recognized them not as limitations to freedom but as a means to gain spiritual wisdom. I especially like the part entitled "Mem":

> Oh, how I love your law! I meditate on it all day long. Your commands make me wiser than my enemies for they are ever with me. I have more insight than all my teachers, for I meditate on your statutes. I have more understanding than the elders, for I obey your precepts. (Psalms 119:97-100)

Allegiance to the laws of the Great Ones produces phenomenal benefits in our lives. The purpose of following these instructions is simply to be the wisest and happiest people we can be. Aren't truly happy, self-contented people living by values close to the great commandments whether they realize it or not? Don't they live by the golden rule? Test this way of life for yourself and I think you will find that the degree of true happiness attained is directly related to adhering to God's basic laws of conduct set out in antiquity. That is because these decrees actually define what loving is all about.

The Rule of Reciprocity

The golden rule of loving your neighbor as yourself has such incredible consequences that God upholds it through spiritual reciprocity. In other words for every positive or negative act we do, a corresponding reaction results: we reap what we sow. With our choices, we bring inevitable results upon ourselves. This concept is stated many times in different ways throughout our textbook.

> *Do not judge, and you will not be judged. Do not condemn, and you will not be condemned. Forgive, and you will be forgiven. Give, and it will be given to you. A good measure, pressed down, shaken together and running over, will be poured into your lap. For with the measure you use, it will be measured to you. (Luke 6:37-38)*
>
> *For in the same way you judge others you will be judged. (Matthew 7:2)*

Even when Jesus gave us an example of how to pray, he reminded us of this principle. When we recite what is known as the Lord's Prayer, we ask God to forgive our wrongs in the same manner as we forgive those who have wronged us:

> *Forgive us our debts, as we also have forgiven our debtors. (Matthew 6:12)*

This reciprocity is immutable. The Great Ones know the intent of our hearts, and that is what judges us just as our thoughts and actions judge others. Are we harsh, critical, and unforgiving? So be it: others will be the same to us. How can we expect any thing different if we are treating other people that way ourselves?

> *A man reaps what he sows. The one who sows to please his sinful nature, from that nature will reap destruction; the one who sows to please the spirit, from that Spirit will reap eternal life. (Galatians 6:7-8)*

Through the choices we make about the way we live, we reap what we have sown in this life. This is true for everyone whether we acknowledge the standards of the Great Ones or not, because the standards of God are like the physical laws of our planet. They are set up to produce results, and they operate regardless of whether or not we know of them or whether we even believe in them.

> *"Do not be deceived. God cannot be mocked. A man reaps what he sows." (Galatians 6:7)*

Allegiance to the Great One's standards is linked directly to positive outcomes in our lives. Our efforts to follow these moral codes are the ways in which we love and honor God. These standards were given to us so we could to learn how to love. Learning how to love by their definition is having loyalty to their codes of conduct.

When one of my sons reached his teen years, he asked me, "Why do we have to follow God's rules anyway?" We sat down as a family to discuss this most important question, and I told him we don't have to follow any rules. But if we want to find real happiness and power in our lives, the instructions are there in a written moral code. In other words, the more diligently we follow God's instructions for living, the more we enjoy a life filled with love and metaphysical empowerment.

Love and being in alignment with celestial law are intermeshing parts of the whole thing. Jesus Christ explained it this way:

> *If anyone loves me, he will obey my teaching. My Father will love him, and we will come to him and make our home with him. He who does not love me will not obey my teaching. (John 14:23-24)*

Integrity in Love

The friends and followers of Jesus understood that by observing the ancient, basic laws of God they were showing their allegiance and love to the God Kind. They found power to "overcome the world" in doing so.

> *This is love for God: to obey his commands. And his commands are not burdensome, for everyone born of God overcomes the world. (1 John 5:3-4)*

Not too many people like the word *obey* in our society anymore. Within the English language, we have come to see it as having a rather harsh quality. Please, don't be misled. The Psalms were not written with any such thing in mind when the author stated his convictions:

> *How sweet are your promises to my taste, sweeter than honey to my mouth! I gain understanding from your precepts; therefore I hate every wrong path.*

> Your faithfulness continues through all generations; you
> established the earth, and it endures. Your laws endure to
> this day for all things serve you.
>
> ...I will never forget your precepts, for by them you have
> preserved my life. (Psalm 119:103-104, 90-91, 93)

If it helps, let's use the phrase, "allegiance to the standards of the Great Ones" instead of the word obey. We can define allegiance as a type of obedience, but the important difference is that it's based on a warm relationship. Allegiance is following someone or something because there is love and honor involved in that relationship. We give allegiance to the Great Ones when we love and honor their ways. Jesus didn't just read or hear the words of the laws in the Old Testament. He lived them and gave his total allegiance to his father and his God by following the mandates of the mission he was sent to do.

> For it is not those who hear the law who are righteous in
> God's sight, but it is those who obey the law who will be
> declared righteous. (Romans 2:13)

The standards set forth by our Great Ones are the way of rightness by celestial definition. It is not expected that we as human beings will be able to follow them perfectly, but they desire us to be conscientious and sincere in our efforts. Otherwise, they won't benefit us in any way. The God Source knows our hearts and asks that we try to the best of our ability. At the same time, God can see when we are not acting with the integrity of which we are capable.

Jesus Christ was also aware of people's lack of sincerity in their worship. In one recorded incident, he was so sick of the hypocrisy he found in the churches of the time that he drove the faithless moneychangers out of the temple with a whip (John 2:15). Again, we are reminded that without love, all our efforts are for nothing. Religious people even then tried to become righteous by meticulously observing all the fine points of the law, but what did Christ actually say about the synagogue leaders during his ministry?

> *Woe to you, teachers of the law and Pharisees, you hypocrites! You shut the kingdom of heaven in men's faces. (Matthew 23:13)*
>
> *...do not do what they do, for they do not practice what they preach.... Everything they do is done for men to see. (Matthew 23:3, 5)*

It's the same today in many ways. The great celestial God family has given us codes of conduct to become godlike and to learn how to love, but the rules *are only a means to an end.* The Pharisees did not succeed when they tried to earn the prize of eternal life in this way. They had their religious way of life bound up so tightly by following the letter of the law that they missed the whole point. When strict adherence is our focus, religion can be thoroughly miserable! We cannot gain approval only by observing the letter of the law. This is quite clearly set out in scriptural verses, for example in the book of Romans: "...a man is justified by faith apart from observing the law" (Romans 3:29).

The word *justified* means that we are made right with God by our repentance and our belief in the love behind his son's sacrifice. Here this word is used again:

> ...we are justified freely by his grace through the
> redemption that came by Christ Jesus. God presented
> his son as a sacrifice of atonement through faith in his
> blood. (Romans 3:24-25)

God's grace is his love toward us, his willingness to erase our sins. For example, while I was growing up my mother had such a loving willingness to erase any misbehavior I may have been involved in, she wouldn't even believe me when I confided in her about the things I was doing. Her saying, "Oh, honey, I know you wouldn't do that" made me strive to live up to her expectations. Her love and belief in me as a young person covered my errors with grace.

When I was faced with my own children doing something wrong, I had no lack of love or pride in them either. Their wrong-doings were simply acknowledged, and together we explored a better way to do things the next time. Now, as adults, they laugh over the dreaded question I used ask them: "Oh dear, that is a problem. How do you plan to fix this?" At one time my youngest looked back at me sheepishly and said, "Can't you just be like some other mothers and give me a spanking for being bad?" As loving parents, we always try to back up our children's integrity. God does the same. He overlooks the past and walks with us into the future.

So does all this mean we can actually do what we want, and disregard any laws that may exist? Of course, we can choose to live this way, however we are accountable for all our choices, and unfortunately there may be real negative consequences that follow. Once God has called us, he would rather have us put away our old natures and follow a better way of living.

We surrender our life in the baptism ceremony in allegiance to him, and in this sense, we put to death our sinful self. It is not that we *have to* follow the laws of God in our lives, but rather it is that we *want to.*

> But now by dying to what once bound us, we have been
> released from the law so that we serve in the new way of
> the Spirit…. (Romans 7:6)

Love Satisfies the Law

This gives us background and an understanding of how the laws of God fit into the picture. We are to follow celestial rules in the new way of Spirit in order to establish the parameters of love. In fact following the two simple laws—loving God and loving your neighbor—will satisfy the requirements of the old order of law. This is exactly what is meant when Paul explains, "Love is the fulfillment of the law." (Romans 13:10)

However, we can't get away with an "oh, I love everybody" attitude and not follow through with actions of integrity. The law judges whether we act in love or not. This is what Christ wanted to get across to us.

> Do not think that I have come to abolish the law or
> the prophets; I have not come to abolish them but to
> fulfill them. I tell you the truth, until heaven and earth
> disappear, not the smallest letter, not the least stroke
> of a pen, will by any means disappear from the law until
> everything is accomplished. (Matthew 5:17-18)

The basic rules for developing the ability to love still exist. Jesus did not struggle to obey his father's laws in order to get rid of them at his death. His death on the cross only did away with the *penalty* of breaking those laws when we have contrite hearts. He paid our penalty for the times we would slip up. He did not abolish the law but he *paid the penalty* for our breaking the law. This was God's love expressed in mercy toward us.

What is the purpose of God's moral standards for us today? Well, what is any society or group of people without law? It is anarchy. When everyone decides for himself what's right and what's wrong, there is chaos. Paul, in the New Testament, struggled with this issue.

> What shall we say, then? Is the law sin? Certainly not. Indeed I would not have known what sin was except through the law. For I would not have known what it was to covet if the law had not said, "Do not covet." (Romans 7:7)
>
> ...through the law we become conscious of sin. (Romans 3:20)

How do we really know what's right and what's wrong when we can so easily deceive ourselves and be deceived by others? God wants us to gauge our actions against solid celestial standards. These standards are not mere rules once written down in the Bible; they are a merciful moral code of conduct created to ensure our happiness. We can hold up the standards of God as we hold up a mirror, to take a good look at our spiritual selves. I love this analogy! It can be found in the book of James:

> *Do not merely listen to the word, and so deceive*
> *yourselves. Do what it says. Anyone who listens to the*
> *word but does not do what it says is like a man who looks*
> *at his face in a mirror and, after looking as himself, goes*
> *away and immediately forgets what he looks like. But the*
> *man who looks intently into the perfect law that gives*
> *freedom and continues to do this, not forgetting what*
> *he has heard, but doing it—he will be blessed in what he*
> *does. (James 1:22-25)*

The standards and laws of God are there for us to hold them up in order to measure our own actions!

The very best of it all is that by following the commands of the Great Ones, we can have confidence in our connection to God and be able to ask for and receive wonderful things. Just as a father trains a son or daughter and hands over the authority of the family business when he or she becomes an adult, God desires to give us authority. The disciple John saw it all very clearly:

> *Dear friends, if our hearts do not condemn us, we have*
> *confidence before God and receive from him anything we*
> *ask, because we obey his commands and do what pleases*
> *him. (1 John 3:21)*

We can think of it in yet another simple way. It's as though we now belong to a powerful celestial family with its own code of conduct. We have been chosen to be adopted into a God-family and are being given specialized sacred training. Like a young samurai or Jedi, our allegiance to these standards sets up a protective and powerful force field around us. We are loved, and we belong to something far greater than ourselves.

With this understanding in place, let's move forward. There is still much to learn in order to master the ways of the Great Ones.

.

activating the power

11

Words OF Power

From the beginning, God created reality by speaking words to that effect. Therefore, God's word is truth because what he utters comes into being. God cannot lie! All this sets the stage for understanding the most powerful tool we have in our possession: the authoritative and creative power we release with our own spoken words.

Strange Titles

The Great Ones have strong integrity. The allegiance and loyalty shown by the Son to the Father, model this. Mastering their ways will require the same allegiance from us. They communicate powerful promises to us, yet their laws are set up and implemented by natural consequences. In everything they do, they keep their word.

The manner in which the Great Ones communicate is the next characteristic we need to explore, because the words they use are extremely important in the celestial realm and in ours. Just as our ability to communicate with language sets us high above the rest of the animal kingdom, the Great Ones' sophisticated means of communication is far advanced in complexity above our own. It is also a key component in how they activate creative power.

Remember back in Chapter Four, Jesus Christ is referred to as the Word? It seems like an odd title, yet this is how he was described in the very first paragraph of the book of John: "in the beginning was the Word, and the Word was with God, and the Word was God" (John 1:1).

The Word is a significant label. In one sense, it was a most fitting description because Jesus was a spokesperson and an ambassador for God. He communicated and fulfilled God's words on earth. As we shall see, words have inherent power just as Christ had power within him, and that's why John called him the Word. Jesus was the amplifier and exemplar of God's words of salvation to humanity. He was the will of God manifested into a living, breathing, and physical state.

The God Source used a specific name for himself also. As we have briefly discussed, it was first communicated to Moses when he came to a burning bush in the desert while tending his flock. He thought this was a very strange sight because the bush was not being burnt up. God spoke to him in a voice coming out of the flames and instructed him to go to Pharaoh and bring the Israelite people out of Egypt and slavery (Exodus 3:2, 10). Moses had the audacity to believe in this metaphysical, invisible presence claiming to be his God! He accepted the great commission that was given to him. However, there were many gods in Egypt, and Moses didn't know if he could convince his people that an authentic God had really sent him. In skepticism he asked:

> *Suppose I go to the Israelites and say to them, "The God*
> *of your fathers has sent me to you" and they ask me,*
> *"What is his name? Then what shall I tell them?"*
>
> *God said to Moses, "I am who I am. This is what you are to*
> *say to the Israelites; I AM has sent me to you." (Exodus 3:13)*

What a strange name! In the original Hebrew and Chaldean language, "I am" is translated from the word *hayah*, which means, "to be," "to exist," "to come to pass." So, when he said, "I am that I am," it was as if he was also saying, "I will be what I will be." The meaning is conveyed when it is put into this active future tense also.

Moses asked for a personal name for the God of his people, and he was given the name hayah. The titles YHWH and Yahweh are derived from this name and personify that same meaning. The original name was written without vowels, but it came to be shortened to Yah. We are still familiar with it in terms such as "hallelujah," meaning literally "praise to Yah" or "praise to God."

What's most interesting is that Mary, the mother of Jesus, was instructed by an angel of God to name her baby Yahshua. When this name—usually translated as Joshua—is translated into Greek, it becomes what we know as the name Jesus. The Y and J are interchangeable when crossing into other languages still today, and the S in Jesus had to be added to keep his name masculine. Most important is that Yahshua also means "Yah is salvation."

Therefore, in English, the name of Jesus literally communicates that God saves. When we are told to believe in the name of Jesus, we are told to believe that God saves us! That's where this term comes from. Isn't this intrinsically wrapped up in Jesus's very purpose in life? In the Old Testament, the Israelites were

promised a messiah would save them (Isaiah 9:6). Mary's intimate promise was that her son would be a savior. It's as if these
words of God somehow took on power, and a living persona
materialized. When Jesus Christ told us he was "the way" to salvation, he was explaining another miraculous fulfillment of God's
word. Another verse states:

> The son is the radiance of God's glory and the exact
> representation of his being, sustaining all things by his
> powerful word." (Hebrews 1:3)

The God Source's way of thinking is so far above our own.
His thoughts and words actually cause things to happen! He is
indeed the "I am/I will be what I will be." Words that proclaimed
a coming savior for the world caused Jesus Christ to be born. This
then is the key to understanding how God creates and how his
power actually operates: his very words consist of creative power!

What Is Truth?

Let's compare God's power to a vast computer network capable
of creating life and all there is, and then maintaining the continuity of this interdependent system of multifaceted realities. The
programmers of the network are the Great Ones. Perhaps the
God Source is like the hard drive. The Old Testament LORD,
who became Jesus the Christ, is like the powerful software. Sacred
Spirit would then have to be the force of activation throughout
the network—the electrical current by which everything communicates and connects.

Just as the inner workings of a computer are purely and powerfully logical, so are the thoughts and words of these Great Ones.

> *"For my thoughts are not your thoughts, neither are your ways my ways," declares the Lord. "As the heavens are higher than the earth, so are my ways higher than your ways and my thoughts than your thoughts." (Isaiah 55:8)*

Imagine someone from the past who had never used a computing tool more complex than an abacus trying to comprehend a modern computer capable of performing more than two million calculations per second. The differences are like the vast chasm between the human mind and the capabilities of the Great Ones.

Our God Source is an entity of omnipotence. He is what he is through no other source of power but his own. His very essence is to be in a constant act of creating. In fact, whatever he explicitly says springs into being because this is how God makes things happen.

> *By faith we understand that the universe was formed at God's command, so that what is seen was not made out of what was visible. (Hebrews 11:3)*
>
> *In the beginning God created the heavens and the earth. And God said, "Let there be light," and there was light. (Genesis 1:3)*

This is not only an opening statement in the pages of biblical history; it demonstrates perfectly how God's creative power works. God said, "Let there be light," and then there was light instantly radiating at his command. Here is another description:

> *As the rain and the snow come down from heaven, and do not return to it without watering the earth and making it bud and flourish, so that it yields seed for the sower and bread for the eater, so is my word that goes out from my mouth; it will not return to me empty, but will accomplish what I desire and achieve the purpose for which I sent it. (Isaiah 55:8-11)*

God creates by projecting out words! He utters thought and personally wills things to happen. "For he spoke, and it came to be, he commanded and it stood firm" (Psalms 33:9). With his spoken word, God created our world, and he maintains it still.

> *By the word of the Lord were the heavens made, their starry host by the breath of his mouth. (Psalms 3:6)*
>
> *He set the earth on its foundations; it can never be moved. You covered it with the deep as with a garment; the waters stood above the mountains. But at your rebuke the waters fled, at the sound of your thunder they took to flight; they flowed over the mountains, they went down into the valleys, to the place you assigned for them. (Psalms 104:5-8)*

Most of us today don't comprehend the inherent creative power in God's words. Yet, all through ancient history, people understood this concept of power in operation whenever God spoke to them in some way.

The prophets of old claimed to be in communication with their LORD. If something was prophesied, the prophet began by announcing: "The word of the Lord came unto me." Often these prophetic announcements forecasted the future. The prophets knew without doubt that what their God verbalized to them would happen.

When we look at the definition of *word*, it means "a matter spoken of." We find in Bible concordances that the prominent root meaning is "to arrange." A second common phrase the prophets in the Old Testament used was "according to the word of the Lord." Here, *word* comes from the original word *peh*, which means "the mouth," so we could literally say what comes from the metaphysical mouth of God arranges things.

Therefore, what God says is true because it is created in whatever way he says the words! Doesn't this actually indicate that God's word is always going to be the truth? This fundamental trait in God's character and makeup is so basic that it is not even possible for God to speak something untrue, because whatever he speaks comes to pass. In a logical conclusion, then, God can't lie (Hebrews 6:17-18). It is foreign to his nature; in fact, it is impossible!

We accept then that God's word in itself is truth. It cannot be otherwise. Jesus Christ stated this most emphatically when he prayed for us: "Sanctify them by the truth: your word is truth" (John 17:17). Consider this: God doesn't speak only *about* what is true; he *creates* truth by speaking! "What I have said, that will I bring about" (Isaiah 46:11).

How vastly superior are God's utterances to that we human beings speak! Most of the time, what comes out of our mouths means so little. Sometimes we say things without even knowing what we're saying. We complain, we exaggerate, we gossip, and we lie about things—though we may call it "stretching the truth."

If lying is unknown to the family of Great Ones, where did it come from? When did it start, and from whom did we learn it?

This was a fascinating part of my research. Jesus spoke to those opposing him, saying:

> You belong to your father the devil and you want to carry out your father's desire. He was a murderer from the beginning, not holding to the truth, for there is no truth in him. When he lies, he speaks his native language, for he is a liar and the father of lies. (John 8:44)

Wow! Telling lies began with our original adversary. The passage states there is "no truth in him." If there is no truth to what Satan says, then there is no creative power to his words! Therefore, he is in fact very limited, for what he says does not cause anything to be created at all. He is not God, nor is he made like God. He cannot create.

No wonder Satan dislikes us—we're the ones with the power! We are made in God's image and likeness, so we as earth-gods are the ones designed to create things in the same way. But what's even more crucial to understand is that in order to compensate for his lack of power in our physical realm, the devil has mastered the fine art of manipulation. This is how he operates: His main tactic is to project his lies to deceive our minds so we end up causing negative things to happen to ourselves. We create what he wants. When we can see his trickery in this light, it almost makes one ill. He is very proficient in his stealth—and ruthless in his intent.

This knowledge of the power in God's words and in our own words has been almost lost in our modern world. Many people can be liars in our societies and still be considered acceptable. Politicians are caught lying outrageously, but often it is just shrugged off as part of the job. Spouses promise loyalty and end up having affairs. Employers promise what they think their workers want and then those expectations are not met. Corporate philosophy is based on financial gain not maintaining integrity. Falsehood is so prevalent in our contemporary world.

For thousands of years in our past, however, moral fiber had a superior strength. A man's reputation and honor lay in keeping the vows, pledges, and covenants he made with others. Even a nod or a handshake was a nonverbal commitment that lasted a lifetime. People of past eras did not need to insist on written contracts when they were involved in important business transactions. One would say, "I give you my word," and out of self-respect the commitment would not be broken.

Liars were once regarded as criminals. In a court of law even today, an intentional lie while under oath is called perjury and carries strong consequences. So it doesn't surprise me that falsely testifying to something being true when it is not, is on a list of detestable practices of conduct in the New Testament.

> But the things that come out of the mouth come from the heart, and these make a man "unclean." For out of the heart come evil thoughts, murder, adultery, sexual immorality, theft, false testimony, slander. These are what make a man unclean.... (Matthew 15:18-19)

Thus our next focus of study is the "things that come out of the mouth" and from the heart. Just as Jesus accepted the words of the God Source as truth for his life, we can begin to accept God's words into our lives.

> *Therefore, get rid of all moral filth and the evil that is so prevalent and humbly accept the word planted in you, which can save you. Do not merely listen to the word, and so deceive yourselves. Do what it says. (James 1: 21-22)*

Why Words Have Power

There is unimaginable power in the words we speak. They are more than just uttered sound but are powerful vocalized thought. This is not a new concept for most of us but it originated from the proverbs of the Bible. The idea that words have intrinsic power ripples repeatedly throughout our textbook.

> *Words of a man's mouth are deep waters. (Proverbs 18:4)*
>
> *A word aptly spoken is like apples of gold in settings of silver. (Proverbs 25:11)*
>
> *Pleasant words are a honeycomb, sweet to the soul and healing to the bones. (Proverbs 16:24)*

The book of Proverbs also instructs us to consider what we say and how we say it. Foolish words bring much different results from the words used by a person who thinks affirmatively with compassion and wisdom. The manner in which we communicate is directly related to how we are actually treated in life:

> *A fool's lips bring him strife and his mouth invites a beating. A fool's mouth is his undoing, his lips are a snare to his soul. (Proverbs 18:6-7)*

> *...his speech is like a scorching fire...moving his lips he brings evil to pass. (Proverbs 16:27, 30)*
>
> *...reckless words pierce like a sword. (Proverbs 12:18)*

Apparently, our mouths can cause profound and sometimes disastrous effects. The contrast is further illustrated when we are wise in the way we use our words:

> *...a gentle answer turns away wrath, but a harsh word stirs up anger. (Proverbs 15:1)*
>
> *...a fool's talk brings a rod to his back but the lips of the wise protect them. (Proverbs 4:3)*
>
> *...the words of the wicked lie in wait for blood, but the speech of the upright rescues them. (Proverbs 12:6)*
>
> *An evil man is trapped by his sinful talk, but a righteous man escapes trouble. From the fruit of his lips a man is filled with good things as surely as the work of his hands reward him. (Proverbs 12:13-14)*

Can we really direct our lives by carefully choosing the directions of our conversations? In all these verses, we see some basic premises. What we verbalize determines whether positive or negative events are produced. This means that when we utter something, creative power is released in one of two directions. From our very mindsets, we are instrumental in making things happen for better or for worse!

The heartfelt words we use are extremely important in our lives. Yes, we need to be conscious of the words we use. Jesus Christ also explained why his own words were so powerful:

> *The spirit gives life; the flesh counts for nothing. The words I have spoken to you are spirit and they are life. (John 6:63)*
>
> *The words I say to you are not just my own. Rather it is the Father, living in me who is doing his work. (John 14:10)*

From this viewpoint, words are not just emitted sounds. They activate things to come into being. Jesus spoke the words of God, and these words carried active celestial spirit. Yes, we ought to speak positive, uplifting words to create positive results in our lives. It will give us great benefits. But what happens if we fine-tune this even more and speak the very words spoken by God or Jesus Christ?

When we accept the words Jesus gave to us, we too can activate celestial power and feel it working through us. In talking with his father, Jesus said:

> *You gave them to me and they have obeyed your word...for I gave them the words you gave me and they accepted them. (John 17:6-8)*

What words did Jesus give us? Could we just memorize those and recite them in our times of trial?

Well, first, God is not fooled by our dramatics. Also, to be effective, the words themselves must be backed by our own belief system. To have any actual power, we must connect in a personal way with what God proclaims, remembering that these spoken things are automatically defined as truth. When we can believe and speak the same words in our lives, then we can create and change our realities.

We do not have to be buffeted by every emotional mood into which we are suddenly thrust. We are not leaves blown about in the wind. We were given choice, and we were given power. By agreeing with God, we can tap into and conduct his current of pulsating, creative energy, bringing about the existence of those particular truths in our lives. This is a skill worth learning, and there are concrete principals we can put into practice.

Conducting the Current

Around the world, the majority of people believe there is a God. But not all of us truly believe what God has said. What kind of power is activated in the words we use in our everyday lives? We utter negative words of helplessness: "Life is tough. This stress is killing me. I feel rotten. I've got a headache that just won't quit." We've all said things like this.

Now, from what force do these words come? God never led us to believe or speak utterances like these. He does not want us to give power to such negative claims. He runs on the positive current. He is the plus; he is for us.

> If God is for us, who can be against us? He who didn't spare his own son, but gave him up for us all—how will he not also...graciously give us all things? (Romans 8:31)

When our negative dialogues sound hopeless, we believe whatever Satan projects for us in our minds—we are in agreement with his lies and we appropriate them into our lives. On the other hand, when our conversations are uplifting and edifying, we are aligned with the very power current in which the Great Ones themselves operate—we are in agreement with God's projection for our lives.

Whether consciously or subconsciously, we conduct power from whatever spirit source we believe in at that particular moment. The real question in our lives is always this: with which source of power do we agree?

Look at our knowledge about positive and negative energy fields on the surface of our earth, right down to the scale of electrons and protons in each atom. There are opposing forces in all of nature. Spiritual forces also magnetize us in one direction or the other. According to the positive or negative energy issued from our own mouths, we reap the corresponding dividends of our words. Just as the God Source created our world with his words, we each create our individual world, and together we create the personalities of our nations, all through vocalized thought!

Logically then, if God's words of promise to us are true (and God can't lie), we should be saying things in agreement with them. These promises are like prized gold nuggets—the same ones that make the Bible, "the Word of God," so valuable. They are the reason the Bible has remained the best-selling book for the last two thousand years. We have to mine these truths out of the Bible like precious metal, sifting through all the nice religious jargon until the nuggets of truth stand gleaming in the sun and our eyes are wise enough to discern them. These gold nuggets contain the words of truth that we need to adopt unconditionally in order to have power in our lives.

Instead of complaining in depressed monologues, we should be asserting powerful, optimistic statements such as, "Spirit lives in me. I trust God and not my own understanding." When our health is down, we can claim God's promises: "By Jesus' wounds, I am healed" (1 Peter 2:24).

We don't have to be in Satan's stranglehold! By speaking God's words, we unshackle the chains that bind and oppress us. You are promised, "no weapon forged against you will prevail.... This is the heritage of the servants of the Lord" (Isaiah 54:17).

Each of us will resonate to different scriptures; the nuggets we find will differ in their relevancy. I have collected pages of gold nuggets that are very meaningful to me. The ones I treasure most are strong foundational pillars for my own thinking processes. I dug them out, and to me they are exquisite! I have ingrained them in my mind, as celestial words of promise must be incorporated into our minds personally and uniquely. My golden words may not shine so brilliantly for your individual needs, so you must prospect to discover your own.

It is not enough simply to memorize the nuggets of truth as we find them, but it is a good place to start. To activate their real power, we must put them into practice. Only then will we understand them for the truths they are. In agreeing with God's promises and verbalizing his words, we establish a reality in our lives where anything is possible. Jesus Christ wanted us to have this kind of empowerment:

> *If you remain in me and my words remain in you, ask whatever you wish, and it will be given you. (John 15:7)*

The content of our conversations, whether positive or negative, will bring corresponding reactions from the world around us. It's not that God is constantly judging us, rewarding us for good vocabulary, and punishing us for bad. Instead, our words to others and even our silent words to ourselves determine which of the two power sources we are activating. Even when we silently talk to ourselves, we activate power and radiate it outward. So in order to mature spiritually, we need to develop godly character from the inside out. Then the words we speak will be a good portrayal of our inner beliefs. The concept of automatically being accountable for our words in this way is an extremely important part of spiritual maturity. Jesus tried to explain it this way:

> As for the person who hears my words but does not keep them, I do not judge him. For I did not come to judge the world, but to save it. There is a judge for the one who rejects me and does not accept my words; that very word which I spoke will condemn him at the last day. (John 12:47-48)

If we reject the words of Jesus Christ and do not accept them as truth in our lives, we condemn ourselves to needless frustration, depression, and self-destruction. God does not wish to judge us, but our words judge us due to the beliefs we choose. Our destiny is in our mindset, for we get what we expect!

The Great Ones want us to control not only our actions but our thoughts as well. Note what Jesus taught in his famous sermon on the mountain:

> You have heard that it was said to the people long ago, "Do not murder, and anyone who murders will be subject to judgment." But I tell you that anyone who is angry with his brother will be subject to judgment. (Matthew 5:21-22)

> *You have heard that it was said, "Do not commit*
>
> *adultery." But I tell you that anyone who looks at a*
>
> *woman lustfully has already committed adultery with her*
>
> *in his heart. (Matthew 5:27-28)*

Why did Jesus want us to control even our thoughts? Because he realized our thoughts will produce words, and our words give power to creative energies. Our words then produce actions, either good or bad. However, it is the thoughts that set things in motion. Jesus Christ tried to make this emphatically clear:

> *Make a tree good and its fruit will be good or make a*
>
> *tree bad and its fruit will be bad, for a tree is recognized*
>
> *by its fruit. You brood of vipers, how can you who are evil*
>
> *say anything good? For out of the overflow of the heart*
>
> *the mouth speaks. The good man brings good things out*
>
> *of the good stored up in him and the evil man brings evil*
>
> *things out of the evil stored up in him. (Matthew 12:33-35)*

Therefore, whatever comes out of our mouths is indicative of our inner attitudes. Our words are representations of the strong, creative forces deep inside us. We usually express what is in our hearts. When we form words, we release the power of these forces. Like the power of deep waters breaking forth from our mouths, they cause good or evil things to happen. Heartfelt words always transmit power.

Control of the Tongue

Words are what actually produce results. When we have negative thoughts but don't speak them, they remain unborn and are not manifested. The object then is to have control over our thoughts before we end up manifesting them in our expressions. When we change our words to be positive, we are able to reap good and bountiful harvests in life.

The place to start is in our daily conversations with our selves and with others. It's a matter of controlling our tongues. That may sound like a strange idea, but even this concept is fully covered in scripture:

> When words are many sin is not absent, he who holds his tongue is wise. (Proverbs 10:19)
>
> Whoever would love life and see good days must keep his tongue from evil and his lips from deceitful speech. (1 Peter 3:10)
>
> Death and life are in the power of the tongue. (Proverbs 18:21)

But the best, the clearest passage is in the book James wrote:

> If anyone is never at fault in what he says, he is a perfect man, able to keep his whole body in check. When we put bits into the mouths of horses to make them obey us, we can turn the whole animal. Or take ships as an example. Although they are so large and are driven by strong winds, they are steered by a very small rudder wherever the pilot wants to go. (James 3:2-4)

We direct our lives with our mouths in the same way! Just as we tack back and forth in a sailboat or rein a horse to gallop down a country lane, when we change the words that come from our mouths we can change the very direction we are going. If we do not have that kind of self-control, then we will be living powerlessly.

> Likewise the tongue is a small part of the body, but it makes great boasts. Consider what a great forest is set on fire by a small spark. The tongue also is a fire, a world of evil among the parts of the body. It corrupts the whole person, sets the whole course of his life on fire, and is itself set on fire by hell. (James 3:5)
>
> All kinds of animals, birds, reptiles and creatures of the sea are being tamed and have been tamed by man, but no man can tame the tongue. It is a restless evil, full of deadly poison. (James 3:8)

That certainly sounds hopeless, and that's why we need a celestial connection of some sort. Thankfully, God has said all things are possible when sacred Spirit is living within us. If we allow Spirit to lead us, we are enabled to use the tongue to articulate sounds that work for our own best interests and for great benefit to others.

There are two uses of the tongue: to speak words that build up or to speak words that tear down. Think of it in this way: Words flow with a current from the demonic or from the celestial forces of the Great Ones.

> *With the tongue we praise our Lord as Father, and with it we curse men, who have been made in God's likeness. Out of the mouth come praise and cursing. My brothers, this should not be. Can both fresh water and salt water flow from the same spring? My brothers, can a fig tree bear olives, or a grapevine bear figs? Neither can a salt spring produce fresh water. (James 3:9-12)*

What are we producing with the words we utter to ourselves and to our families and friends? Do we give out pure, clean, cool, living water or stale, salty stuff that slowly poisons those around us? Jesus Christ said,

> *If a man is thirsty, let him come to me and drink. Whoever believes in me, as the scripture has said, streams of living water will flow from within him. (John 7:37-38)*

What a beautiful analogy. We have to create our own deep well of living water and let it overflow in sparkling clarity to produce a pure, powerful kind of living. The words of God have to be comfortable and acceptable to us. For this to happen, it is necessary to reprogram our minds so God's words become our words, so his words become our default mode of communication. Only then can we speak from the heart with power.

In the book of Proverbs, Solomon wrote:

My son, pay attention to what I say; listen closely to my words. Do not let them out of your sight, keep them within your heart; for they are life to those that find them and health to a man's whole body. Above all else, guard your heart, for it is the well-spring of life. (Proverbs 4:20-23)

All these concepts prove one important fact: words from the heart and uttered from the mouth, will transmit power! They conduct forces of energy. If we align our verbalization to that of the Great Ones, our hearts will be attuned to the most-powerful, affirmative, creative forces in the universe!

In summary, when our creator vocalizes his thoughts, he creates. Because we are made in his image and likeness, when we speak our thoughts, we also create. This means we are intimately involved in producing our own realities. We are masters of our own fates, whether they are dark and hopeless or filled with the awesome joy of growing strong and being spiritually alive. Just as God swept away the darkness in the very beginning of our creation story and said, "Let there be light," we too can brighten our dark circumstances with the words we say. Now, we know our expressed thoughts are the building blocks of our very own reality.

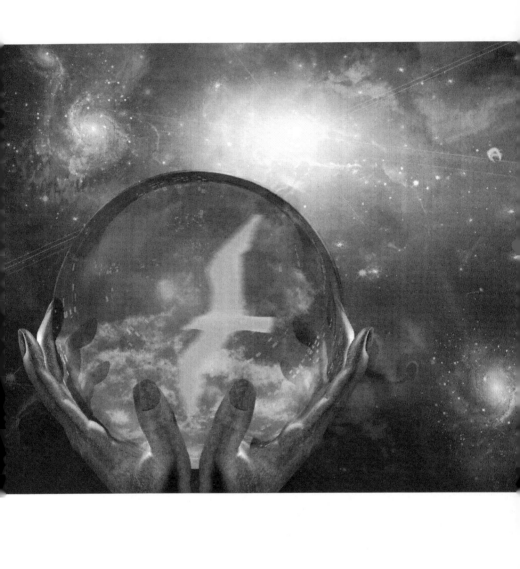

12

a quantum leap belief system

Faith is defined as a source of power. In order to access this creative force, certain components need to be in place. A quantum leap is then necessary to connect to Spirit, for we are required to believe absolutely in the supernatural.

The Extraordinary Definition

If this book were a fictional work, this chapter would be the climax. The first chapters were written because they were necessary for laying the foundation. Then the celestial plan for the human race was detailed to give us the framework for developing spiritual truths. Now, after understanding the characteristics of the Great Ones, we can finally discuss the spiritual definition of faith and how we each can make it operable in our own life.

In Chapter One, we briefly touched on the idea that in traditional Christianity the word, *faith* means "a belief in God," and each denomination states this in its doctrines. Yet, faith is a lot more than just a belief in God; it is a belief that the power of God is available to us through a unique connection.

My personal experience while ranching in the wilderness of central British Columbia in western Canada required that I build just this kind of faith to withstand the physical trials and concerns of safety for my children, my husband, and myself. We qualified as one of the very last ranch holdings under the Canadian Homestead Act. The ranch was one hundred miles from any town, with no water, sewer, electricity, or paved roads. There was no social network on which to rely. It was there in the harsh but beautiful wild alpine forests and meadows that I searched for the meaning of life and a personal source of power to endure the hardships. Tested sometimes to what I felt were my utmost limits, I desperately needed to be in connection with a higher power of some sort. I developed a deep understanding of a metaphysical kind of faith and began to see it as a tangible source of power situated just at the edge of my physical reality.

In our contemporary world, countless people believe there is a God. Many of these are Christians who believe that Jesus Christ lived and died for us. But how many people today actually believe in the concepts Jesus proclaimed? By now, we understand that he said some incredibly bizarre things!

Let's look at this from a personal viewpoint. If we believe in a good friend, we don't just believe he exists; we also believe in what he says. If our trusted friend says that something happened, we are certain it's true. If he promises to help us with something, we expect him to follow through for us. Jesus is offering this kind of relationship. Why would we expect anything less of him?

Christians claim to believe the promise that we can be saved from death by entry to a spiritual existence afterward. Shouldn't it be easier then to believe that we could be saved from all manner of trials and troubles in our current daily lives? This too is part of the core message Jesus Christ brought to humanity. He gave us access not only to the eventual reward of eternal life but also to the ability to overcome all kinds of hardships in everyday living.

I decided to take this Jesus/God-person at his word. I took a large, green concordance and became determined to read all the words defining faith directly from a Bible. What I read was so extravagant in empowering implications that it shocked me. I had already proved to myself that God's words couldn't be anything but true. So, when I cried out and needed courage and endurance, it was as though Spirit spoke these strange words directly to me:

> If you remain in me and my words remain in you, ask whatever you wish, and it will be given you. (John 15:7)
>
> I will do whatever you ask for in my name, so that the Son may bring glory to the Father. You may ask me for anything in my name, and I will do it. (John 14:13-14)

I started testing these verses and asking for the things that I needed. Then I began to witness magical and amazing things! My personal deep faith started developing simply out of necessity.

These Bible passages state something phenomenal. Jesus told us to ask him anything in his name and he would do it for us. "But what's the catch?" we might ask. God doesn't lie and Jesus was very sincere when he gave us these marvelous promises, but the difficulty has always been in *believing*. We must believe wholeheartedly so that spiritual forces can come into play. If Spirit from the God Source is inside of us, we can do all things because the power to do so is readily available—if we believe. So now when

I read this one verse, I can rest in full assurance: "Everything is possible for one who believes" (Mark 9:23).

Our belief system is the whole key. We cannot gain the spiritual power of faith by our own strength or mental willpower. It is necessary to yield to God's powerful presence in order to override the old circuits of our negative thought patterns. That's why we are encouraged to "trust in the Lord with all your heart and lean not on your own understanding" (Proverbs 3:5). For when we align each manufactured thought with what we know to be the ways of the Great Ones, where truly anything is possible, our own creative power springs forth in quantum leaps and bounds.

Taking a quantum leap of faith means, we actually believe there will be metaphysical changes to our physical reality in life. Faith has to be accepted as a metaphysical process. Again, from chapter one, let's recall the surprising definition of faith:

> Now faith is being sure of what we hope for and certain of what we do not see. (Hebrews 11:1)

That is an extraordinary description. In other words, authentic faith has to have an element of unexplainable certainty. It is like a quantum leap of understanding. I use the word *quantum* to describe the fundamental uniqueness in the activation of faith. From the book entitled *Quantum Enigma* by physicists Bruce Rosenblum and Fred Kuttner, I have come to understand that in physics, this word describes the mechanism governing the behavior of atoms. In today's physics, the quantum theory states that the behavior of an atom can be changed by a quantum of what can be described as the tiniest existence of expectation from a conscious thought. Our expectation is the catalyst that makes it happen.

This concept is emerging in contemporary thought through many channels. Michael Luckman, in his recent book *Overpowering Fear—Defeating the #1 Challenge in Sales and Life,* refers to it as the

Universal Law of Deliberate Manifestation. I love this present-day definition because it incorporates the necessary element of deliberate expectation into the formula for your desired outcome.

Likewise, I think, we can view faith as an imperceptible amount of mental energy required to jump the synapse between our human belief system and the luminous consciousness of celestial Spirit. This quantum transfer enables our connection to creative power from another dimension of reality. We must make the leap in order for the process to work. If we want to activate faith, we must be "sure of what we hope for and certain of what we do not yet see" (Hebrews 11:1).

When this synapse connection to Spirit happens, there is recognition of a power greater than our own working in our lives. We ask with full confidence, and we're certain that what we ask for will eventually happen. It's like we know that we know what we know. But we don't quite know *how* we know it. We just have the assurance and the conviction that what we have faith in—will be. Each time we stretch our faith enough to make this leap, it becomes easier. Eventually our faith in the quantum leap principle becomes a powerful mindset.

In the Western world we say "seeing is believing," but there are other cultures on our planet where things must be believed in order to be seen. There is growing evidence of this phenomenon in the quantum theory of physics. Passive acceptance of a sole physical reality requires very little effort and gives no empowerment over our physical world whatsoever, whereas when we enact a personal belief system upon our environment, we affect our reality, and expanded possibilities are opened to us.

Two Components of Faith

We all have trials in life, so exploring faith, as a method to activate power to overcome these trials is exciting. How does this process work? When we cannot see the things we hope for at all, how can we be sure and certain of them? Few of us are really sure and certain about anything. So how do we go about strengthening a weak belief system?

First, if we are sure and certain that something will happen, it means we will not exactly be surprised when it does. Instead of doubt, we hold fast to the mindset of expectation. In the New Testament, the disciples were not surprised when they asked for healing and it immediately happened. We don't hear them exclaim, "Hey! It really worked!" They were certain of God's power to heal and perform the miraculous, and because Jesus commissioned them, they were sure of their own right to use that power. They understood that they were accessing a spiritual law, and so were both sure and certain that in some way a celestial source of power would be activated.

Gravity is unseen deep in the earth. It is a law of the physical world that we often take for granted. The Bible gives us a passage that describes the law of faith similarly. It even tells us where this "word of faith" is located.

> "The word is near you; it is in your mouth and in your heart," that is, the message concerning faith that we proclaim.... (Romans 10:8)

Now we even know where to find its location! Faith is found deep in our hearts and in our mouths. Faith is not something outside of us but a law we activate from the inside. This principle stands consistently in place, just like the law of gravity. We don't have to go out and find gravity; it is activated whenever we throw something up in the air—in fact it operates constantly, whether we are thinking about it or not. Faith works the same way. It is already in place, and we activate it with the heartfelt words we speak. It is our belief system expressed by our actions.

These two simple instructions are the basic components of faith. They are also the requirements to obtain the vital promise of salvation:

> For it is with your heart that you believe and are justified,
>
> and it is with your mouth that you confess and are saved.
>
> (Romans 10:10)

These ingredients are the building blocks of faith. When we believe with our hearts and confess with our mouths, heartfelt words give creative, manifesting power.

I remember a time when I was driving with my two small children through a blinding snowstorm to visit a family friend. It was late, and I was on a dark, unfamiliar road that zigzagged through the farmlands. As I peered through the frosted window, the snowflakes seemed to come straight at me. We crested a small hill, and I saw yet another corner, but it was too late to slow down. I thought we were going to crash. But my belief in the power of God's words surged up in my mind and I shouted, "Jesus, save us!" This is the meaning of his name—God saves. My small car made the ninety-degree turn in a microsecond, and we were again driving straight down the road. I continued in the solitude of the snowy night, driving much slower with shaking hands and mumbling a continuous stream of "thank you God, thank you God." When you think about it, many of us have had similar supernatural experiences. Whether we realize it or not, this is the law of faith taking place.

A Formula for Faith

In the last chapter, we learned that the words of God are truth. He calls things into being because whatever he says comes into existence. Therefore, when we proclaim what God says to be true, there is a metaphysical reaction to our use of the words.

We were designed and made in his image and likeness, so it is not so difficult to conceive that this function of speaking things into being can be self-activated by each of us. That is the essence of the quantum leap analogy to faith. In the following odd story, Jesus clearly demonstrated to us how to make it work using the two vital components of activating the heart and the mouth.

> *The next day as they were leaving Bethany, Jesus was hungry. Seeing in the distance a fig tree in leaf, he went to find out if it had any fruit. When he reached it, he found nothing but leaves, because it was not the season for figs. Then he said to the tree, "May no one ever eat fruit from you again." And his disciples heard him say it. (Mark 11:12-14)*
>
> *When evening came, Jesus and his disciples went out of the city. In the morning, as they went along, they saw the fig tree withered from the roots. Peter remembered and said to Jesus, "Rabbi, look! The fig tree you cursed has withered!" (Mark 11:19-21)*

Perhaps Jesus was showing the half human side of his nature when he cursed the fig tree. I like to think he was not just being petty but giving his disciples a memorable lesson, with the result of his strong language. He adequately demonstrated that spoken words of conviction have the power of life and death. Thankfully, in this case, it was simply a tree. The disciples were perplexed and asked him what it all meant.

> "Have faith in God," Jesus answered. "I tell you the truth,
> if anyone says to this mountain, 'Go, throw yourself into
> the sea,' and does not doubt in his heart but believes
> that what he says will happen, it will be done for him.
> Therefore I tell you, whatever you ask for in prayer, believe
> that you have received it, and it will be yours." (Mark
> 11:22-24)

This outrageous passage is the simple formula for faith! It is stated with clarity again in another bold scripture: "If you believe, you will receive whatever you ask for in prayer" (Mathew 21:22). This formula is in every Bible ever printed, and it is the premise for all the powerful, ancient mysteries. It still forms the basis of positive thinking, the power of prayer, the idea of manifestation. It was famously renamed in *The Secret*, a popular book by Rhonda Byrne.

The formula simply requires that we *believe what we ask for*, to be so sure of what we hope for and certain of what we do not yet see (Hebrews 11:1), that we haven't a doubt it will take place. Then it does take place. That is the means of activating faith. Focused intent from our thinking capacity really is this powerful! Our minds are like organic computers designed with high-level programming to create—just as the celestial Great Ones create.

Proving Faith with Action

Therefore, when we desire to activate faith as an energized creative force, the two components—heartfelt belief and confident words—must be there. However, it's all well to say that we believe in something wonderful, but if we never take the first step to accomplish it, how valid are our words?

There is yet another condition that usually has to be met. Activating faith is not quite as easy as the black-and-white promises on the page because whenever we speak, our words are automatically tested for authenticity against our belief system. Sometimes our words have to be accompanied by some kind of action in order to prove (maybe even to ourselves), that we truly believe in what we say. This is expressed in the second chapter of the book of James:

> Suppose a brother or sister is without clothes and daily food. If one of you says to him, "Go, I wish you well; keep warm and well fed," but does nothing about his physical needs, what good is it? In the same way, faith by itself, if it is not accompanied by action, is dead. (James 2:15-17)

If we want to harness the power of faith, we have to live out our beliefs. It is not enough to just believe in God and talk the talk.

> You believe there is one God. Good! Even the demons believe that—and shudder.... In the same way, faith by itself, if it is not accompanied by action, is dead. But someone will say, "You have faith; I have deeds." Show me your faith without deeds, and I will show you my faith by what I do. (James 2:18-19)

The strongest desire of the Great Ones is that we develop this kind of active faith in order to overcome and accomplish worthwhile goals. Our life game has been designed and set up so that learning how to activate faith will happen by the necessity of overcoming life's hardships. Both the Old and New Testaments illustrate authentic faith in action through stories recording the life events of courageous men and women. These stories have resisted the decay of time, so let's assume they may have actually miraculously happened.

There is the account of three Jewish government officials who, in honor of their LORD, refused to follow the king's new edict to bow down and worship his image in gold. Their faith was tested severely when they were thrown into a fiery furnace. But then they were seen walking about within the flames unharmed. This sight convinced the great pagan king, Nebuchadnezzar, that the one true God had ultimate power and could be accessed by mere men (Daniel 3:12-30). These people proved their faith by their courageous actions, and God honored them by saving their lives.

Daniel was another hero. He was put into a den of lions for a similar refusal under King Darius. Throwing slaves into an arena to combat lions was a national sport at the time. But Daniel was not harmed (Daniel 6:1-27).

In both cases, God sent protective angels to preserve the lives of these heroes. In their faith, they dared to trust in a metaphysical source of power. These famous, historical figures pledged allegiance to God over and above even the scientific laws of nature—including fiery furnaces and hungry lions!

A most-incredible example of faith was the actions of a man called Abraham, who unquestionably put his faith in the supernatural essence of an otherworldly power. His is a strange story for many reasons. When I first read these passages, I was troubled and in awe of their implications.

God promised Abraham he would have a son and, through him, have numerous offspring. He became an old man, and his wife, Sarah, was well past childbearing years when this promise was fulfilled. When Sarah was told she would become pregnant, she laughed (Genesis 18:9-15). Abraham thought about the physical realities of their circumstances:

> *Without weakening in his faith, he faced the fact that his body was as good as dead—since he was about a hundred years old—and that Sarah's womb was also dead. Yet he did not waver through unbelief regarding the promise of God, but was strengthened in his faith and gave glory to God, being fully persuaded that God had power to do what he had promised. (Romans 4:19-21)*

He and his wife finally did have a son in their extreme old age. Then God told Abraham to do something quite unthinkable: to sacrifice his son Isaac on a ceremonial altar. Sacrificing animals as a financial offering to God was a cultural norm at that time, but this was a horrible request. God had miraculously given them a son and then wanted Abraham to end the life of the child in this grotesque way? But Abraham knew the voice and the nature of his invisible deity. He trusted him wholeheartedly. God's words had promised him abundant offspring from this child. Abraham also knew that life itself was composed of more than just X number of years on earth. He must have reasoned that if God had the power to create his son's life in the old age of his wife and himself, he could again recreate life for this same son if need be. He set out to do what he was asked to do. What actually happened on the wilderness mountain where Abraham took his son for the sacrifice?

> *Then he reached out his hand and took the knife to slay his son. But the angel of the Lord called out to him from heaven: "Abraham! Abraham!"*
>
> *"Here I am," he replied.*

"Do not lay a hand on the boy," he said. "Do not do

anything to him. Now I know that you fear God, because

you have not withheld from me your son, your only son."

Abraham looked up and there in a thicket he saw a

ram caught by its horns. He went over and took the ram

and sacrificed it as a burnt offering instead of his son.

(Genesis 22:10-13)

In this dramatic story, we are relieved Isaac's life was saved and that he was not slain at the altar by his father. Years passed, and during Isaac's lifetime, he had a son named Jacob, who had twelve sons who developed into the twelve tribes of the ancient nation of Israel. These huge tribes of people, living by the standards of a celestial God, changed the pages of history. The best-known tribe of Judah, along with parts of the tribe of Levi, is still intact and marches down through the years in the current nation of Israel. The other ten tribes have been scattered and absorbed into powerful kingdoms throughout the world.

According to Wikipedia, diverse nations around the world identify with the original twelve tribes descended from Abraham, the European, and Western nations especially. There are many other tribes of people as well, as evidenced by DNA testing, oral history, word similarities to Hebraic-Semitic root words, and traditional customs paralleling religious practices of Judaism. These pockets of humanity come from surprising places, such as the Chiang Min people of China and the Lemba people of Africa, and to the tribesmen of Afghanistan, where many claim with pride to be descendents of the first twelve tribes. All this came to be according to the words exchanged in Abraham's encounter with the presence of celestial beings.

> And the angel of the Lord called to Abraham from
> heaven a second time and said, "I swear by myself,
> declared the Lord, that because you have done this and
> have not withheld your son, your only son, I will surely
> bless you and make your descendants as numerous as the
> stars in the sky and as the sand on the seashore. Your
> descendants will take possession of the cities of their
> enemies, and through your offspring all nations on earth
> will be blessed, because you have obeyed me." (Genesis
> 22:15-18)

What is even more interesting is that Abraham, known as the Father of many nations (Romans 4:18), had an elder son by Hagar, who was a handmaiden to his wife Sarah. Earlier in her life, she had given consent to this union, thinking it wasn't possible for her to become pregnant. This son's name was Ishmael (Genesis 25:1, 6). God gave Abraham promises concerning Ishmael also:

> ...I will surely bless him. I will make him fruitful and will
> greatly increase his numbers. He will be the father of
> twelve rulers, and I will make him into a great nation.
> (Genesis 17:20)

The followers of Islam are the actual descendants of Ishmael. While today the Middle East is consumed by cultural and religious conflict, it is ironic that every side still traces their understanding of faith back to this great historical figure named Abraham. The belief in one powerful, omnipotent God Source and the confidence to trust the promises and honor the imperishable standards of this deity are historical concepts brought to the human race through this one man.

Abraham's sons, Ishmael and Isaac, were half brothers; they each had twelve sons, and each fathered a great nation. When Abraham finally died at 175 years of age, "[h]is sons Isaac and Ishmael buried him in the cave of Machpelah..." (Genesis 25:9). These brothers had their differences, but they were still family, and as such they honored their father together. Oh, if only the religions in the nations of the world today could still remember that we are all related and believe in the same God!

However, this biblical story about a possible child sacrifice still bothered me greatly. Did Abraham's willingness to act in faith prove something to the God Source? Did the "father of us all" (Romans 4:16), establish for humanity some kind of higher status in allegiance to the species of the God Kind?

Abraham's loyal actions confirmed that man could surrender to a presence greater than himself, that he could be sure and certain of what he could not yet see or understand.

When we read about Abraham's unquestioning faithfulness, an extraordinary parallel clicks into focus. God's perverse request leaves us feeling very unsettled. But upon closer examination, it becomes rich in symbolic meaning and purpose. Abraham's faithful actions may have been the very event that convinced the God Source to sacrifice *his own son*—Jesus—for humanity!

In both the celestial and human species, each was willing to sacrifice a peace child so an alliance could be formed. The death of Jesus Christ seemed to be God's reenactment and fulfillment of the same event, for he allowed his only son to be sacrificed on man's altar. God demonstrated his love and belief in humankind through the same action that Abraham had shown God. Each had faith in the other. The invisible Great Ones communicated their intent to adopt and mentor the human race through this extraordinary, historical event!

Once again powerful concepts and spiritual covenants were being established through events on the human timeline. In the book of James in the New Testament, this story of Abraham's incredible belief system was passed on to the followers of Jesus Christ:

> *Abraham is remembered because of his great faith. This account of Abraham's faith through works comes down to us from thousands of years of history. You see that his faith and his actions were working together, and his faith was made complete by what he did. (James 2:22)*

Thousands of years later, we are still reading the same account of how Abraham activated great faith. He could not have lived as he had without a core-deep, heartfelt belief in a supernatural God. He repeated to himself the promise, in the words of God, that he would be blessed with many generations of descendants from his son Isaac. He told his young boy that God would provide a lamb for the offering. Yet, when his faith was tested for authenticity, he immediately acted on God's bizarre request. Here were the components of faith: the belief, the words, and the action. Then God reciprocated thousands of years later with faith in the human race by offering his son in the very same manner.

Developing the ability to activate a powerful faith is an ongoing process. It does not happen instantly or automatically. It took great courage for the heroes of old to conquer their fears and stand up to the accepted realities of their world. The first

Christians also must have activated great faith to go against the whole structure of organized religion and believe that a strange, dynamic carpenter was only half human and in fact the Son of the one true God. Today it takes the very same kind of courage to take the quantum leap of faith and connect with celestial Spirit in our world. But now we have the formula.

13

activating the law of faith

The innate qualities of the law of faith are examined.

Confidence Is the Key

Today there is a hunger for empowerment wherever we reside. A sense of helplessness has darkened our world, and it seems that what we most need is nowhere to be found. Many outsiders looking into Christianity see only the history and the hypocrisy. Insiders acknowledge an omnipotent God in the doctrines of their churches but struggle to implement powerful faith in their daily affairs. Hasn't this formula for activating faith as a power source been there in print for all these centuries? Is this same supernatural power available right now to every one of us here in our contemporary world? In a bittersweet way, it may be a new and surprising concept to many who believe in God.

Christ proclaimed our access to God's unlimited creative power when he announced the good news of the kingdom of God because every kingdom has its own laws. This surely was good news—that celestial laws will work for us during our lifetime on earth. Jesus Christ was affirming that we too have the capacity to be empowered. Like a strong electrical current, creative power can be channeled through our lives by our own faith-filled thoughts and words.

However, even when we grasp the principle of faith and understand the activation formula, it is hard to put it into practice. Activating faith is a skill to be mastered. Besides the two major components—our belief and our heartfelt words—other things can be put into place that will help build our confidence to tap into this powerful, metaphysical current.

First, if we want the current to be conducted through us at all, we have to believe we are truly connected to the God Source. Jesus never doubted the Father's ability to override earth's physical laws. It's recorded that he walked on water (John 6:19)! We too are required to have enough confidence in our connection to the Great Ones to believe that metaphysical things will occur. When we come to terms with the otherworldliness of the God species and the whole realm of powerful forces in existence, we realize life is not what it actually looks like on the surface of our reality. We have to take our idea of inanimate faith out of the passive, little religious rooms of our hearts and see it instead as an active current of power flowing through the corridors of our minds.

The first step then is to believe not only in God but also in what he says—*to trust him explicitly.* Jesus taught us that there is no power at all without this belief. The following is an account of a persistent man who struggled with his faith but desperately wanted his son to be healed.

> *Teacher, I brought you my son, who is possessed by a spirit that has robbed him of speech.... I asked your disciples to drive out the spirit, but they could not. It has often thrown him into fire or water to kill him. But if you can do anything, take pity on us and help us.*
>
> *"If you can?" said Jesus. "Everything is possible for him who believes." (Mark 9:17-23)*

At this point, the man's lack of faith could have prevented his son's healing. The whole matter hung on the man's mindset, expressed by the words "if you can." Christ pointed out the problem by repeating these words to the man.

The primary condition for activating metaphysical miracles never ever rests with God's ability but with our own capacity to believe in the miraculous. This is probably the most important thing to remember. The God Source obviously has the ability, but do we have the capacity to believe? That is the distinction. When this father looked deep into the eyes of Jesus the Christ, he saw the depth of self-confidence and assurance. Then he cried, "I do believe!" and, glancing at his poor, warped son, uttered, "Help me with my unbelief."

If we can trust in the source of a higher power, it overrides our difficulty in believing the specific details of what must happen. Believing in God's provision for us is the key. According to all the recorded scriptures, it has always been the will of Jesus, the one anointed with celestial authority, to help and to heal us. He was tortured and murdered for that very reason, and that was the purpose of his life. Saving people was inherent in his name. However, he can't heal or save anybody if we don't believe in his power to do so. This is why only a few miracles could be accomplished in the town in which Jesus grew up. The residents found it hard to believe that someone they knew could actually do supernatural things (Matthew 13:54-58).

In our example, though, the boy was healed quickly before the crowd could influence the small amount of faith the father had. This child had probably been mentally ill from early childhood, and the father's understanding of medical science in that day led him to believe there was no cure. We too have so many incurable forms of disease today. When our medical experts tell us something is inoperable, we shake our heads, and say, "It's hopeless. Isn't it sad?" But how does God want us to speak? The apostle Paul encouraged us:

> We have not received the spirit of the world but the Spirit who is from God, that we may understand what God has freely given us. This is what we speak, not in words taught us by human wisdom but in words taught by the Spirit, expressing spiritual truths in spiritual words. (1 Corinthians 2:12-14)

You see, Paul didn't depend on his own understanding, nor was he known for his great preaching ability. He simply spoke powerfully about what he had received from God. Here is how he explained it:

> My message and my preaching were not with wise and persuasive words, but with a demonstration of the Spirit's power, so that your faith might not rest on men's wisdom, but on God's power. (1 Corinthians 2:4-5)

God wants us to speak with words of Spirit! We do not have to be especially talented or wise. When we quote spiritual truths with the words we say, we can create the answers we desire. We can initiate miracles by decisively believing in the words of great celestial beings. We actually have to come to the point where we believe in the metaphysical Great Ones more than we believe in our own senses.

Understandably, this is very difficult, because in whatever hemisphere we live, we have already been programmed to accept this world's miserable state of existence. Thus, we are limited by our own logical acceptance of only "normal" solutions. This area of the supernatural is the biggest hurdle we must leap over. While others may tell us to be practical and "get real," we in fact have to think the impossible to access the power given to us by an extraterrestrial, paranormal kind of God!

> ...the God who gives life to the dead and calls things that are not, as though they were. (Romans 4:17)
>
> So we fix our eyes not on what is seen, but on what is unseen. For what is seen is temporary, but what is unseen is eternal. (2 Corinthians 4:18).

Therefore, the first condition to activate the law of faith is to put implicit trust in God's way of doing the impossible. If ever there were a nugget of truth worth memorizing, this is it:

> "I can do everything through him who gives me strength."
> (Philippians 4:13)

Stepping Out in Faith

The second condition to activate the process is to take a leap in faith—take a step in the direction we want to go. We spoke of the quantum leap factor in the last chapter, and often some kind of action needs to validate our words.

People in Jerusalem and the neighboring countryside had heard of the man called the Christ and the strange, miraculous occurrences that seemed to surround him. Many people with a multitude of needs made extensive and perilous journeys just to find him. For their belief and action, they were healed. Some of them even climbed trees to see him pass. One group lowered their friend through a rooftop to get him in front of Jesus Christ so he could be healed. Would these people have seen miracles if they had dismissed or laughed at what Jesus had to say? I don't think so. If we say we believe something but fail to take even the very first steps to accomplish it, do we really believe in it at all?

We often think we must take a huge leap of faith and believe in something unthinkable. However, if we start trying to have faith at that level in the midst of so much doubt, the power doesn't work for us at all. We have to choose something we can almost believe in, and then maybe, with a stretch of will, we can begin to visualize it. Remember, we don't need to understand *how* God will do something; we just have to accept in our hearts that what God promises can be manifested in our lives. Then, by using the definition of faith, we believe it, we state it with words, and then we take the first step toward our goal. The connection with a power source greater than our selves will orchestrate it.

To a certain degree, we already access the power of belief through our thinking processes, but most of us don't realize where the power comes from. Popular success manuals have adapted the sentiment by saying that *if you can conceive it and believe it, you can achieve it,* but they cannot explain how or why it works. However, it is fascinating to find this profound truth to be a celestial principle mirrored in the pages of our Bible:

> If you believe, you will receive whatever you ask for in prayer. (Matthew 21:22)

Yet how detrimental our disbelief is. If we don't really expect it to work out, we will never achieve it. Unfortunately, doubt erases all activation of power. There is a need then to prove this principle in our lives starting with small, personal steps. These increments develop and strengthen our ability to act confidently in faith. Expecting a favorable result is the very first part of activating faith, and relying on Jesus Christ is the foundational cornerstone for building our new belief system.

> "See, I lay a stone in Zion, a chosen and precious cornerstone, and the one who trusts in him will never be ashamed." (Isaiah 28:16, 1 Peter 2:6)

We can depend on our belief and trust in Jesus as a celestial ambassador because he will never go back on his word. What can we count on him for? Can we trust him to see us through that long talk we put off with our partner? Can we trust him to help us make that important, life-changing decision? Can we trust him to give us satisfying employment or a successful job interview?

I really encourage you to choose something for which you would like his help. I dare you to set a personal goal! Find a celestial promise you can believe in, state it aloud, and wait for the results with expectation. Just take that first step! If you expect something to happen, then your very expectation proves you believe in the power of God. Nothing is more supernaturally exciting than to watch God's invisible, celestial power in action upon your own reality. You can prove to yourself that he exists. You can feel his presence. But keep in mind that God has a sense of fun, for some-times things work out in very strange and humorous ways!

When we implement the components that activate faith, the formula actually does work. As we trust God, he provides for us in ways even greater than what we originally asked for. There's an awe-inspiring account that illustrates how simply taking the first small steps in faith can bring us to a huge miracle. It starts with a poverty-stricken mother sharing the last of her food with a stranger.

There was once a poor widow at Zarephath in the land of Sidon near the seashore. During a severe drought and famine, a strange man appeared at the gate, asking for water and a piece of bread. She gave him water but then she explained, "I don't have any bread—only a handful of flour in a jar and a little oil in a jug. I am gathering a few sticks to take home and make a meal for myself and my son that we may eat it—and die." (1 Kings 17:12)

She thought this stranger acted rather odd but there was something powerfully confident about him. The stranger named Elijah told her not to be afraid but first go and make him a small cake of bread and then some for her and her son. He said his God had told him that she would be taken care of.

For this is what the LORD, the God of Israel, says: "The jar of flour will not be used up and the jug of oil will not run dry until the day the Lord gives rain on the land." (1 Kings 17:14)

In her dire situation, God didn't give her a one-hundred-pound sack of flour and a gallon or so of oil. No, in her personal faith, she had to reach in her little jars of precious flour and oil every day and decide to share it with yet another person.

> *She went and did as Elijah had told her. So there was food every day for Elijah and for the woman and her family. For the jar of flour was not used up and the jug of oil did not run dry, in keeping with the word of the Lord spoken by Elijah. (1 Kings 17:15-16)*

Having faith is not supposed to be easy. It will push us out of our comfort zone. Activating the power of God requires effort on our part. The process of believing is the work we must do, and our actions prove those beliefs. Sometimes even more effort will be required so we learn to activate faith powerfully.

In our story of the poor widow, the famine drew on and her son grew ill, then died. In anger she spoke out:

> *What do you have against me, man of God? Did you come to remind me of my sin and kill my son? (1 Kings 17:18)*

Now it was Elijah's faith that was severely tested. Aghast, he carried the son into his room and cried out to the Lord, asking for a miracle not only with words but also through proof of action. With deep, heartfelt belief, he stretched himself out beside the boy and cried, "Oh Lord, my God, let this boy's life return to him!" But nothing happened. Now, most of us would have given up, saying, "See? It didn't work!" or "I guess God's answer is no." But Elijah didn't give up. Instead, he actually stretched out beside the boy and cried out to God three different times! After that, God heeded his belief and poured life back into the son. Elijah took the boy to the widow, saying:

> *"Look, your son is alive!"*
>
> *Then the woman said to Elijah, "Now I know that you are a man of God and that the word of the Lord from your mouth is the truth." (1 Kings 17:21, 23-24)*

When the woman had first started to share her food, she had taken a leap in faith. Despite her reality she held belief in her heart and kept doing the action of dipping into her meager supplies a few times each day. As the miracle continued day after day, the food was somehow never consumed. Elijah finally activated his faith by taking a number of steps also. He did not pray over the boy once. He stretched himself out beside the boy and requested a miracle a total of three times before he saw any results. In all those "failures," he held his faith steadfastly.

This story vividly portrays the next principle we must understand: our thoughts, our words, and our actions all work together. When we activate faith, they all have to be in place no matter how small those first steps may seem. This whole example is exemplified by the last verse: "The word of the Lord from your mouth is the truth!" (1 Kings 17:24). We are not talking about small, hopeful prayers here. We are talking about the authority to speak God's words with the power to change the reality of life and death. We are talking about persevering in our beliefs to cause metaphysical things to happen!

Fighting against Doubt

When I tried to apply faith to my own trials in life, there were many opportunities for doubt to set in. Just like everyone else, I have had my share of personal crises and disasters. My life experiences became valuable experiments to test and develop a powerful personal faith. In addition, I found a third condition for activating strong faith. It can be discovered when we look in depth at the faith principle.

Jesus mentored his apostles in the use of spiritual laws. Sometime during the teaching process, they finally recognized faith as a source of power, and they wanted more of it.

> *The apostles said to the Lord, "Increase our faith!"*
>
> *He replied, "If you have faith as small as a mustard seed, you can say to this mulberry tree, 'Be uprooted and planted in the sea', and it will obey you." (Luke 17:5-6)*

What a strange answer!

Another time the apostles tried to heal an epileptic and found their words did not work. When the boy was brought to Jesus and healed, they asked Jesus afterward:

> *"Why couldn't we drive it out?"*
>
> *He replied, "Because you have so little faith. I tell you the truth, if you have faith as small as a mustard seed, you can say to this mountain, 'Move from here to there' and it will move. Nothing will be impossible for you." (Matthew 17:19-21)*

Now, a mustard seed is one of the tiniest seeds there is. Does this mean we only need a small amount of faith? Not exactly, because according to Jesus the disciples actually did have a little bit of faith, but still they could not heal this boy. Instead Jesus showed them just how powerful faith can be in the absence of doubt. He clarifies the principle with this verse:

> *"Have faith in God," Jesus answered. "I tell you the truth, if anyone says to this mountain, 'Go throw yourself into the sea,' and does not doubt in his heart but believes that what he says will happen, it will be done for him."* (Mark 11:22-23)

These passages about moving mountains and uprooting mulberry trees are always overlooked in the Bible because they seem so outrageous. You seldom hear them spoken about from a church pulpit. Yet here is the key to understanding the quantum-leap characteristic faith has.

The core of it is this: either we believe something will happen or we don't. Either we have faith or we don't. If we don't have faith, then we do have doubt. This is a fundamental principle in activating the celestial law of faith.

Remember the original definition: "Now faith is being sure of what we hope for and certain of what we do not see" (Hebrews 11:1). There is no "maybe" in this formula! There is no room for doubt because doubt and faith are antonyms! They can't be mixed. If they are both present, they cancel each other out, becoming neutral and powerless.

A passage in the book of Matthew shows another occasion when Jesus specifically taught how faith and doubt oppose each other. The centurion in this story was not affiliated with Jesus's disciples, but he had such an abundance of faith, even Jesus was impressed.

When Jesus had entered Capernaum, a centurion came to him, asking for help. "Lord," he said, "my servant lies at home paralyzed and in terrible suffering."

Jesus said to him, "I will go and heal him."

The centurion replied, "Lord, I do not deserve to have you come under my roof. But just say the word, and my servant will be healed. For I myself am a man under authority, with soldiers under me. I tell this one, 'Go,' and he goes; and that one, 'Come,' and he comes. I say to my servant, 'Do this,' and he does it."

When Jesus heard this, he was astonished and said to those following him, "I tell you the truth, I have not found anyone in Israel with such great faith."

Then Jesus said to the centurion, "Go! It will be done just as you believed it would." And his servant was healed at that very hour. (Matthew 8:5-13)

Jesus was amazed to find there was no doubt in this man at all. The centurion knew how to activate the faith formula flawlessly! He believed in his heart and stated as much with his words. He was certain that Christ held this kind of authority by the reputation he had, and told him "just say the word, and my servant will be healed." That same reality was created because his belief was not shadowed by any doubt. The words he spoke authenticated his belief and therefore released the power of God.

From these examples, we can see that the law of faith is either activated by our belief or deactivated by our doubt. Because of this have or have-not nature of faith, our confidence will be under constant attack. All kinds of reasons will occur to us as to why something won't work. It is Satan, our adversary, who brings these reasons to our minds in order to keep us in a state of oppression. If he can cause us to doubt, that stops our faith from creating anything miraculous. He fights hard to convince us we cannot connect to the powerful current of the Great Ones, but the power still exists and is always available to us. Most importantly, we are the ones who get to activate the power switch! We turn faith on and off with the level of our beliefs.

Doubt stops the current of free-flowing faith. First, we have faith, and then we don't; then we do, then we don't. We think something might happen, we hope it will happen, we ask God for it to happen, but most of the time we don't really think it will happen. This is a wavering kind of faith and it is also quite clearly explained in scripture:

> If any of you lacks wisdom, he should ask God, who gives generously to all without finding fault, and it will be given to him. But when he asks, he must believe and not doubt, because he who doubts is like a wave of the sea, blown and tossed by the wind. That man should not think he will receive anything from the Lord: he is a double-minded man, unstable in all he does. (James 1:5-8)

To look at it another way, isn't it somewhat insulting to ask God to intervene on our behalf and then not believe he will? Either we doubt his ability or we don't believe his abundant love for us. Yet, the God Source cares about our unique needs so personally. He gave up his own son to ransom us, and he sent sacred Spirit to empower us. He now wants to teach us how to manifest our needs as the godlike children he wants us to become. That is ultimate love! So why do we doubt him?

We doubt because we don't trust the unknown. We trust the world because we think we know how it works; it's familiar. The answer then is really to know who the God Source is so we can totally trust him. As we get to know his integrity, his honor, and his unfailing love for us, our belief in God's ultimate authority over all things will become consistent and strong. Then our faith can override what we see in the natural world.

This point was made perfectly clear when Jesus sent the disciples out in their boat while he stayed behind to pray alone. Late in the night, when he had finished his meditation, he walked out to them *on the water*. Why did he do this phenomenal and crazy thing? They thought he was a ghost!

> "Lord, if it's you," Peter replied, "Tell me to come to you on the water."
>
> "Come," he said.

Jesus was inviting Peter to take a stroll with him on the top of the lake. Peter believed so much in the integrity of his friend Jesus, he actually had the faith to throw a leg over the side of the boat, step out on the water, and walk on it!

> But when he saw the wind, he was afraid and, beginning to sink, cried out, "Lord, save me."
>
> Immediately Jesus reached out his hand and caught him. "You of little faith," he said, "Why did you doubt?" (Matthew 14:28-31)

What is so awesome is that for a short time, Peter had enough faith to walk on water. It wasn't just Jesus who accomplished it. What did that feel like? I wonder. When Peter took his eyes off the power of overriding celestial laws, he noticed the wind and waves around him. That was his undoing. When we allow our view of the real world to hold us back, it is difficult to have a powerful faith. We become afraid. Although we might not realize it, our fear is acknowledging Satan's dominion over us. Remember, those dark forces on our planet do not want us to be empowered!

Facing Fear

The fourth condition to activate strong faith lies in conquering our fears. Fear is the principal tool Satan uses to destroy our faith. Whether it is fear of consequences, fear of failure, or even fear of being laughed at, this emotion will stop miracles from happening.

In fighting our fear, we can again look to Jesus's example. On one occasion, a synagogue ruler pleaded with Jesus to heal his dying daughter, while his colleagues ridiculed him.

"Your daughter is dead," they said. "Why bother the teacher anymore?"

Ignoring what they said, Jesus told the synagogue ruler, "Don't be afraid; just believe...." He went in and said to them, "Why all this commotion and wailing? The child is not dead but asleep." But they laughed at him. After he put them all out, he took the child's father and mother and the disciples who were with him, and went in where the child was. He took her by the hand and said to

> her, "Talitha koum!" ["Little girl, I say to you, get up!"]
> Immediately the girl stood up and walked around.... (Mark
> 5:35-42)

Jesus was not afraid to be laughed at. He and the girl's parents were not afraid to put all their friends out of the house. They quieted their fear of death, and then their belief in the supernatural conquered the fear.

We are created to be powerful, but fear weakens us. What is fear, anyway? It is simply a lack of faith! Worry can be seen as its cousin. Having fear is disbelieving God's ability and desire to handle things for us. Fear is actually giving allegiance to Satan and accepting his influence over us. In extremes, it can even be a form of satanic worship. The demonic angels enjoy when we cower in fear because it makes them feel godlike. We even seem to enjoy cowering in fear as proven by the popularity of horror movies in western society. But in truth fear is the method Satan uses to subdue and manipulate us in order to feed off our power to creative things his way in the physical world. Remember, he can only create things to happen through our beliefs and behavior. In fear, Satan is able to influence our thoughts so negatively that we can commit great atrocities. In fear we also build huge mental prisons that lead our minds step by step down into dungeons so deep and dark that all we want to do is to die. We call it suicide then. But I believe no dungeon is so deep that the presence of God can't pierce it with light. We can overcome fear by replacing it with a stronger belief in a higher power.

To fight fear we need to feel God's love for us deep inside. We have to be able to hear his words of promise so we can take action. This we can do no matter what situation we find ourselves in or where we live. Physical location does not matter because Spirit is spirit and able to live within us. It is there, internally, that God gives assurances for whatever fears we might have.

> *I took you from the ends of the earth, from its farthest corners I called you. I said, "You are my servant"; I have chosen you and have not rejected you. So do not fear, for I am with you; do not be dismayed, for I am your God. I will strengthen you and help you; I will uphold you with my righteous right hand. (Isaiah 41:8-10)*

How truly loved we are! No matter what our circumstances, we can put our fears aside simply by keeping our focus on God's invisible but real presence of love toward us. Then we can activate faith strong enough to overcome any trials in our perceived reality!

Feelings of Unworthiness

When we stand on these gold-nugget scriptures and grasp how especially precious we are to God, we feel more confident in our relationship with him. That is the fifth condition to activating the powerful faith formula: we need to establish in our own minds that our self-worth to God is of great value. Our adversary will always try to make us feel unworthy to receive the promises that were given to us. Therefore, feelings of inferiority and guilt have to be eliminated for us to become bold with the necessary confidence.

We may think God is too busy for our trivial little needs, or maybe that we are just so insignificant God won't bother. What fallacies! They're not even logical. Those trains of thought come from the one who is the accuser and the originator of lies.

Haven't we been given sacred Spirit because the Great Ones respect us so much? We are so valuable to them that the God Source offers us a powerful Spirit to live inside our minds! They have so much compassion for the human species that an ambassador was sent to earth to ransom us from Satan's tyranny. God is so much better, than we have ever dared to dream. Their greatest desire is to spoil us with gifts of empowerment! Jesus tried to express this:

> Which of you, if his son asks for bread, will give him a
>
> stone? Or if he asks for a fish, will give him a snake?
>
> If you, then, though you are evil, know how to give
>
> good gifts to your children, how much more will your
>
> Father in heaven give good gifts to those who ask him!
>
> (Matthew 7:9-11)

Jesus once asked God, his father, to feed a huge group of people who had come to listen to him. From two meager fish in a basket and a few pieces of bread, he was able to replicate uncounted bushel baskets full of fish to feed the whole crowd. God's extravagant intent toward us goes much further than simply meeting our needs, however.

As the old saying goes, God doesn't want just to feed us with fish; he would much rather teach us how to fish so we can feed ourselves! He chooses to empower us and celebrates our sense of accomplishment when we learn for ourselves how to manifest the good things we need and desire. Jesus stated:

> You did not choose me, but I chose you and appointed you
>
> to go and bear fruit—fruit that will last. Then the Father
>
> will give you whatever you ask in my name. (John 15:16)
>
> I have come that they may have life, and have it to the
>
> full. (John 10:10)

We have to see the God Source as a kind and awesome father figure whose only desire is to bless us with good things. Obviously, in his eyes, we are worthy enough to ask him for any good thing!

Perhaps we waver in our beliefs because our guilty consciences convince us we do not deserve to forgive ourselves. It is difficult sometimes to pardon ourselves for whatever we've done, but a guilty conscience will not help spiritual growth in any way. Maybe we haven't been "good enough" in the past, but that is what Christ died for—to pay the penalty for our sins. If we could become perfect by our own efforts, why did God have to send his son down here at all? To be forgiven and set free from our guilt was the whole purpose of Jesus's death!

> *...For all have sinned and fall short of the glory of God, and are justified freely by his grace through the redemption that came by Christ Jesus. (Romans 3:23)*

Of course, we cannot measure up to all the celestial standards. How presumptuous to think that we might! We are only humans struggling to develop our spiritual maturity. We are like beloved but immature children, and not yet perfect. When we mess up, we simply need to apologize from our hearts and then continue learning and activating faith through true and godly kinds of action.

> *Dear children, let us not love with words or tongue but with actions and in truth. This then is how we know that we belong to the truth, and how we set our hearts at rest in his presence whenever our hearts condemn us.... [W]e have confidence before God and receive from him any thing we ask, because we obey his commands and do what pleases him. (1 John 3:18-20)*

If we can humble ourselves, God forgives all our faults. This love from the Great Ones is so vast. Who are you to think he can't forgive you? After all Christ befriended prostitutes and thieving tax collectors! Even the highly respected apostle Paul was originally instrumental in having the very first Christians put to death! He was accountable for having them killed; yet, he was forgiven and became a great Christian leader.

Our sins do not keep us apart from God, but our attitude toward our sin can be a big obstacle. There is a way to erase all feelings of inferiority and guilt. Through the process of accepting Jesus's payment of the penalty for our sin, we can be free of it! This is how highly we are valued, and how greatly we are loved.

Knowing the Will of God

There is one last condition for activating powerful faith. Knowing the will of God is perhaps our greatest struggle yet. If we have met all the other conditions, there is one last way that our adversary will keep us weak and grounded in the patterns of our world: if we question the will of God.

How do we know that what we want to happen is what God wants to happen? What if we ask for something that God doesn't approve? In order to truly understand God's will, there has to be changes made in our minds.

> Do not conform any longer to the pattern of this world, but be transformed by the renewing of your mind. Then you will be able to test and approve what God's will is— his good, pleasing and perfect will. (Romans 12:2)

If we ask for something and don't know if it is within God's will, there is a simple way to find out. We can align our request to stand up to the two great laws of love because ultimately God is love, right? Does our request line up with loving God with all our heart and mind and soul? Does the request conform to loving our neighbor as our selves? If so, what we ask for is acceptable; it is a godlike request! Therefore, it is within God's will.

> *This is the confidence we have in approaching God: that if we ask anything according to his will, he hears us.*
> *(1 John 5:14)*

In an overview of the recorded miracles Jesus Christ performed in his lifetime, some things are apparent. Of all the hundreds, maybe thousands of people who were healed, he never said to any of them, "I can't help you." This was never his attitude. In every example where there was faith, his will was to heal and to overcome the problem. Such was the willingness of his heart, as his examples show.

> *"Lord, if you are willing, you can make me clean." Jesus reached out his hand and touched the man. "I am willing," he said. "Be clean!" (Matthew 8:2-3)*
>
> *...The blind men came to him, and he asked them, "Do you believe that I am able to do this?"*
>
> *"Yes, Lord," they replied.*
>
> *Then he touched their eyes and said, "According to your faith will it be done to you"; and their sight was restored. (Matthew 9:28-30)*

"Do you believe?" was the only conditional question Jesus Christ ever asked. If faith was there, he was willing and able to perform his miracles. It's not that God decides whether or not to perform miracles on a whim or as favors to us. The activation of faith by each person determines whether a supernatural event occurs. As discussed earlier, we are the ones in control of the power switch! It is always Jesus Christ's will to save, heal, and to give us peace.

> But he was pierced for our transgressions, he was crushed for our iniquities; the punishment that brought us peace was upon him, and by his wounds we are healed. (Isaiah 53:57)

Jesus willingly went through all he did because it was his will to free our minds and to heal our bodies. His will is the same today as always (Hebrews 13:8)!

The unique key here is that Jesus sacrificed himself not only to give us eternal life but also to heal us from our physical sicknesses and tragedies. He sacrificed himself for us; we do not need to sacrifice ourselves in sickness for him. Sometimes, however, spurred on by our desire to serve God and the twisted idea that we might earn the favor of God, we see our poor health or dismal situation as a sacrifice we must carry. Then, when the burden gets too heavy, we end up making excuses for why God wouldn't want to heal or help us. Sometimes this makes us want to blame God for our ill health and times of trial. Our belief in the will of God wavers because we don't recognize there is a dark force working against us. This destructive power is from Satan. It is Satan, who wants us willing to sacrifice ourselves.

The Great Ones do not need our sacrifices. Jesus Christ's will was to empower us.

> He himself bore our sins in his body on the cross, so that
> we might die to sins and live for righteousness; by his
> wounds you have been healed. (1 Peter 2:24)

Yet, notice this! What seems outrageous is that these last two verses do not say we might be healed or even that we will be healed. They say we *have been* healed—in the past tense! By this example, Jesus taught that we have been healed as soon as we decide that the Son of God's death on the cross was endured for the very purpose of giving us that personal healing.

We don't need to wait around until God is ready to heal us. Jesus was ready to heal us in the garden of Gethsemane and proved it on the cross. The Son of God was sent for that purpose. Instead of saying, "God will heal me when he is ready," we have to realize that God and Jesus Christ were ready more than two thousand years ago! It's already been done. Our belief system must get into alignment with that truth, and then the miraculous will happen!

Another scripture states, "Now is the day of salvation" (2 Corinthians 6:2). Right now is when we can be saved from all manner of negative things. God promises to be there and to save us when we truly believe he has saved us. The power in Jesus's name is the meaning of his name: God saves. This is the will of God; to save us from every kind of trouble we encounter.

When we think these things through in a logical manner, nothing should stop us from believing and asking God for help and for healing because we have been given it already. It's like a wonderful gift waiting to be opened. We only have to accept the gift that's been given to us and believe. Wow! What an extraordinary legacy.

the implications

14

Developing spiritual maturity

We continually use our mindsets in two different directions, resulting in opposite consequences. The reason for human suffering is explored.

A Learning Process

I am convinced that creating positive events in our lives is a skill the Great Ones desire us to learn. Our lives are set up so our belief systems will engage with our environment, and the results will be in direct correlation with exactly what is being projected from our minds. It's true that our environment influences us, but by connecting to the realm of Spirit, we can also influence the reality of our environment.

Vast and powerful possibilities can be opened to us if we program our mindset to be one of positive expectation. The Book of Hebrews stated it simply: if we can be "sure of what we hope for and certain of what we do not see" (Hebrews 11:1), then it will be done for us. Winning over the negatives in our lives requires knowledge of the metaphysical nature to the law of faith. We experience trials in order to gain skill in using faith in the supernatural to overcome them. Thus, we grow to become more spiritually mature. Through the struggles we endure, we develop godlike character and transform into formidable opponents to our adversaries.

However, acquiring spiritual maturity is a growth process. When we are born, we leave our existence within the near-perfect water world of the womb to enter a completely different realm. In our new world of open space, our needs are not taken care of automatically. Our infant minds expand rapidly to sponge up as much knowledge as possible for survival. Through the years of childhood, we develop mentally and physically, and learn how to get our needs met. Then adolescence gives us autonomy, and we break away from the structure our parents set up. At this time, we begin to determine right from wrong, but we are still influenced by family and the cultural norms with which we have been programmed. Within these parameters, we choose our own answers to the questions presented in our personal lives, and our morals are formed. Most physically mature adults attain some level of mental and emotional maturity. That is considered a human being's normal cycle of moral development.

But how does our spiritual development occur? At what age does it start? The seed of sacred Spirit enters us and begins to develop at the precise moment when we recognize and want to honor a higher power and authority in our lives. As we align ourselves to celestial standards instead of choosing right from wrong for ourselves, the real journey to spiritual maturity begins. And how long does this process take? It depends on the experiences we encounter on our personal pathways through life and how we react to them. I have found there are old-wise young people, and very immature old people.

I believe this conception of spirituality can happen in all cultures and any country, and under any standard of living. The ability to believe in a God Source of the highest power does not rely on affiliation to any one religion. There is no advantage to being educated or wealthy. Actually, we in the modern nations sometimes seem to struggle more with spiritual development because of our dependence on monetary definitions of success.

A Christian family I met in rural Mexico once taught me something profound. In broken Spanish, I told them I would continue to pray for relief from their situation of poverty and physical need. They told me they would continue to pray for me as well, that I might resist the temptation of personal decadence that was part of my country's moral deprivation! The struggles people face may be individual, but they are all result in teaching us to rely on God.

Imagine trying to raise a family in a poverty-stricken third-world country. Trials in such places are never-ending, and a person's sole drive is to stay alive. Compare this reality to our carefree living and self-indulgence. Which would more easily influence us to call on God and desire an alliance with him for empowerment? Which one would motivate us more to develop our spiritual maturity?

The populations of the third world have such great faith because there is so little access to any other source of power. In these nations, survival depends on a very strong belief system, and that type of character development is most important to the Great Ones. From a celestial viewpoint, that is the ultimate purpose to the game of life. Only the godly characteristics we are able to acquire in this world have true eternal value.

We must consider a much bigger picture. God's goal for us is not to see how powerful we can become in our society. It is not important to his eternal plans for us if we have two cars, two bicycles, or even two healthy legs to walk on. Yes, he wants to give us health, wealth, and happiness in our physical lives, but that is not his main priority. More than any other thing, God wants us to gain maturity. He wants to give us the skills to activate faith in order to have celestial empowerment. He knows this power can easily change all other physical situations. God wants us to be godlike—to be like him and have unlimited power to create the things we really need.

Your biological father may want to give you wonderful gifts but he does not want to spoil you. He expects you to grow up eventually and be able to get the things you need for yourself. Parents hope their children will mature with intelligence and develop self-control. It is the same with God. What the God Source passionately desires is for us to grow in spiritual maturity by using the deposit of celestial Spirit he has given us. God wants to see his character grow and flourish in us.

Good training of any kind does not come easily. It takes self-disciplined endurance. Look at the great athletes who willingly suffer pain to obtain their goals. These are serious, hardworking men and women challenged by their own passionate drives toward excellence. The "no pain, no gain" ideology suggests it takes time and practice to develop muscles and skills. It's the same for spiritual strength. Our earthly lives have been set up for us as specialized training grounds. We are in boot camp here on earth! The books of James and Romans describe it in this way:

> Consider it pure joy, my brothers, whenever you face trials of many kinds, because you know that the testing of your faith develops perseverance. Perseverance must finish its work so that you may be mature and complete, not lacking anything. (James 1:2-4)

> *And we rejoice in the hope of the glory of God. Not only so, but we also rejoice in our sufferings, because we know that suffering produces perseverance; perseverance, character; and character, hope. And hope does not disappoint us, because God has poured out his love into our hearts by the Holy Spirit, whom he has given us. (Romans 5:2-5)*

The hope this verse talks about is integral in activating the law of faith. On an individual basis, we can sometimes use pain and suffering as signals that we are playing the game of life in the wrong direction. Just as pain teaches a small child not to touch something that's hot, our suffering is meant to instruct us in wisdom. Among the nations of our planet, if there is violence, oppression, war, or hunger, it should signal to us that those political systems are tragically straying from the standards of the Great Ones—standards that were designed to bring about optimum human performance. If we find these symptoms exist in ourselves as well, we are breaking the rules God set up for living in love and abundance. In other words, the hurt we experience is necessary so we discover that what we are doing does not benefit us. To alleviate the pain, we need to grow, change, and align ourselves to celestial standards. Oh, if the nations of the world would only consider this!

While I was working with troubled teens as a youth-care worker at an inner-city school, a teacher explained something that has stuck with me. He said students learn quickly and easily when a teachable moment occurs. That precise time happens for them when they are faced with a crisis and they desperately need knowledge and answers. Only then are they able to accept advice and redirection in life. Real steps toward maturity can then be made. Like being on a game level, when teenagers learn self-discipline, they start to become mature adults. It's the same for all of us; the pain or discomfort we experience during trials provides the teachable moment, and we seek out wisdom, resulting in spiritual growth. We can take correction best when we directly see its spiritual value. This too is covered in our resource book:

> *Endure hardship as discipline; God is treating you as sons. For what son is not disciplined by his father? If you are not disciplined (and everyone undergoes discipline), then you are illegitimate children and not true sons. (Hebrews 12:7-8)*
>
> *Moreover, we have all had human fathers who disciplined us and we respected them for it. How much more should we submit to the Father of our spirits and live! Our fathers disciplined us for a little while as they thought best; but God disciplines us for our good, that we may share in his holiness. No discipline seems pleasant at the time, but painful. Later on, however, it produces a harvest of righteousness and peace for those who have been trained by it. (Hebrews 12:9-11)*
>
> *My son, do not despise the Lord's discipline and do not resent his rebuke, because the Lord disciplines those he loves, as a father the son he delights in. (Proverbs 3:11-12)*

Our spiritual development requires discipline. But who wants to be disciplined? Who wants the hard work, the sore physical or mental muscles? Who has the time and focus anyway? It's not an easy thing to face our faults and overcome them, but there has always been a high price to pay for attaining any great goal.

Taking Accountability

I spent many years coaching teenagers in life skills. They were in transition from being children to becoming young adults, and their biggest hurdle was accepting accountability for their actions. Many of them had very desperate childhoods, and learning to become personally responsible for their lives regardless of the past was often a terrific struggle. Invariably they blamed their teachers, their parents, and anyone in authority for the situations they were in. One student stated the epitome of his life philosophy by exclaiming, "But I didn't ask to be born!" How sad that he couldn't conceive of life as a gift and saw no purpose in living it. He knew nothing of his powerful potential and had yet to begin his own search for life's purpose.

Often we lose track of the awesome value of the one-time ticket we have been given to play the game of life. If we don't put value on the game itself or put forth any effort, how can we expect to win in anyway? If we don't take responsibility for our own lives, that certainly makes it easy, but then there's no point in playing the game.

In other words if we're not behind our own steering wheel on the road of life, is it any wonder we don't enjoy the journey? Who can we blame for that? If we don't choose the direction in which we're going, then we are allowing someone else to take over and direct our lives.

There will always be people who negatively influence us. Where we err is in allowing that to keep happening. How they treat us may be wrong, but we can't change the way others choose to play their life games. We must simply play ours in the most positive way possible, and sometimes that means it has to be played out somewhere else entirely. This is our right and our responsibility.

Being a Victim

It's so much easier to blame somebody else for our weaknesses. Instead of being accountable for our decisions and actions in life, we open our mouths and say negative things to attack those who offend us. We seem to find a false sense of importance by blaming, but does this benefit us at all? Does it rectify any situation? When we blame other people, we focus only on their faults and not on growing our own potential. In fact blaming others is simply a verbal acknowledgment that we are victims. We create our own victim mentality.

Actually, when we feel sorry for ourselves, our thoughts and actions activate the law of faith in an unfavorable direction. We say negative, harmful words of doubt, and these heartfelt words, by the very definition of faith, create the wrong things for us. Pessimistic self-talk can result in very destructive patterns. This is how we become caught in vicious circles of self-fulfilled prophecy. Whenever we feel like victims in our lives, we blame whomever and whatever we can, but really, aren't we the only ones who have the power to make changes in our lives? We are able to do this through the way we think and talk. Even if we can't actually change our reality right away, we can at least change the ideas we have about our circumstances.

It may come as a surprise, but God is not impressed with our suffering as victims. We do not earn any respect for our discomfort. Think about this: If we have accepted Spirit to live inside of us, would this celestial entity enjoy living with the pain, sorrow, and misery to which we so often subject our physical bodies when it isn't necessary? God has promised many times that he will never leave us or forsake us (Hebrews 13:5-6, Joshua 1:5), but can Spirit exist in a body saturated with negative power from the enemy? How could that be God's will? After all Jesus went through to ransom us, it is just not rational.

God never wants us to be victims. However, sometimes we just don't know what else to do when we think we are all alone. The wonder of it is, once we have invited sacred Spirit to live in us, we are not alone. Through our connection, we belong to a God-family and we have a whole group of angelic celestial beings backing us, urging us to activate faith as a source of metaphysical power for our lives. We are in Christ and he is in us (John 14:19-20).

I urge you not to be a victim. It does you absolutely no good to play this role. It merely makes you look like prey to the enemy. Did you know that Satan is like a roaring lion always looking for weaknesses in his victims?

> *Your enemy the devil prowls around like a roaring lion looking for someone to devour. Resist him, standing firm in the faith, because you know that your brothers throughout the world are undergoing the same kind of sufferings. (1 Peter 5:8-9)*

When we act like victims, there is no forward momentum to help us overcome trials. On the other hand, when we connect and allow Spirit to guide us, we are shown how to make a situation better. With Spirit working from within, we are in alignment with celestial power and can overcome all the worldly things that try to oppress us. God is greater than any negative situation.

> *You, dear children, are from God and have overcome them, because the one who is in you is greater than the one who is in the world. (1 John 4:4)*

The Purpose of Suffering

At some point, we have all tried to sort out the reasons for the problems we have in our lives. We still wonder why there is so much suffering in the world. We wonder the *why* of this because we forget and we don't acknowledge the dark force in existence on our planet. The Bible clearly defines and personifies an evil force working intently against us. Our trials were not created or even condoned by our God of love. Why would a God of love cause us pain, misery, and violence and then sacrifice his son to ransom us from them? It's not logical to believe that God is responsible.

The Great Ones entered our realm to save us from the pain and misery found in our world. Sometimes our trials are natural consequences from not being in alignment with godly standards and sometimes trials come from being swallowed up by a culture engulfed by immorally. But when we end up *accepting* long-standing trials in our lives, it may be an indication that we are suffering for the wrong reasons. The distinction lies in understanding that adversity does not need to last forever.

> ...Now for a little while you may have had to suffer grief in all kinds of trials. These have come so your faith—of greater worth than gold, which perished even though refined by fire—may be proved genuine and may result in praise, glory, and honor when Jesus Christ is revealed. (1 Peter 1:6-7)

The key to suffering is the phrase "for a little while." Our God of love does not condone a lifetime of constant pain as a tool for perfection.

Sometimes we become convinced that our bad habits, sicknesses, problems, and afflictions are things we have to suffer in life. We are forever carrying our troubles around with us like excess baggage, as though we were martyrs. It's like we take pride in the problems we have and brag about just how bad we have it.

Let's question this. In the way we deal with our own misery, to whom are we giving honor? Which powerful spirit entity does our suffering edify? Satan wants to steal our health and happiness, and above all else destroy our minds; Jesus came to bring about the very opposite—to give us hope, strength, and positive power. He stated this quite clearly:

> *The thief comes only to steal and kill and destroy; I have come that they may have life, and have it to the full. (John 10:10)*

To be given life and to live it to the full! By justifying our afflictions, addictions, or sicknesses as crosses we have to bear, are we giving honor to God? Emphatically no. Jesus Christ carried his cross and shed his blood to honor God, but he was not a victim. Actually, he knew he had the power to stop what was happening, but he went through with it to empower us. This was the purpose of the cross. If we still bear our own crosses of suffering, then what was the purpose of Jesus's cross?

How can our sickness, troubles, or enslaving bad habits possibly bring honor to God? How can they help us or anyone else in any way at all? While our trials oppress us, they give control to the author of destruction, the one who holds us in bondage. The trials we suffer only honor God when we are in the process of overcoming them! We have to stop martyring ourselves. We have to quit suffering with Jesus, because Jesus Christ no longer suffers. He lives jubilantly! He has already conquered Satan and wants us to do the same: to conquer our enemy, to live life and to have it to the fullest! It is then we bring honor to God. The apostle Paul wrote:

> *...We urge you not to receive God's grace in vain. For he says, "In the time of my favor I heard you, and in the day of salvation I helped you. I tell you, now is the time of God's favor, now is the day of salvation." (2 Corinthians 6:1-2 and Isaiah 49:8)*

Now—right now—is our day to be saved from affliction! Right this minute, each of us can overcome trials by believing in the metaphysical power of God, by stating it with our mouths, and by stepping out into action. Only when we refuse to remain a victim is it possible to stop being a victim.

Gaining a Victory

The Great Ones do respect one type of suffering we may choose to endure. This comes when we hold fast to celestial standards and are persecuted for doing what is right. The first disciples of Jesus Christ suffered much persecution for their new beliefs. Peter gave them strong encouragement:

> *Dear friends, do not be surprised at the painful trial you are suffering, as though something strange were happening to you. But rejoice that you participate in the sufferings of Christ, so that you may be overjoyed when his glory is revealed. If you are insulted because of the name of Christ, you are blessed, for the Spirit of glory and of God rests on you. If you suffer, it should not be as a murderer or thief or any other kind of criminal, or even as a meddler. However, if you suffer as a Christian, do not be ashamed, but praise God that you bear that name. (1 Peter 4:12-16)*

The followers of Jesus underwent great trials, but they were not caused by a lack of faith or by being a victim. These first believers willingly suffered in this way because of their loyalty and allegiance to Christ. They were persecuted because their beliefs were different from their cultural norms. The scriptures known as the Beatitudes portray this very well:

> *Blessed are those who are persecuted because of righteousness, for theirs is the kingdom of heaven.*
>
> *Blessed are you when people insult you, persecute you and falsely say all kinds of evil against you because of me. Rejoice and be glad, because great is your reward in heaven, for in the same way they persecuted the prophets who were before you. (Mathew 5:10-12)*

The apostle Paul lived a horrible life of suffering because he was affiliated with a new, fervent religion and believed that the man named Jesus was the actual son of a omnipotent, celestial God. Paul was beaten with rods, stoned, shipwrecked, and imprisoned. He was scourged five times, with thirty-nine lashes on his back made by leather whips with metal barbs on the ends; there must have been very little normal skin left. In those days, just one flogging to the maximum sentence of thirty-nine lashes often resulted in death. Paul did not give in but endured it repeatedly because he was convinced of the otherworldliness of Jesus Christ. Paul lived by the integrity of his convictions even when they brought him intense suffering. Yet, he believed he was the strongest when his own emotions made him feel weak.

> *That is why, for Christ's sake, I delight in weaknesses, in insults, in hardships, in persecutions, in difficulties. For when I am weak, then I am strong. (2 Corinthians 12:10)*

God often allows us to endure trials we think are more than we can handle. In experiencing hardships, we learn how to rely on God. We realize we cannot do everything ourselves and we're reminded that we need to plug in to God's power outlet. Paul was strong in the midst of his weakness because it was during those times that he allowed supernatural power to flow through him. He recognized he was connected to the source and that very connection brought him joy.

> *So we say with confidence, "The Lord is my helper; I will not be afraid. What can man do to me?" (Hebrews 13:6)*

The book of Job also has a unique perspective on trials. This book has had many interpretations, but all agree that Job went through a mess of afflictions! Throughout it all, he didn't accuse others, and he didn't blame God. He didn't give up or give in to the pessimism of his friends. In the end, he learned to be a little less arrogant and a lot more humble in his own integrity. Afterward, God blessed him with even more abundance than what he originally lost. He scored a huge victory over Satan. That's what this form of suffering is all about.

If we must suffer, let's do it by denying Satan when he tries to convince us we need to martyr ourselves and be victims. Enduring a trial can be challenging yet exciting, especially when we understand that power is available to overcome the trial. We look for that power to intercede. We expect it!

Even when the ordeal results in physical death, is it still possible for us to go through it without being a victim? Yes, we still can triumph over Satan. Jesus Christ died a physical death, yet his resurrection was the biggest defeat of the demonic world that has ever occurred. It was a great show of victory. Death is not the enemy here! We all eventually die a physical death; our victory is the entry into the realm of the celestial kingdom. Just as we fall asleep and leave this world, we'll awake to a celestial reality.

> *Brothers, we do not want you to be ignorant about those who fall asleep, or to grieve like the rest of men, who have no hope. We believe that Jesus died and rose again and so we believe that God will bring with Jesus those who have fallen asleep in him. (1 Thessalonians 4:13-14)*

But now is not the time to sleep. There is an adversary to conquer and a victory to win!

Spiritual Tools

How do we achieve victory when fighting against the dark strongholds that threaten to destroy us? We have to start looking beneath the surface at the deeper things in life. There are always both positive and negative spiritual forces in operation, and though we may want to fight evil with human efforts, there is a much better way.

> *For though we live in the world, we do not wage war as the world does. The weapons we fight with are not the weapons of the world. On the contrary, they have divine power to demolish strongholds. We demolish arguments and every pretension that sets itself up against the knowledge of God, and we take captive every thought to make it obedient to Christ. (2 Corinthians 10:3-5)*

It always goes back to the way we think and the way in which we express these thoughts. In order to break strongholds, we first have to change the way we think. Even if we can't change the situation immediately, we can change our ideas about that situation. Every big change in life begins when we look at our circumstances from a new perspective:

> *Do not conform any longer to the pattern of this world,*
>
> *but be transformed by the renewing of your mind.*
>
> *(Romans 12:2)*

Effective ways to renew our minds include prayer and meditation because these establish contact with Spirit. It works whether we address the God Source, Jesus Christ, or Spirit because they are all in unity, in and of each other. We are simply talking to God and then quietly listening as truth is revealed in a positive form.

In the midst of chaos, we can also establish spiritual grounding by asking, "What is God's truth about this?" When we meditate on what God tells us is true, we see the important considerations from a celestial viewpoint. Only then, can we cut through our negative feelings and perceive our creator's incredible promises for an abundant life.

The God Source sent Spirit into our world to empower us. If we have invited Spirit to reside in us then we have a very effective built-in personal guide. According to Jesus, Spirit was given to us as our counselor. We can talk to this confidante as a respected and powerful friend because Spirit knows everything about us and loves us anyway! However, the friends we most respect do not let us go on and on complaining about our troubles. While they may commiserate for a time, they challenge us to rise above our circumstances. After respectfully listening they ask, "So what are you going to do about it?" A true friend will not see us as a victim. He will see our weakness but know our strengths.

Why would Spirit want to hear all kinds of negative words? If we end up only complaining about how impossible our difficulties are, it would be like accepting a valuable gift and then not using it at all. The power in Spirit is there waiting; the onus is on us to access it. The question is, in which direction are we going to direct it?

What we believe in our hearts and voice with our mouths is the force that either saves us or allows our destruction. If we can fill our hearts with a strong belief in God's power and love for us, and proclaim positive words of faith, we will create good things in our lives. There is validity to the idea of positive thinking. We are asked to think precisely in that way!

> *Finally, brothers, whatever is true, whatever is noble,*
>
> *whatever is right, whatever is pure, whatever is lovely,*
>
> *whatever is admirable—if anything is excellent or*
>
> *praiseworthy—think about such things. (Philippians 4:8)*

The Flip Side to the Law of Faith

Here is something else to consider. The words we speak, coupled with our beliefs, are the components to implement faith, but wouldn't the inverse of the faith formula hold true as well? When we construct negative thoughts and belief systems within our minds and vent our anger in frustration, we verbally speak out and act upon our feelings. The components of faith then work in the wrong direction. This is how we create a negative reality for ourselves.

Here are a couple of strange passages of scripture:

> *What I feared has come upon me; what I dreaded has*
>
> *happened to me. I have no peace, no quietness; I have no*
>
> *rest, but only turmoil. (Job 3:25-26)*
>
> *What the wicked dreads will overtake him; what the*
>
> *righteous desire will be granted. (Proverbs 10:24)*

These verses show the other side of the faith formula. They imply that by our expectations, the negative words and actions we use have already created the reality in which we currently live. Most of us have at least some corners of chaos in our minds, filled with banked embers of anger we have simply built up over the years. We can develop such destructive thinking patterns that we, not only destroy ourselves, but also like a black hole in outer space we subconsciously pull down and suck the life out of everyone around us. The proverbial dark cloud lies at our shoulder. If we are angry or if we feel hopeless about things, we may be using our minds in the wrong manner. Our troubles stem from our mindsets and the way we speak. As the King James Version of the Bible states: "For as he thinketh in his heart, so is he" (Proverbs 23:7).

It is a difficult task to reprogram the mind, for those dark, negative forces influence us. Remember that the rebellious and demonic angels have perverted their original purpose as messengers. They try to make us believe their deceptive messages so we use the law of faith negatively! These entities want us to believe the worst is going to happen. If they can subtly influence us to believe we have unsolvable problems, then these situations seem beyond our control. We will see no way out. If we can be convinced that life is hopeless, disease incurable, and hunger to be expected, then that too is our reality. Demonic entities whisper lies. When we repeat them to ourselves, we end up creating the harmful outcomes we are so afraid might happen. Don't buy the lie! Satanic power is but a mirage.

When we align our thoughts to what God says is true about our circumstances, we can access celestial power to overcome all things. Our own beliefs and words are so potent! But how do we protect ourselves from ourselves? When my daughter first read and edited a draft of this manuscript, the formula for activating faith became clear in her mind. Her own quest for spiritual understanding led her to describe it as simple equations for aligning our beliefs and words with corresponding outcomes. She perceived faith like a current of negative or positive power and expressed it in this way:

Negative beliefs + negative words =
hazardous things happening

Negative beliefs + positive words =
negative current blocked

Positive beliefs + negative words =
positive current blocked

Positive beliefs + positive words =
marvelous things happening

As you can see, even if we have doubts and can't change our negative beliefs right away, we are still protected if we use positive words. In fact, our positive words have a way of giving insight and gently changing our beliefs about those things. If we have positive beliefs and use careless, negative words, the current is blocked from creating anything. The real damage to our lives comes when we have a negative mindset and express our feelings with negative words as a way of venting our emotions.

Our faith doesn't activate the current unless both our beliefs and words to ourselves and to others line up. Unfortunately, the law of faith works both negatively and positively with these two components in place. This principle is intrinsic to the power of choice God gave us from the very beginning. Our individual choices activate either positive or negative results.

The Power Source

Every day we are challenged to grow spiritually and to use the authority God has given us in our own lives. Our words can act as weapons or they can be our magical wands. Just as it would be foolish to flail around a razor-sharp sword, so also is it dangerous to fling about negative and derogatory words, even to yourself.

We are instructed to think and dwell on the positives. Used with love and wisdom, our words can create beautiful worlds in which to live. If we put ourselves in agreement with God's word in any matter, then we will speak with authority and overcome impossible hurdles, for "the prayer of a righteous man is powerful and effective" (James 5:16). I believe if we visualize a favorable outcome and take steps with words and actions, any goal we want to achieve or anything we want to overcome has a way of working out. Unique solutions will find us. When we live with a certainty of what we hope for, then the game of life becomes very exciting!

Years ago I read about a very small boy who was diagnosed with a rare kind of cancer. He couldn't be treated by normal radiation or chemotherapy, so his parents told him that God could work through his mind, and his own thoughts could kill the "bad guy" cells in his body. He was to imagine the white blood cells as a strong army, dividing, growing, and conquering. They were to flow throughout his body, to seek out, surround, and destroy all the bad-guy cells. He spent a certain amount of time each day visualizing this. He became actively involved, and told his parents of his progress every day. Not knowing the deadly aspect of the disease, he visualized success. Through his own words and positive belief system, this little boy was cured of cancer!

After reading this account, I was curious about the power of visualization. I enlisted my ten-year-old daughter to activate the process in a similar but much less serious way. She had a terrible case of children's warts that plagued nearly all her finger joints for a number of years. They kept returning even after many doctor's appointments for tearful and painful removal. We decided that each night before falling asleep, she would imagine that she could attack these growths from the inside out. In her mind, she entered a cell-like capsule and travelled through tiny blood vessels to fire positive energy into the funnel-like roots of each wart. She visualized them turning black. Within months, she was cured of the affliction and has not suffered from it since. Now, as a mother herself, she has taught her six-year-old son to use the same technique for a plantar wart on his small foot and it too was gone within a few weeks.

Taking a leap of quantum faith is very simple for children to do. Perhaps it is because little children believe whatever we tell them is true. They trust us! If we take God's words literally and his assurances as true, we too can receive from God what he promises us. We can trust him, and process the operational principals of the kingdom of God into our lives.

It's not that *we* have to create miracles. Spirit does the work. Creating what we desire is not done by our efforts but by sacred Spirit that lives within us. All we are required to do is plug in to that power to activate faith according to the celestial laws God laid out for us. We are like animated clay figures until we bridge the gap, make the quantum leap, and connect to the authority of the Great Ones. Then we can be powerful. "But we have this treasure in jars of clay to show that this all surpassing power is from God and not from us" (2 Corinthians 4:7).

The secret to powerful living is a powerful connection to the Great Ones with corresponding intensity. We do not have to fear dark entities trying to oppress us. If we have accepted and allowed the seed of celestial spirit to enter and live within us, then we are in fact hardwired to the God Source.

> *Be strong and courageous. Do not be afraid or terrified because of them, for the Lord your God goes with you; he will never leave you nor forsake you." (Deuteronomy 31:6)*

Then with conviction you too can say, "I can do everything through him who gives me strength." (Philippians 4:12-13)

15

welcome to the kingdom!

The kingdom of God is near us in a very surprising way. Various analogies describing this kingdom open new doors of understanding. Loud is the battle cry to align our selves with the Great Ones and take back authority to reign over earth.

The Unique Location

More than two thousand years have passed since Jesus Christ, the ambassador of the Great Ones, walked on our planet, and still new concepts about God and Spirit are being released in contemporary books. I feel one last important topic is needed in this book before we can finally understand the true celestial proposal put forth to us. This final topic is the concept of the kingdom of God.

The word *kingdom* refers to "the highest classification of plants, animals, or things," according to one of its dictionary meanings. It is also "a realm of influence or a sphere of government by the monarch of an area." Looking in a Bible concordance, we find that the English word *kingdom* in the New Testament translates from the Greek word *basileia,* meaning "the realm or reign of a great ruler." So we can say the kingdom of God is a realm of existence that is governed by the spiritual laws of the Great Ones. This is highly significant when we are told God wants to give us his kingdom (Luke 12:32). But where is it? When we understand the kingdom's most governing principles, we will know where it is and how to get there.

The very first reference we see of God creating his reality on earth is in a simple statement in the opening paragraph of the Bible. The great book begins with these words:

> And God said, "Let there be light," and there was light.
> God saw that the light was good and he separated the
> light from the darkness. (Genesis 1:3-4)

When God stated these words, light was created. It's significant that he created light even before he created the sun and the moon (Genesis 1:3, 14-17). The kingdom then has the properties of light; in the realm of the Great Ones, nothing can be hidden.

To personally experience this aspect of a celestial kingdom, I suggest that you sit in a pitch-black auditorium or other very large room, and then light a single candle and see what happens. You will find that no matter how vast the darkness may be, light always overcomes it. There is no darkness that can't be overcome! That is because "God is light; in him there is no darkness at all" (1 John 1:5). This is a powerful awareness.

When we reprogram our minds according to God's truths, we begin to see things by the light we let in. The brighter the light we allow into our lives, the less the darkness can overtake us. The more we increase light's voltage, the clearer things become. With light, we can clearly see where we need to go next.

Jesus Christ claimed to have come from the kingdom of God, and he gave many analogies to describe it. However, not everyone believed in the enigmatic new teacher from Galilee who addressed the huge crowds. He presented a new way to think about things in a strange, spiritual philosophy. The people were accustomed to a strict religion requiring material offerings and sacrifices to obtain righteousness. In simplicity, Jesus Christ taught that the basic governing principle in God's kingdom was to love. Some of the new believers grasped this concept, and one of them spoke up from the crowd.

> "Well said, teacher," the man replied. "You are right in saying that God is one and there is no other but him. To love him with all your heart, with all your understanding and with all your strength, and to love your neighbor as yourself is more important than all burnt offerings and sacrifices."
>
> When Jesus saw that he had answered wisely, he said to him, "You are not far from the kingdom of God." And from then on no one dared ask him any more questions. (Mark 12:32-34)

In a broad sense, both light and love can define the powerful attributes of the kingdom and how all pervasive they can be.

The governing realm of God's kingdom is vastly different from other earthly governments with which we are familiar. In order to enter this kingdom, we must be able to accept the reality of a new and different kind of world. Jesus urged us to accept the kingdom of God as little children do when they take at face value the reality their parents teach them.

> ...Jesus called the children to him and said, "Let the little children come to me, and do not hinder them, for the kingdom of God belongs to such as these. I tell you the truth, anyone who will not receive the kingdom of God like a little child will never enter it." (Luke 18:16-17)

Young children rely on their parents for every basic need, and begin their life with ultimate faith that what their parents tell them is true. Sometimes they come up with strange and wonderful wisdom because they take things so literally. Their perspectives are unpolluted by doubt! We also need to trust in our celestial father for his providence in the same way.

One of my favorite analogies of the kingdom of God came from a precocious three-year-old girl. She was the daughter of a Christian friend of mine, a single father. One time in a conversation, she unexpectedly wanted to talk about God and solemnly explained to her dad, "We live in God's tummy." He had no idea how she had come up with this concept, but after talking to her decided she had profound insight. She had somehow perceived that God surrounds and nurtures us. We exist in him and he flows into us (John 14:20)! Is it that perhaps she, at such a young age, sensed the spiritual realm that we have all forgotten as adults? Even at three, she was comforted by the truths of her personal belief system. When we are willing to embrace God's governing standards of love and light with this same kind of childlike acceptance, we too can experience the kingdom.

The things of God just can't be understood within our physical limits, and we have long been at fault for expecting them to conform to human reality. Jesus came into the human realm from an other-dimensional existence—perhaps even an extraterrestrial world. His words do not come from an ordinary man but one born from human egg and celestial seed. Jesus clearly stated that his diplomatic proposal to us from the Great Ones comes literally from a governing kingdom that's out of this world.

Jesus stood before Pilate, the Roman governor, before sentenced to be crucified. It was only at this point near the end of his life that Jesus made it very clear that his government was not from earth.

> *My kingdom is not of this world. If it were, my servants would fight to prevent my arrest by the Jews. But now my kingdom is from another place. (John 18:36)*

The kingdom is not of our world because, as previously discovered, Satan has dominion over our planet and is presently the "god of this age" (2 Corinthians 4:4). Yet even though we live in a world clearly affected by that dark dominion, Jesus also said, "The kingdom of God is near you" (Matthew 3:2, 10-7, Luke 10:11, 21:31). That's the puzzle: How can the kingdom of God be "not of this world" and still be near us?

Let's think this through. If the God Source wanted to hide something on the face of the earth, something he thought was highly valuable, where would the best place be to conceal it? Where would it be safe from the demonic influences controlling the planet yet accessible to everyone? The answer is in the book. Jesus clearly told us where it would be. He explained that the portal to the kingdom of God is—within us!

> Once, having been asked by the Pharisees when the
> kingdom of God would come, Jesus replied, "The kingdom
> of God does not come visibly, nor will people say, 'Here it
> is', or 'There it is,' because the kingdom of God is within
> you." (Luke 17:20-21)

Inside our minds is the only place that Spirit can have dominion and where it can be safely guarded from the enemy. We are all certainly near to the kingdom of God—not necessarily in time, but certainly in location. We can access celestial benefits from our minds even though Satan holds our earth captive. That is because our minds can be connected to the kingdom of the Great Ones. We are linked to a line of authority that activates our thoughts into words, our words into creative actions, and our actions into positive reality. By accessing the governing principles of the kingdom from the inside of our minds where Spirit lives, we humans can do amazing, miraculous things.

Jesus sent his original twelve disciples out and instructed them:

> As you go, preach this message: "The kingdom of heaven
> is near." Heal the sick, raise the dead, cleanse those who
> have leprosy, drive out demons. Freely you have received,
> freely give. (Matthew 10:7-8)

What authority these first believers displayed in their lives! The occurrence of supernatural things took place in miracles, in healings. "But those were the days of miracles," we might say. Why do we compartmentalize the power of the God Source according to the physical limits of time? God doesn't live in time like we do. Through their writings all these years later, these same men instruct us. Why would Jesus Christ empower them back in history but not want to give us that same authority now? It is being given. Actually, there are miracles constantly happening around the world.

We too have the keys to the kingdom! Our contemporary world has the same opportunity for miracles. Let's not underestimate the power of God we can access for our lives. Jesus urges us to use it!

> I tell you the truth, my Father will give you whatever you ask in my name. Until now you have not asked for anything in my name. Ask and you will receive, and your joy will be complete. (John 16:23-24)

With confidence in implementing the governing principles of the kingdom from within the portals of our minds, we can then simply ask and receive.

Descriptions of the Kingdom

Now we are beginning to understand what the kingdom of God looks like. Jesus also used many parables to describe it, but this is one of my favorites:

> ...What shall we say the kingdom of God is like, or what parable shall we use to describe it? It is like a mustard seed, which is the smallest seed you plant in the ground. Yet when planted, it grows and becomes the largest of all garden plants, with such big branches that the birds of the air can perch in its shade. (Mark 4:30-32)

I have a huge, shady, beautiful walnut tree in the backyard of my home. So many walnuts fall to the ground that it takes many weeks to harvest and dry them. But I can hardly bear to throw them away because they are so healthy and delicious. The inside nut looks like the two hemispheres of our brain—they are works of celestial art. These seeds of life give us sustenance rich in abundance. What a wonderful analogy for the kingdom that grows from a small, single seed! When a celestial seed is planted in us, it too has the potential to grow and become a huge, beautiful tree with outstretched branches to shelter our friends and family. It produces wonderful fruit and provides healthy nourishment for all whose lives we touch.

> That person is like a tree planted by streams of water, which yields its fruit in season and whose leaf does not wither—whatever they do prospers. (Psalms 1:2-4)

Jesus wanted to convey the concept of an invisible kingdom, so he also compared it to something his friends and followers knew very well in the area around the Mediterranean Sea.

> I am the vine, you are the branches: If a man remains in me and I in him, he will bear much fruit, apart from me you can do nothing.... If you remain in me and my words remain in you, ask whatever you wish, and it will be given you. This is my Father's glory, that you bear much fruit, showing your selves to be my disciples. (John 15:5-8)

In order to produce fruit, we have to be grafted into something greater than ourselves. As a part of the vine, we are connected to God, and Spirit can flow through us. Through the life force of the vine, we can produce rich, spiritual fruit, and the intrinsic characteristics of this fruit are wonderful attributes to have!

> But the fruit of the Spirit is love, joy, peace, patience, kindness, goodness, faithfulness, gentleness and self-control. (Galatians 5:22)

There are many more simple analogies for the kingdom of God. Belonging to this kingdom also gives us an opportunity to be grafted into a powerful royal family with members all over the world.

> Yet to all who received him, to those who believed in his name, he gave the right to become children of God—children born not of natural descent, nor of human decision or a husband's will, but born of God. (John 1:12-13)

We are chosen to be children of the kingdom though we do not yet know exactly what celestial form we shall have when God appears. Each human being from every race and nation who has accepted Spirit to live in them now is our brother or our sister. Jesus entered our world that "he might be the firstborn among many brothers" (Romans 8:29).

Belonging to the kingdom is like being linked to a family bloodline only it is a sacred line of Spirit that flows through all of us. Jesus understood this spirit-line and stated with clarity, "who ever does the will of my father in heaven is my brother and sister and mother" (Matthew 12:50). In the spiritual sense, we are not alone in this world at all. We have some powerful relations!

> *The Spirit himself testifies with our spirit that we are*
> *God's children. Now if we are children, then we are heirs—*
> *heirs of God and co-heirs with Christ, if indeed we share in*
> *his sufferings in order that we may also share in his glory.*
> *(Romans 8:16-18)*

Right now, we may live among ugliness in the world, but we belong to a new division of humanity that is fighting the dark forces that try to destroy our species. Already, many of us have formed an alliance with a cosmic foreign family of immense power. We have rights and benefits as heirs to the kingdom of God.

> *...do not set your heart on what you will eat or drink; do*
> *not worry about it. For the pagan world runs after all*
> *such things and your Father knows that you need them.*
> *But seek his kingdom, and these things will be given to you*
> *as well. Do not be afraid, little flock, for your Father has*
> *been pleased to give you the kingdom. (Luke 12:29-32)*

Never forget the Great Ones want to give us the kingdom. Their codes of integrity in that other dimension are the best traits ever to be found in our human qualities—justice, charity, honor, perseverance, and endurance—they all originate from the celestial standards of the Great Ones. It is to these standards we must rally.

> *But you, man of God, flee from all this, and pursue*
> *righteousness, godliness, faith, love, endurance and*
> *gentleness. Fight the good fight of the faith. Take hold of*
> *the eternal life to which you were called.... (1 Timothy 6:11-12)*

When we employ these spiritual laws, we draw closer to the reality in which the Great Ones exist. So even in this life, we too can become a part of the kingdom and enjoy its benefits on a grand and powerful scale.

How to Get There

Every kingdom has its own unique governing laws, its own cultural standards. When a person chooses to immigrate to a foreign country and take its citizenship, they want to know about the existing laws of that nation because the government defines a person's rights and privileges. The kingdom of God just happens to be the ultimate in having an altruistic government. The kingdom of God is the government of God!

Just as God created this world's physical laws, there are spiritual laws equally as binding. Incredibly, the invisible spiritual laws of God override the physical laws of earth. This celestial priority explains why miracles can and do still happen in our contemporary world. At any time, we can choose to live according to these higher celestial principles and begin living in the kingdom, just as Jesus invited us to do.

Jesus walked in these celestial laws. He lived by his conviction in the standards of his kingdom. By application he was empowered to heal incurable diseases and even brought people back from the dead. Jesus was not the only one who was able to do this; his disciples displayed the same power after he was gone. Right up into this present age, uncounted miraculous healings have occurred in every culture around the world because these godly principles of faith have been activated. Quite ordinary people have done amazing things by applying these laws—sometimes without even knowing them—to what they wanted to happen.

Many examples highlight the use of the quantum-leap connection in activating faith even outside of a religious format. For centuries, we believed it was physically impossible for a human being to run a four-minute mile. Then, in 1954, Roger Bannister broke this world record, and within a few years, many others did the same. The Wright brothers were laughed at and told that the machine they wanted to power through the air couldn't be built. But they persevered. Other people begin to think it might just be possible and this expanded their vision. Now we travel on airplanes and take them for granted all the time.

Thomas Edison conducted more than one thousand experiments that failed. His family and friends called him crazy and wondered if he should be put away. Now with a flip of a switch we light our homes! Beethoven became deaf but still continued to create powerful music, becoming one of the world's great composers. How do people do all these impossible things? Even though they may have been unconscious of celestial principles in operation, they connected to Spirit and believed things into being!

The celestial ambassador who entered our world came to give us an extraordinary gift we can use right now in our physical lives. He opened doors to celestial wealth. These are his words to us:

> I will give you the keys of the kingdom of heaven;
>
> whatever you bind on earth will be bound in heaven and
>
> whatever you loose on earth will be loosed in heaven.
>
> (Matthew 16:19)

The keys to the kingdom! That sounds incredibly magical. Yet this was the very purpose for Jesus to be on earth: to make the kingdom of God accessible to mortal human beings. The keys are the governing principles of the laws of faith—making the things we "hope for and do not yet see" (Hebrews 11:1), actually come into existence through our heartfelt words!

Successful people succeed mostly because of the way they think. They work diligently and expect success because they believe their goals are possible. They have already created success in their minds, and the world around them responds. This is how our minds were designed to function, just like the cognitive processes of the God species. When we begin to think like God-beings, we begin to create as they do. Then all things truly become possible. Our beliefs define the highest level in the game of life we are able to achieve.

The ultimate question is always: just what are we going to believe? Are we going to believe what everyone else believes? Are we going to believe the limiting lies that Satan wants us to believe? Are we powerless victims in life, or are we spiritual activators? Our mindsets are what limit us. They can also wildly expand the parameters of our reality.

Let's relate the whole concept of the kingdom of God to one last analogy with which the modern world is very familiar. The Internet is cosmic and diverse in its complexity. It is also like a vine flowing in power and connection. No matter what nation we are in, we can contact and communicate with each other via e-mails, blogs, and websites on the World Wide Web. Pictures, movie clips, and real-time voices are zapped around the earth, all invisibly and seemingly without effort. Immeasurable transactions of wealth instantaneously take place through the touch of a key in business investments, online banking, and stock trading. Most of us don't quite know how it works, but we accept this as a normal way of connecting and take it all for granted. We are sure and certain of its mode of operation even though sixty years ago, this medium for communicating would have existed only in science fiction.

With this in mind, the invisible realm of the Great Ones is not really such a difficult concept for us to imagine. What if celestial Spirit is a supernatural software program by which we can access spiritual properties? What if we authorize its download when we request Spirit to be installed in our minds? We already have built-in connection ports because we have been created in the likeness of the Great Ones!

However, there is a requirement: we must defragment our hard drives to free up space for the installation of this new software for human beings. Downloading this updated, powerful version can override the current operating system by interfacing directly with a celestial network. To initiate the program, we need only to agree to the conditions in fine print, and then click "Yes, I accept"!

The best part of this new operating system is the expansion of our minds to run with even more megabytes of boundless power, allowing us to download infinite wisdom from the celestial grid. Downloading installs the components of love and compassion for others and becomes the basis for every relationship. Spinoff effects of human joy and happiness are the result.

Best of all the upgrade is free! Remember, we have been given life, and it's a ticket to play a multiplayer, interactive, celestial game of life. This game is set up with all kinds of trials to be overcome in each level of difficulty. It is specifically designed to develop the spiritual skills possessed by the Great Ones. In every level, we are offered keys to understanding true greatness, helping us to conquer evil in countless battles of engagement.

There is a strange distinction here, though: achieving a high score in the celestial game of the Great Ones does not come from battles of violence and aggression toward others, but in the complete opposite manner. Obtaining spiritual maturity by activating celestial principles is the only way to activate the highest levels of this game. What is the goal? Empowerment in this physical life and the ultimate reward—full citizenship into the immortal realm of the Great Ones!

Entrance to the Celestial Realm

Welcome to twenty-first century Christianity. Looking at religion from a present-day perspective in no way diminishes the magnitude of God's omnipotence; rather it enables a better framework of understanding. If we have experienced the joy of having our minds fused with celestial Spirit, we know that this life on earth is but a growth process to the real purpose of existence. Biological life is simply not all there is. Nature is full of parallels for understanding this metamorphosis. For the tree to live, the seed must die. The caterpillar is lost to form a butterfly. Vegetation decomposes for the rebirth of spring. Should it be otherwise on the greater scheme of things?

A friend of mine used to sing a mournful melody with this chorus: "Everybody wants to go to heaven but nobody wants to die." We can't live in the old way of the flesh and still enter an invisible dimension of Spirit. In the end, we all have to change physically into something else. When we accept this truth, we can lay down our corporeal lives knowing that death is simply a short birth canal. It is not an ending but an entry!

> I consider that our present sufferings are not worth comparing with the glory that will be revealed in us. For the creation waits in eager expectation for the children of God to be revealed.... We know that the whole creation has been groaning as in the pains of childbirth right up to the present time.... [W]e ourselves, who have the firstfruits of the Spirit, groan inwardly as we wait eagerly for our adoption to sonship, the redemption of our bodies. (Romans 8:18-19, 22-23)

Then death is actually the end goal of life. It is simply a necessary component in the process. Here is another passage to explain it:

> I declare to you, brothers, that flesh and blood cannot inherit the kingdom of God, nor does the perishable inherit the imperishable. Listen, I tell you a mystery. We will not all sleep, but we will all be changed—in a flash, in the twinkling of an eye, at the last trumpet. For the trumpet will sound, the dead will be raised imperishable, and we will be changed. For the perishable must clothe itself with the imperishable and the mortal with immortality. (1 Corinthians 15:50-53)

Our minds will then be housed in a different imperishable substance! Just as Jesus was transformed back into a celestial being of spirit form, we too shall see our bodies change from flesh into spirit. The following verses shed more light on this:

> There are also heavenly bodies and there are earthly bodies; but the splendor of the heavenly bodies is one kind, and the splendor of the earthly bodies is another. (1 Corinthians 15:40)
>
> And just as we have borne the likeness of the earthly man, so shall we bear the likeness of the man from heaven. (1 Corinthians 15:49)

We don't know exactly what it will be like to exist in the shape of spirit on the other side of biological death, but we do know we will be grafted into the powerful, cosmic family of the Great Ones. The author of the book of Revelation saw a vision of what he thought to be heaven:

> *And I heard a loud voice from the throne saying, "Now the dwelling of God is with men, and he will live with them. They will be his people, and God himself will be with them and be their God. He will wipe every tear from their eyes. There will be no more death or mourning or crying or pain, for the old order of things has passed away." (Revelation 21:3-4)*

There is no pain in paradise!

Here is another astonishing concept: there aren't any scriptures saying we will go to heaven. The Bible only speaks of the "kingdom of heaven" and says this kingdom is "coming down from heaven."

> *Then I saw a new heaven and a new earth, for the first heaven and the first earth had passed away, and there was no longer any sea. I saw the Holy City, the new Jerusalem, coming down out of heaven from God.... (Revelation 21:1-2)*

God's kingdom is coming down from the celestial sky or in other words, down from a location in extraterrestrial space!

Many of us are familiar with the Lord's Prayer. Even in this most famous of Christian supplications we pray that "your kingdom come, your will be done on earth as it is in heaven" (Matthew

6:10). Undeniably, the Great Ones want to establish their kingdom on earth. This is the proposal they present to us. To develop a utopian world on our planet was the purpose of the sacrifice of their ambassador, Jesus Christ.

> *And with your blood you purchased men for God from every tribe and language and people and nation. You have made them to be a kingdom and priests to serve our God, and they will reign on the earth. (Revelation 5:9-10)*

They want us to model their government and reign on the earth! When will the implementation of this government take place? It didn't happen two thousand years ago, when Jesus became one of us. Some factions expected Jesus to head a rebellion and overthrow the Roman government in order to become their new king. Politically the society he was born into was only an occupied territory in the great Roman Empire. But Jesus explained that his kingdom would not come in this manner. He would return later to earth to establish his government, not as a human leader of a rebellious movement but as a God.

Heaven being located on earth is almost shocking, isn't it, when so many believers think we are *going to* heaven. This whole science-fiction thriller of our existence ends with a completely different kind of climax from what we've thought for all these centuries! We do not have to go up to heaven to find God. Just like the first time, the very presence of God will come to us. They will return for the same reasons as before: to save us from the evil influences of Satan's dominion over our world. For now, we have polluted much of our planet, and with the state of the current world affairs; we still desperately need to be saved.

Remember when Jesus came the first time around? The Jewish religious leaders ridiculed the idea of a Son of God/Son of Man. What will happen when the persona of Jesus Christ returns? When he comes to reign as King of kings, it is said he will rule with an iron scepter and with great power (Revelation 19:15, Psalms 2:9).

> For the Son of Man in his day will be like the lightning, which flashes and lights up the sky from one end to the other. (Luke 17:24)
>
> At that time the sign of the Son of Man will appear in the sky, and all the nations of the earth will mourn. They will see the Son of Man coming on the clouds of the sky, with power and great glory. And he will send his angels with a loud trumpet call, and they will gather his elect from the four winds, from one end of the heavens to the other. (Matthew 24:30-31)

How will our world's media, the political powers, and the religions in our contemporary world perceive it? How will they deal with that bright spectacle in the sky, the arrival of the Son of Man/Son of God coming in the clouds? This arrival will quite likely be viewed as a worldwide, catastrophic event. All the nations of the earth will mourn this event because their governments will seem to be in jeopardy of an imminent extraterrestrial invasion!

The Son of God will come once again, but this time he will save us by taking over the world's corrupt governments—those operating under the dominion of the dark forces. Then he will set up the governing laws of his kingdom over the earth, just as he must have longed to do during his first visit here. Today's national superpowers will not easily surrender their sovereignty to a mysterious force that's seemingly from outer space. Will they try to make war with our creator? How tragic that would be, when all along God has been nurturing humanity to evolve into powerful members of the God family. How ironic when the highest honorable intelligence existing in the universe is attempting to teach us celestial laws of love. The stage on earth is set. The curtain waits to be parted on this final act in the spiritual evolution of the human species.

A Call to Spiritual Warriors

In God's plan for humanity, the next great memorable day to be reenacted is symbolized by a loud trumpet call. This is the call for the final confrontation against evil to take place, the event that will emphatically oust demonic forces from our planet. Spiritual warriors will gather from all over the earth. Our weapons will be our words, convicted with power, aligned with the celestial presence in the sky. It will not happen in the human way of world war, for this very event has been planned by the Great Ones for eons of human time.

We no longer have to escape into science fiction for thrilling plots of action. We need to recognize that the battle of good and evil has been played out on our planet and with its inhabitants for a very long time. Satan and the dark forces of evil have long ago invaded earth and we have been battling against them since our time began. They have no respect for our species. They want the human experiment to fail. They hope humanity is wiped out by hunger, disease, and violence. Isn't this the very world we live in? Our world is oppressed and infested by these insidious forces. Instead of labeling satanic influences as imaginary paranoia, let's consider them the real enemy of our human species.

Meanwhile, how do we mere earthlings do battle with the dark forces of evil and begin to solve today's world problems? We are formidable opponents only when we give allegiance to the Great Ones and align ourselves with their operating principles. By activating our most-powerful weapons, those spiritual laws that operate above the physical limits of this world, we become invincible spiritual warriors! Although it may sound melodramatic, the true blueprint for humanity requires that we *fire up the grid* and unite to "overcome evil with good" (Romans 12:21).

You are being offered a celestial proposal from a great, heavenly species, and you are needed! Even now, you're being called to recognize the spiritual power lying dormant within you and to discipline yourself. You're invited the take up the weapons of the Great Ones and join the forces that will save humanity from destruction by an ancient enemy.

Learning how to use our weapons and shields effectively takes courage, perseverance, and practice, for we must know how to hold up our shields of faith even in the midst of great battle.

Finally, be strong in the Lord and in his mighty power. Put on the full armor of God so that you can take your stand against the devil's schemes. For our struggle is not against flesh and blood, but against the rulers, against the authorities, against the powers of this dark world and against the spiritual forces of evil in the heavenly realms. Therefore, put on the full armor of God, so that when the day of evil comes, you may be able to stand your ground, and after you have done everything, to stand.

Stand firm then, with the belt of truth buckled around your waist, with the breastplate of righteousness in place, and with your feet fitted with the readiness that comes from the gospel of peace. In addition to all this, take up the shield of faith, with which you can extinguish all the flaming arrows of the evil one. Take the helmet of salvation and the sword of the Spirit, which is the word of God. (Ephesians 6:10-17)

The earth is under the siege of Satan, and only when we put on the whole armor of God are we prepared to fight as spiritual warriors. God's word is truth, and this needs to be belted tightly around us to hold everything in place, so we don't fall into agreement with the lies of our adversary. With plates of armor over our hearts and shields in our hands, we can deflect the fiery darts from the forces of darkness. Knowing intellectually that Jesus came to ransom and save us is the helmets on our heads. We have plenty of defensive shielding. But where is our weapon? What will we use to attack our enemy?

The formidable sword of Spirit is our only aggressive weapon. It is wielded when we voice with authority the words of God. Powered by the precision of our speech, it cuts with laser accuracy to manifest what we declare. It is the only possible weapon capable of subduing the enemy. We create with it and that is where we get our power!

> For the word of God is living and active. Sharper than any double-edged sword, it penetrates even to dividing soul and spirit, joints and marrow; it judges the thoughts and attitudes of the heart. (Hebrews 4:12)

Our ultimate challenge is to learn how to wield the sword of the spirit without violence. The components of faith—pure, heartfelt words of God coming from our mouths—have to be confirmed by our action, which is symbolized by the swords in our hands. They alone can slice through the walls of our physical reality and open the realm of spiritual truth. Jesus instructs us to put on the whole armor of God and then hands us the swords so we can do exactly what has been planned from the very beginning: to seize back our planet from Satan and live forever!

Earth was once given to us as our dominion. We are earth-gods and our planet does not belong to satanic forces any longer.

Spirit has conceived us for this purpose, and collectively we grow ever stronger. Already many people around the world have tapped into this spiritual life force, and they recognize it. In my travels to other nations, I have discovered the same celestial spirit active beyond the borders of different cultures, religions, and dialects. We are all brothers and sisters within the human race. Regardless of which denomination, organization, or ideology we belong to, there is but one true God who holds these celestial standards and freely offers us this kind of power.

> But you are a chosen people, a royal priesthood, a holy nation, a people belonging to God, that you may declare the praises of him who called you out of darkness into his wonderful light. Once you were not a people, but now you are the people of God.... (1 Peter 2:9-10)

Our God Source is big enough to encompass us all and revels in our diversity. These concepts have been understood in multiple languages and shared with those who dare to believe, for our allegiance is to God and we are members of *one powerful earth family.*

Let us dare to believe in the great, awesome, and far-reaching plans for our humankind to take its place among celestial, immortal beings. Fused with Spirit in a symbiotic relationship, our minds have unlimited potential, and nothing is impossible to us.

And so, my brothers and my sisters, I recognize you by your fruit, by how you play the game. Your eyes meet mine directly with light and acceptance. You radiate love! I feel your spirit because it's the same Spirit from the same vine. It runs through all those who have given their allegiance to God for we have accepted celestial Spirit into our minds and are already connected. We are seriously playing the Game of Life and our words bear fruit.

And now, dear children, continue in him, so that when he appears we may be confident and unashamed before him at his coming. (1 John 2:27-29)

Come, my friends, let us stand together strong and confident. The realm of the kingdom has already begun in we who believe. Let's blow the trumpets to wake up the world. Let's sound the battle cry. When the Great Ones come to establish God's kingdom "on earth as it is in heaven," we will be eagerly waiting—for we have accepted their awesome Celestial Proposal.

fictional epilogue

A New Age Begins

"Excuse me, please... Excuse me," I mumble, jostling for a better viewing position among the throng of world representatives inside the huge amphitheater. Live media screens show the faces of famous leaders from around the world. The room is packed with apprehension.

Dr. Joe Callahan has just finished his speech to the somber Federation of Nations assembly. As one of the world's leading astronomers, he has been called in to give a carefully considered analysis. But there is still very little information to answer the main inquiry: What is that pulsating cube of light that radiates through dense, shimmering cloud? It appeared instantaneously on the edge of earth's ionosphere and has been resting there for the last twenty hours. Right now its softly illuminating earth's population all along the west coast of the Americas. Harmlessly repelling all airborne intrusion, it simply remains motionless. Is it the cutting-edge ultimate weapon from one of the world superpowers? No government or other terrorist group has announced any challenge or threat, and beside this mysterious, glowing entity is just too big.

The recent decades of world devastation have been so complete there is little need for another type of weapon. Chaos and confusion lie over every continent. Disease grows in epidemic proportions, and outbursts of new, mutated germ infections are rampant. Earth's fragmented population is devastated, and the planet's darkened atmosphere has taken all it can handle. Oceans are swamped with pollution, and since the alteration of earth's orbit following the hit from Meteorite A-12; the dead may easily outnumber the living. No, there is no need for weapons anymore. The planet is saturated in calamity.

National emergency instructions from leaders around the world are being broadcasted on all media sources. Calming false words in every known language flow out smoothly in an effort to maintain the fabric of a quickly disintegrating human society. Even the new, more-conscientious politicians are finding the illuminating cube phenomenon a most difficult situation. So little is known about it, yet it's impossible for the media to cover it up. We all can look up and see it for ourselves! Bizarre theories are being tossed around. It's thought that it might be an after-effect, square-type rainbow of chemical gases from the planetary shift. Still others are sure it's an immense UFO, visibly announcing an extraterrestrial invasion.

That's why an extended security council of the fragmented World Federation has been called together. The almost-hysterical ambassadors have come to report on their ravaged countries and to confront a new menace that has seemingly come from outer space. Ironically, humankind is finally experiencing an aura of true unity against an unknown adversary.

Inside the vast assembly, the chairperson calls upon the eminent Dr. Loran Kitchner. A nervous, fidgety, little man, Kitchner is the head of Ibex, a world crisis-solving think tank. Held in high regard, Ibex searches vast data banks from scientific communities around the world and bypasses national agendas and the idiosyncrasies of diverse governments to develop completely rational solutions. Indeed Ibex is one of the last hopes for humanity's multitude of problems. All agree that some of the previous solutions presented by Ibex to halt the world's madness should most assuredly have been put into action. If Ibex can't come up with an answer then the world is without hope, and whatever is waiting at the edge of its atmosphere will be able to neatly consume it.

Weary and bloodshot eyes throughout the hall now move only half expectantly toward Dr. Kitchner. He rises, adjusts the microphone, clears his throat, and begins. "In the questionable limit of time we may have before a possible final cataclysmic end to our world as we know it, I will simply read in layman's terms the key points of the Ibex report."

Shifting from one foot to another, he slowly begins, "'Summary Report of the Unidentified Cube Phenomenon. Characteristics: Composed of an unknown class of energy, there is no mass within it, yet it radiates from its center. It has power in excess of all known and combined nuclear weapons and is capable of spontaneously altering its structural makeup at any moment. Currently it is not emanating on full power, but is instead allowing for visualization only.'"

Kitchner hesitates and looks about for a moment. "Ibex states that the cube is ancient and"—he pauses—"it is alive!"

Breaths are drawn sharply across the room, and there is a buzz of muted conversation. Dr. Kitchner waits solemnly until the chairperson quiets the assembly and asks him to continue.

"Although all probes have been rendered neutral, it has unquestionable indications of supreme intelligence and it may be offering some sort of invitation. Ibex itself is rather in a quandary."

The president of a Western nation asks, "Dr. Kitchner, what statement did Ibex give as to the question of identification?"

Dr. Loran Kitchner looks intensely at the chairperson, then hesitantly out across the floor at the many diverse representatives of the major nations left on the ravaged earth. He straightens his papers and clears his throat again.

"Ibex states that it might be humanity's...alien God," he says.

Hearing this, I turn to see how his statement is received. Low chuckles and scornful side-glances are sprinkling over the majority of the distinguished ambassadors. In minutes, the media screen of each country will broadcast alternative, more-believable headlines. I will see it on the corner flat screens when I get out on the streets: "WORLD LEADERS UNITE IN DEFENSE OF ALIEN ATTACK."

But I too have seen with my own eyes that great, immovable light in the sky, and it has filled me with many unnamed emotions. How do I feel about this new looming, supposedly catastrophic event? Most of my colleagues and acquaintances seem to flinch with fears of even more unknown disaster. Some are consumed by anger at what they perceive as an invasion they can now blame for all the recent world catastrophes.

Me? I'm feeling wild ecstasy inside my heart! My pulse races deep in my soul like a distant jungle drum. Vibrating in the very air I breathe, I become aware of a penetrating slow musical scale playing the notes of a vast trumpet chord. I look upward then, remembering a passage from some preserved archaic literature—Revelation 1:7-8—and I whisper it to my self softly:

> *"Look, he is coming with the clouds, and every eye will see him.... The Alpha and the Omega.... Who is, and who was, and who is to come..."*

about the author

Jane Catherine Rozek spent ten years in the alpine meadows of the Canadian wilderness where she shaped a unique spiritual belief system that enabled her to thrive in that harsh isolated environment. Challenged by necessity, she learned how to activate faith as a creative force that can actually change reality.

She dedicated herself to an eighteen-year career as a Life Coach for high-risk teenagers. Rozek also co-managed an Alcohol & Drug recovery home, foster parented troubled teens, facilitated for Parents in Crisis groups and church youth groups. She has used the concepts exposed in her book to help others create positive changes in their lives.

Photo taken by Kris Zerr

After decades of effort to conform to mainstream Christianity, Rozek now writes as an independent Christian trailblazer, leading us on a twenty-first century trail to the celestial realm of eternity. She currently divides her time between her Canadian home in beautiful Kelowna, BC, and traveling to distant parts of the world with her laptop in hand, for spiritual *grand adventures*.

Made in the USA
Charleston, SC
29 November 2013